Praise for **Love Now**

"In *Love Now*, Jan and Alan share their marriage, their professional expertise and their wisdom. The result is down to earth, inspiring—and full of humor. It will change the way you deal with the people you love."

–Suzanne Braun Levine, author of *Inventing the Rest of Our Lives* and 50 *Is the New Fifty: Ten Life Lessons for Women in Second Adulthood, Ms. Magazine* Editor Emerita

"*Love Now* is beautifully written with such gentle humor and real and accessible clarity. This book offers straightforward tools for developing deeper intimacy in our relationships."

–Lesley Ann Warren, Academy-Award nominated actress

"*Love Now* is an accessible, delightful yet powerful book that provides a map for individuals and couples to free themselves from the blame-shame dynamics, uneasiness and conflict that are so often part of relationships. Jan and Al demystify relationships and show us the way to attain clarity, self-empowerment and the emotional freedom to love again!"

–John P. Elia, Ph.D., co-author of *Sex and Relationships: An Anthology*, Professor and Associate Chair of Health Education San Francisco State University

"*Love Now* is a remarkable book—remarkable in its simplicity and with its ease in unraveling issues that seem impossibly complex. Delivering wisdom with humor and compassion, Al and Jan help us unlock the potential for deeply gratifying connections with others and with ourselves."

–Kelly Christopher, M.S., Department of Sociology, University of Georgia

"*Love Now* gives practical advice from the heart that will help you to negotiate the minefield that is love."

—Katia Loisel-Furey, co-author *How to Get the Man You Want /*
How to Get the Woman You Want

"*Love Now* offers a fresh perspective on how to uncover greater self awareness, aiding the reader in separating themselves from the paralyzing emotions of anger, hurt, fear and frustration, while re-directing them toward conscious communication, emotional responsibility, and celebration. These authors offer a liberating approach toward learning how to live in rewarding, loving, relationships."

—Tara Crocitto-McCreery & Crash McCreery, President and
CEO Production Designer Calypso Productions Inc.

"*Love Now* is an intelligent guide for creating loving, compassionate and joyful relationships. The authors generously share anecdotes from their own lives to illustrate their concepts, making this book enjoyable to read and often humorous. I found myself nodding in self-recognition, and sighing with relief to find such practical solutions to the challenges that can occur in any relationship."

—Carol Gray, Professor, Directional Psychology,
Ananda College of Living Wisdom

"*Love Now will change your life.*"

—John Austin, host of *The Book Club* radio program, Florida

"*Love Now* is not one of those 'quick fix' self-help books. When I read this book, I felt like I had come 'home' to a reality I knew instantly was the truth, but one I had never known even existed. The approach is so simple, and yet so powerful—and will guide you not only to the relationship you want to have, but through the deep, transformative, soul wrestling, turn yourself inside out process of creating a new and amazing life."

—Annie Eadie, CFO, The Naumes Corporation

LOVE NOW

untangling relationships

jan harrell
alan robins

White Cloud Press
Ashland, Oregon

White Cloud Press books may be purchased for educational, business, or sales promotional use. For information, please write:

Special Market Department
White Cloud Press
PO Box 3400
Ashland, OR 97520
Website: www.whitecloudpress.com

Cover design by Ron Taft
Interior design by Christy Collins, Constellation Book Services

First edition: 2017

Printed in the United States of America
17 18 17 18 19 20 10 9 8 7 6 5 4 3 2 1

Library of Congress Cataloging-in-Publication Data

Names: Harrell, Jan, author. | Robins, Alan, author.
Title: Love now : untangling relationships / Jan Harrell,
  PhD, Alan Robins, PhD.
Description: Ashland, Oregon : White Cloud Press, [2017]
Identifiers: LCCN 2017028649 | ISBN 9781940468570 (pbk.)
Subjects: LCSH: Man-woman relationships--Psychological aspects. |
  Couples--Psychology. | Interpersonal relations. | Interpersonal conflict.
Classification: LCC HQ801 .H3279 2017 | DDC 306.7--dc23
LC record available at https://lccn.loc.gov/2017028649

Contents

THE END

Birthday Flowers

Jan

The first time Al ever brought me flowers was after I had a minor surgery. They finally let him into my room after I had a long bout fighting nausea from the anesthetic I had been given. I lay there, exhausted and nauseated, sweaty and wretched. He came in clutching a by now quite beat-up-from-his-nervous-anxiety-and-worry bunch of flowers that he strangled as he held them to his chest. In his shock and agonized fear, he blurted out, "You look awful!"

From that time on, he would periodically bring me flowers—though the successors to that first bouquet were never tortured so thoroughly before landing in my hands. Birthdays, anniversaries, sometimes "just because," I would come home to find beautiful arrangements or clusters of blossoms.

The funny thing, though, is that I have never really been a fan of flowers as a gift. Now, don't get me wrong. I like them. I am not impervious to the glory of the Earth. It's just that they never make me faint or swoon or melt in romantic ecstasy, as other women seem to do on receiving what to them must represent the proof of their man's devotion.

I knew they came from his love and deep desire to make me feel special, so I always appreciated his gift of beauty, knowing that Al was really offering me his heart in a rainbow of colors and petals. Year after year, decade after decade, he brought me flowers.

. . . And then came the birthday that he forgot. Of course, it wasn't actually a real birthday—I was born on Leap Day, and this wasn't a

Leap Year. And it wasn't exactly that he forgot. He was battling cancer, and his pain was so compelling that every waking moment was spent trying to manage it, to find some comfort or ease or distraction. For the first time, my birthday passed without a hug—he couldn't hug me anymore with his arms, only with his eyes. Without a birthday wish—our communication consisted mostly of instructions from him about how to help him and offers from me of what I could do or fix or feed him. And for the first time, without birthday flowers. I was bereft. I cried myself to sleep, so lonely, knowing that he wouldn't even be here for my next birthday, my "real" birthday, that there would never again be those flowers that always made me secretly smile about the sweet innocence of my husband.

The next morning, having scolded myself for not speaking up, for empathically "understanding" his reality so absolutely that I made myself disappear unnecessarily into silence and self-denial, I told him, "Tell me Happy Un-Birthday!" And, loving me as much as he does, of course, he told me. And told me that it broke his heart that he has no energy to give me the attention he loves to give me. That I deserve so much and he can give me so little.

I went to work for a bit and he had company come over. When I returned, there was a dozen beautiful deep red roses near the bed where he lay visiting with our friend, Jill. I admired them, and he said, "They're for you." At first, what he was trying to tell me didn't register. Confused, I asked, "From Jill?" When he said, "No," I still didn't realize what was going on and asked, "From Jill for you?" He just repeated, "They're for you." And then I understood . . . and thought I had never seen such beautiful flowers before in my whole life. He asked, "At four this morning, did you hear what I said to you?" I shook my head, and he continued. "I said, 'Happy Birthday, Jani. I love you so much.'"

I love those damn flowers. Those exquisite flowers. Those deep red and from his heart breathtaking flowers. I have never seen such wonderful flowers in my whole life. I am drying those flowers. And I am going to keep those flowers for the rest of my life. I am going to take those flowers with me through the purifying fires of cremation that will send my soul up in a torrent of smoke to the Heavens, where I will find my Al. And I am going to stand there, clutching those deep red roses of our love to my chest and tell him, "You look beautiful."

Don't wait.

Love. Now.

I will love you forever, Al.

Alan Leslie Robins

April 11, 1951 ~ May 12, 2015

THE BEGINNING
The Premise of This Book

Jan

Epiphanies. Life-changing illuminations. They are different from those comfortable little awarenesses that make our life easier, like "Oh! I'm out of milk. I'd better remember to buy some." No. Epiphanies challenge us. They demand growth and change of the deepest kind. The kind of change that feels like we're turning ourselves inside out so we can grow in totally new directions that we never dreamed even existed. Like a physicist discovering a new dimension, we suddenly have a whole new world opened up before us.

I've had several in my life. They're not easy to deal with. They have come out of nowhere and have totally and irrevocably shattered my comfortable notion of reality. They have each come in an electrifying blast that exploded my known world, replacing it with a revelation that is instantly both clearly self-evident, true and undeniable, yet shocking in the total reversal of all that I have imagined, totally contrary to how I have been living.

The first epiphany I had was when I was in graduate school. I was lying in bed, ready to fall asleep, when that bolt of electricity entered the top of my head and charged down the length of my body. "I'm not learning a profession," I realized. "I'm learning POWER!" I recognized immediately that if I didn't use that power to grow and to free myself from my issues, I could become skillfully manipulative!

I was stunned. I already knew that when I was frightened, I wasn't direct, and didn't speak from my heart with vulnerability and honesty. I was pretty good at this. No one ever seemed to realize what I was doing.

Now in school to be a clinical psychologist, I was learning tools that would make me dangerous if I didn't face my fears and issues. I had received a directive—the imperative to work, to grow and to purify myself. I knew that if I didn't, I would be even better at hiding my true self and it impossible to be the person I wanted to be or to have the kind of relationships I wanted to have—and I would never be able to feel at peace or good about myself.

My latest epiphany occurred only recently. It has given rise to this book . . . .

It was during our regular morning walk—Al, the puppies (Cassie and Maya) and me—that it occurred. Al said something that instantly created irritation in me. That's when it happened—that rarely experienced but absolutely familiar electricity that stopped me dead in my tracks. I couldn't move. In that instant, I knew that my anger was my demand that he be just like me so I didn't have to feel our differentness. It was my demand that he be a grown-up so I wouldn't have to be. I literally couldn't talk. My new revelation far exceeded my level of development. I could see it, but I could not live it. I stood there and thought with shock, "I've just glimpsed what real maturity is."

And then I really got mad. I got mad that I couldn't just get mad anymore. I got mad that I was so undeveloped that I was getting mad at Al in the first place. And I bit my tongue. (Not really—I don't like pain. But in my mind, I bit it.) I couldn't talk, because my anger was no longer valid, even to me. I had nothing to say. I was too young in my awareness. All I could do was be mad and resolutely "bite" my tongue.

There is theory and then there is being. Let's be honest—one is fairly easy to grasp with our intelligent and well-developed left-brain. The other is a whole different story. I can know and understand and often even sound evolved, wise and mature . . . but inside, I struggle with sudden and powerful emotions that overwhelm me. What really stopped me in my tracks is that I suddenly understood that this whole marriage struggle is about separateness—being different (as opposed to him just being messed up). I know it's not him. It's me. I was angry because he is just human. He is not perfect. He is in his own struggle to deal with his own issues. He is not all evolved and grown up. Again, I realized that the bottom line is that I want *him* to be grown up so *I don't have to be!* I had a secret project throughout our marriage. While I was aware of my behaviors, I never fully realized the secret purpose behind them. I had been enduring, waiting, patient, suggesting, critical, helpful, loving, hopeful, tolerating, suffering, giving, raging—everything I could think of to get him to change (*Grow Up!*) so I wouldn't have to!

I began to share this insight with friends and clients. We no longer focused on superficial complaints or communication dynamics. Any argument or problem became the signal for each of us to look into our own feelings and behavior, as opposed to looking at what the other person did "wrong" that we were "justifiably" upset about. Hurt, anger and the physical experience of tightness in my body became the signals for introspection, not accusation.

This focus on separateness is a stunningly different perspective and approach to the tangle of relationships. I find that other people are affected the same way I was—they are speechless and in shock. Their desperate complaints and accusations, aimed at getting their spouse to change and be just like them, no longer have validity to them, either. Not yet having learned what was triggered in themselves or what to do about it, they also tend to sit with "deer in the headlights" faces—caught in awareness, not yet able to move.

It is to all of us, Al and me included, that this book is dedicated. We are all trying to find our way to love, but because we do not even understand the emotions and reactions we have, we have no idea how to deal with them. Desperate to be understood and loved by our spouse, we try to get them to see what they "did" to us and all we do is hurt each other more—then we feel even more alone, misunderstood and hopeless. Equipped with the tools in this book, we will each be empowered to grow up, to find the adult, mature "me" that we find easily in so many other relationships. We will be able to learn how to bring that mature Self into our marriage and create the loving closeness for which we all long.

Al

My story is a story of survival. I'm not complaining about that, nor do I feel as though I am a victim, but that's primarily what my life has felt like. I grew up in a house with a mother and a father who did not talk to each other much. They didn't fight—probably because that would involve talking! They rarely talked to me, either. My brother escaped to the Navy when he was seventeen and I was two. My sister escaped to her biological father's house when she was a teen. I was five. I was a sweet and shy boy, a good student and a great athlete (as well as always being extremely modest!) My father had his first heart attack when I was three and my mother contracted a terminal liver disease when I was eight. I thought everyone's life was like mine.

Relationships were, to me, functional. I needed my parents to provide food and shelter. They smiled at me a lot, so I believed they loved me. I could tell that my mother desperately needed me and that my job in life was to anticipate what she needed and provide it. I didn't know this at the time, but she demanded that I fuse with her—her needs and my needs had to be the same.

My mother hated all my girlfriends in high school. When I was nineteen, she moved away from her other children, family and friends on the East Coast to California, to live close to me so I could take care of her while she was dying . . . and I did. I am not feeling sorry for myself, but because of all this, I learned to live a separate, lonely life. Relationships felt dangerous. I had no sense that I could have any of my own needs met in a relationship. I put my girlfriends' needs before my own in high school . . . and then I met Jan. I started the same behavior pattern with her, but she did something weird and uncomfortable for me . . . and it changed my life forever.

She asked me what I wanted and needed on a regular basis. I didn't know what I wanted and needed. All I knew was how to attend to the other person's needs. I am still very bad at knowing what I need, but I am hopeful that in writing this book with Jan and in sharing my story, others will find their way to a loving relationship sooner. For me, it all started with recognizing, with Jan's loving help, that I have my own wants and needs—that I exist as a separate independent entity.

An Essential Introduction
(In other words, don't skip to chapter 1!)

How to have a good relationship is a subject that preoccupies our thinking. With all of our ability to break down matter into the tiny quark and to peer deep into the enormity of the Universe, we simply have not been able to understand the intricacies and the mystery of significant relationships, especially the relationships between men and women.

Differences between the brain functions of men and women have been charted and analyzed. The impact of culture on each gender has been widely researched and traced back to ancient times. Popular quizzes and how-to manuals have been offered, endless books of relationship techniques have been written, advice columns appear in countless magazines and newspapers and nuances of behavior are explored in film and literature, but nothing has given us a complete and satisfying understanding of what actually happens in a significant relationship and how we can meet the challenge of achieving and maintaining lasting emotional closeness.

Perhaps the answer to this bewildering puzzle does not lie in dissecting the differences between men and women but rather in understanding the essential commonalities that we all share simply because we are human beings. Our common human experience and the issues we all face in our lives are far greater than any of the differences that distinguish us from each other. We are the same species. We have the same challenges and desires. We all share basic needs and feelings. We all want to feel love and connection. We all want to feel free and safe. We want our feelings to matter and to be able to determine our own fate. We want to feel accepting of ourselves and of the people we love.

1

The unique way each of us has learned to cope with our common human issues determines the types of relationships we establish and the way that we handle the situations and dilemmas that come up in those relationships.

The purpose of this book is to share with you a very simple, though certainly not easy, approach to something very complicated—how to have a good relationship, without anger and without blame. This book will serve as a guide to how to separate and untangle our minds so we can be cleanly and non-reactively connected to each other. In order to be successful in a relationship, it is necessary to understand our own Self and learn how to deal with our human issues. It is necessary, therefore, to explore what it means to be a human being.

There are many relationship books with simple and obvious techniques and suggestions that might make logical sense, yet they just do not work. If they worked, people would not keep buying more books, searching for the right answer. The authors of these books do not go deeply enough into exploring the real issues behind the feelings that come up for each of us in important relationships. They tell us to make sure we have fun together (and how do you have fun together if you are feeling angry or desperately hurt?), to "mirror" what the other person is saying (when we feel that we know what they are saying, but they are totally missing our point!) and how to say the right words (without helping us understand why the wrong words come out in the first place). These techniques often make us feel even more despairing about our relationships because something keeps us from being able to use them effectively, and so we fear there is no hope. The causes of the powerful feelings that overwhelm us and render logical behavior impossible are never addressed.

The cultural illusion that everything can be resolved with logic and willpower persists despite all the evidence that it is false when it comes to the realm of emotions and relationships. We need to explore why we are not being logical and why our willpower is not working. Logic and willpower are inadequate tools simply because they are not the appropriate tools for resolving the issues that come up in relationships. In our ignorance, we either blame ourselves or blame the other person—"It's all *my* fault!" or "It's all *your* fault!" If we do not have the correct tools for a job but try repeatedly to get that job done, we may come to the incorrect conclusion that the task is impossible and we might as well give up. This is not just unfortunate—it is a tragedy. People enter into relationships— marriage, parenthood, friendships, work—with the highest of hopes and intentions, yet face terrible disappointment and heartbreak simply because they are applying the wrong tools to the task. Our incredibly high divorce rates reflect this terrible misunderstanding and ignorance.

We all have complaints about our husband or wife, our mother or father, our sisters or brothers, our boss or co-worker—all of us feeling stuck, helpless, hurt, angry, victimized and at a complete loss as to what to do. All of us wonder what terrible misfortune, ignorance, short-sightedness (or downright deception on the part of the other!) landed us in such uncomfortable and "dysfunctional" relationships. All of us unhappy, but baffled about how to make those relationships better.

In this book, we are going to explore the mysteries of these close, important and bewildering personal relationships. We will be address-ing these issues in terms of a marital relationship, whether it is a con-ventional legal marriage or another arrangement in which two people choose to go through life together. The same principles, however, apply to all important relationships, for we are all triggered by similar issues in any relationship that matters. If we can find a way to talk about these issues, we can apply it to every relationship in our life.

Feel free to substitute the terms that apply most accurately to your situation: husband, wife, significant other, partner, boss, teacher, mother, father, son, daughter, brother, sister, checker at the market or driver in a nearby car! (Even the behaviors of a stranger may stir up strong feelings.) Whoever triggers us is a vehicle for our growth.

The language we use in this book primarily addresses creating emotional closeness in an important relationship, but the concepts of this book can be applied to any relationship that triggers your issues. You can think of using these concepts as tools to create a more successful, less stressful relationship with whomever you find yourself involved.

For the purposes of simplicity, we are going to refer to the person with whom our feelings and issues get stirred up as "our Other." "Our Other" serves as the catalyst for our learning.

Responsibility equals **power**, not fault!

Jan: I don't know about you, but I don't like the thought of being a victim. I don't want to be dependent on my Other being centered and adult. I like to think that there is always something I can do, or could have done, to make a situation better. Not that I should have known to do it—sometimes it takes a difficult situation to wake me up and teach me more than I knew before it occurred.

People tend to mistake responsibility for blame. Responsibility, to us, is power. Fault does not exist. Everyone is doing the best they can with the knowledge they have.

We will seek to help you empower yourself by helping you understand your own emotional dynamics and reactions. This understanding and the tools we will give you in this book will help you become more knowledgeable and more at peace with who you are. While our Other is the catalyst for this learning and growth, no one need be blamed. But, we can all become more empowered by focusing on our Self. The wisdom that is available to each of us will allow us each to become the person we would like to be.

We are going to dive deep beneath the surface of relationship strife to get a true understanding of what is really going on. Only when we can identify and understand the issues that get stirred up in our own Self will we be able to apply logic and untangle the issues that occur in our most important relationships. This understanding will allow us to grow beyond the confusions and hurts we all experience in relationships so we will be free to love.

While the answers are really quite simple—you will be surprised!—applying what we learn will be challenging. But not too challenging.

CHAPTER 1

I Have the Right to Exist

All of us want love. It is a cultural passion. Did you ever notice how much our movies, songs, products and the advertising used to promote them are based on the theme of love with the goal of increasing our attractiveness and our ability to find and keep a mate? We dream of that magic moment where our eyes meet those of a gorgeous stranger and we can fall deeply, deliriously and permanently in love. We long for a marriage that will last forever, bringing us all the happiness and satisfaction we could ever hope for . . . . *Is that asking for too much?*

Oh, and by the way, it should also happen naturally and easily. No struggles, no misunderstandings—just peaceful, effortless, passionate bliss and love. Forever.

Which brings us to the difference between a person and an ice cream cone. (We will pause here for you to double check the cover of this book . . . . Yes, it was written by two doctors of psychology! Now, back to that difference.) We human beings do fall in love. With many things. Who has not exclaimed passionately, "I loved that movie!" "You'll love the food at that restaurant." "We just love our new couch!" Things can bring up a feeling of bliss, even if only momentarily. The difference (are you ready?) between love of an object and love of a person is that objects are static. They have their loveable qualities but little else. There are few surprises with *things*. If you eat your favorite chocolate ice cream, you experience a feeling of bliss. Chances are that the next time you eat it, you will have that same feeling. The ice cream has not changed. You can count on it being exactly the same as it was the last time you ate it. You can safely experience your bliss without any shock of surprise.

A person, on the other hand, is ever changing and multi-dimensional. We each have aspects of ourselves that even we do not know about. Throughout our whole life, we will continue to learn about ourselves and discover feelings and thoughts that have been previously unrecognized. Although these feelings and thoughts lie beneath our conscious awareness, they are extremely powerful and direct our behaviors—especially in important relationships—more than we realize. This fact will not be a problem if we understand and accept it. So before we can even begin to understand marriage and other significant relationships, we must start at the very beginning and try to understand ourselves and the nature of our life as a human being.

I am the only constant in my life, the center of my Universe

> ### Exercise
> Here is a physical experiment to prove that you are the center of your Universe: Stand up. With your eyes open wide, turn around in a full circle. What is the center of that circle? Do you notice that everything in the entire Universe stretches out before you, no matter which way you look?

One thing is absolutely clear—even if we do not feel this way, we are each the center of our own personal Universe. People and experiences come and go, but we always remain. We are each the one constant in our life, the one element that never goes away, from the moment of our conception to the moment of our death. No one else is here forever. This does not mean that we are the only important person in the world. We are, however, the center of our own experience.

When we come together in a relationship, this will still be true. We are each the center of our own experience. Even if we are each adamantly clear about our own "reality," it may not occur to either of us that we are not experiencing exactly the same thing. We are each in a different body, with different personal experiences and histories, different tastes and different connotations and meanings to words and events. While it tends to be surprising that we may each have a different reality, it is unavoidably true and not up for argument.

I have the right to exist

Just as it is a given that we are the center of our own experience of reality, every human being has the right to exist—we were born and like every living being, it is our turn to walk this Earth and have a life. This is not something we have earned or need to work to deserve—it is simply a reality. Life on this planet, from the amoeba to the elephant, includes you and me. Does the amoeba ever think, "I don't deserve to be here. I have to help other amoeba and accomplish great things or else I am worthless"? If you throw a ball to a dog, does that dog ever think, "I am not worthy of having a ball. I don't deserve to chase it"? Why, then, should we have those kinds of thoughts? Are we less deserving and valuable than amoebas or dogs?

For whatever reason, we are alive now. Whether or not we will ever make sense of our existence, the irrefutable fact is—here we are! Just as a baby has value, so do we. A baby must do nothing to earn our love. Our hearts instinctively respond with tenderness to babies. Our natural, innate, inherent value never changes, regardless of how old we are, the struggles we have or the knowledge we gain. We will always have the same basic right to be here as we did when we were born.

A baby's job

All life grows from smaller to bigger, from less whole to more whole. Animals (of which we are one species) seek safety and comfort and also grow from ignorance to knowledge. We come into life as babies and grow toward wisdom and maturity.

When babies feel safe, they naturally are curious and want to learn and try things. They delight in their discoveries—the sights and sounds of the world around them and the movements and experiences of their body. Babies do not think about accomplishing tasks. They do not evaluate their progress. They simply experience life and grow. They do not have a "purpose" of proving themselves valuable, helping others or accomplishing goals.

Babies are naturally the center of their own life.. It is a given. They have not been shamed or trained that it is "selfish" to think of themselves. They are immersed in their own experience. Their job is to discover themselves and to discover the world.

As adults, we can remember that just like babies, we are here journeying from birth to death, having lots of experiences and learning lots of things. Just like babies, we are naturally growing and evolving in consciousness and wisdom, becoming as whole and complete a person as we can. Every new situation we encounter as adults takes us right back to the experience of being a baby, for we are once again ignorant, not yet having had the actual experience that would educate us. Remembering this, we can have the same patience and acceptance for ourselves that we have for babies. Even in the midst of struggling, we can accept the rightness of our efforts. "Oh, look how cute! I'm trying to learn_____."

Knowing that we are evolving, growing beings, we can work toward dispensing with anger, judgment and hurt, putting in their place curiosity about the world and our own experiences and reactions. We can each become a compassionate scientist with our life and development the subject of our observations.

Babies are born to imperfect parents

> Jan: I used to be very critical of parents. I identified with children and was often upset when I observed parent-child interactions. And then, I became a parent . . . Suddenly things were very complicated. Emotionally involved with my children, nothing seemed simple anymore. Everything tugged at my heart and logic was hard to find, let alone follow.

If every new experience brings us back to being a beginner, or a baby, then parents are babies, too, having never been parents before. Babies raising babies. We can forgive ourselves and our parents, for we are all doing the best we can. While we do not need to blame anyone, it is important to understand how we are affected by our childhoods.

> Jan: I have always liked being able to talk with my kids about things that happened in their childhood. It always feels like a gift to them to help them understand how some of their struggles or misperceptions about the world exist because of my limitations as their mother. I tell them that they were babies and didn't know any better, so they

can't be critical of themselves. I was the adult, but I didn't know any better, either. Together, we can look at not only the helpful and unhelpful things that I did and that I taught them, but also at how to understand what they still have to learn. I know that by giving them this foundation of making sense of their history, feelings and reactions, I am helping them let go of any judgment they might have of themselves, replacing it with the reality that for all of us, forever, life is about continuing to grow.

What our parents did in their ignorance impacts what we learned and how we feel about ourselves. We do not have to blame or be angry with our parents, but it is important to be clear about why we have the patterns and feelings we do, or we will think something is wrong with us.

If you are alive, you are vulnerable

The fact that we are evolving, developing beings means that none of us has everything about ourselves or our lives in perfect order. Because we will always be growing and evolving, we are vulnerable—visible in our humanness. There is no way that we can prevent ourselves from the reality that anything could happen to us at any time. Vulnerability is a fact of existence for all living beings.

Al: When I was eight years old, I was riding my bike home from a baseball game I had just played. Thinking about the game, I pulled into my driveway and ran into a large rock that I hadn't noticed. As I fell off my bike and hit the pavement, I screamed bloody murder and began to cry. My mother came rushing out and asked me where I was hurt. I told her I was okay, but the reality was that in that split second when I hit the ground, I had realized, for the first time in my life, how vulnerable I was. I could have hit my head and been killed. As small an event as this was, I was never the same afterward.

We instinctively try to avoid the feeling of vulnerability. No one likes the thought that it is an inevitable part of being alive. Each of us has developed a strategy for how it can be avoided.

Exercise: Have you ever had any thoughts like these?

- If I please everyone, they won't get mad at me and I will be safe.
- If I never get upset or angry, people will like me.
- If I don't make any mistakes, people will not criticize me.
- If I take care of everyone, I will have a place in the world and people will want to be with me.
- If I never show my feelings, people won't be able to judge me and I will feel safe.
- If I remain overweight, no one will want to date me and I won't get hurt.
- If I act intimidating, people won't see my fear.
- If I smile all the time, people won't see how I really feel.
- If I criticize people first, they won't criticize me.
- If I am quiet, people won't notice me.
- If I eat all the right things, exercise, and think positively, I won't get sick.
- If I am a perfect driver, I won't have a car accident.
- If I dress well and have my hair (and make-up) just right, no one will see how insecure I am.
- If I make a lot of money, people will see me as important and won't judge me.
- If I am really outgoing and funny, people won't see how inadequate I feel.
- If we follow the right parenting rules, our children won't have problems.
- If I am a good person, nothing bad will happen to me.

All of these thoughts reflect our desire to protect ourselves from being vulnerable. Because being vulnerable is a fact of existence, as is being the center of our own experience, any attempt to avoid it will result in the distortion of reality. It is impossible to have a solid life if it is based on a distorted reality. Reality tells us that we must accept ourselves in all our humanness because although we may continue to learn and grow throughout our life, we can only be who we are at this point in time.

Jan: Al's sister came to visit us. We were so excited, and cleaned and shopped to prepare for her. Shortly after arriving, she announced that she wanted to take a bath. I decided to call a friend while she bathed, but it was only moments before she was back upstairs, rummaging in our closet. Next thing I knew, to my horror, she was marching downstairs, arms laden with cleaning supplies, to better clean our tub. She never said a word. I clutched the phone like a lifeline, describing to my friend what was happening. I was in an absolute agony of shame. It was all I could do to not rush downstairs to apologize and tell her I'd clean it for her. I felt so exposed and embarrassed that my standard of "clean" wasn't good enough for her. I didn't know how I could ever face her again.

An animal senses his vulnerability as danger. Like all animals, we experience being vulnerable as a threat that we will be killed. How many times have you said and heard other people say, "I thought I'd just die!" when something happened that exposed our humanness? Our logical minds know that we will not really die if we get a traffic ticket, get passed over for a promotion, have acne, trip and fall down . . . . but when these things happen, we usually feel exposed and experience a deep sense of shame. We can tell ourselves that these kinds of things happen to everyone, but that does not make the embarrassment, shame, or sense of vulnerability go away. Like an animal separated from the herd, we feel exposed, helpless and endangered.

Our search for perfection is an attempt to control our world in order to avoid feeling helpless and vulnerable. We have made up the concept of perfection—it certainly does not exist in the real world!—as the answer to how we can keep ourselves from ever feeling vulnerable again. But because we can never attain perfection, what we think will be the armor that will protect us becomes a plague that constantly makes us feel more vulnerable. We are guaranteed to fail at being perfect and this increases our sense of inadequacy, vulnerability and fear. Only by accepting our true state of humanness can we put "perfection" in its place. It is a concept to inspire us, not a condition we will ever attain. Whatever our culture or family might tell us and expect of us, however sincerely we commit ourselves to follow a life path of growth and change, to really think that we will ever become perfect is stepping outside of what is humanly possible.

Our desire to conform and not be noticed is also just an attempt to control our world in order to avoid feeling helpless and vulnerable. We try to not exist, to not stick out, from the same fear of feeling exposed and endangered. In response to the danger of our world, we disappear deep inside of ourselves so we do not attract negative attention. The threat of being judged feels like the threat of death.

Our world is judgmental

We live in a judgmental world. Even if our parents and friends are accepting and loving, we still are affected by the world in which we live. Our culture tells us that the right to exist is conditional. For some of us, the condition is some ever-shifting standard of adequacy that always leaves us with the sense that we have fallen short. Others of us fall prey to the cultural myth that it is possible to be perfect and so we feel judged for our imperfections. Even if no one else knows, each of us is intimately aware of how imperfect we are and how inadequate we feel, so we live in terror of being discovered, exposed to the world as the worthless beings we fear we truly are. Even if we escape judgment one time, there is always the next. We are not good enough and so we hide our true selves in shame and fear. It is hard to feel that we have the right to exist.

What makes life even more terrifying is that everyone else seems to be just fine. No one else talks about problems in their marriages or with their children. They seem so self-confident and sure of themselves. Wanting to believe that it is possible to avoid the experience of vulnerability, we accept their presentations as reality and pretend to be just like them. We cover our private struggles with public faces, smiling that we are just fine, too, and so are our marriage and our family. Everyone walks around hiding and disguising their vulnerability to protect themselves. It is one of those private secrets—each of us, side by side, suffering with self-judgment and fear of the judgment of others.

We worry about how we look and try to bolster our self-image so we do not sink into the fear that eats away at us any time it gets the chance—something is wrong with me. I am not okay, not good enough, pretty enough, handsome enough, smart enough, rich enough . . . the list is endless. "I have a pimple" = "My life is over." We criticize and blame each other, trying to find ways to reassure ourselves that things are not our fault so we will not feel the shame and worthlessness of not being good enough. We spend day after day in the pursuit of trying to feel as though we have the right to be alive.

Our culture does not help us to understand and accept individual differences and the wide range of human looks and behavior. Instead, it presents us, through the media, with a clear idea of what is considered "normal": actors, athletes and models who enact the cultural role of being "together." There is only one little problem—they portray make-believe people, fabricated out of our hope that if we try hard enough, it is possible to attain perfection. But we have no script to read to guide us. Unlike our heroes, we face life armed with no prompters feeding us every line, every action. Comparing ourselves to these smooth and practiced beings, we feel worthless, as though there is something shameful about just being who we are.

Our culture plays on our fears and insecurities. We have been trained to follow. We have never been trained to look into our own Self and trust what is there. We go to school and learn all about the thoughts and discoveries of the past thousands of years. But never, ever, are we taught to look inside of ourselves. We do not learn about our emotions or how to take care of them. We are emotionally ignorant. And so, of course, we are scared of our emotions. Like little children who are scared of the monsters that lurk in the dark, we are frightened of what lurks inside of us. And because it is never talked about, we cannot understand it. We feel as though something must be wrong with us so we do not dare reveal this inner darkness to anyone else.

We are disconnected from our deepest, truest Self. Our culture does not know to support us in being conscious. Our species just has not evolved that far yet, so there is an incorrect assumption about what it means to be human. The reality is that we have no limit to what we can learn emotionally, intellectually and spiritually—we have endless potential.

Judgment is based on a profound misunderstanding about what it means to be alive. It does not accept our right to exist exactly as we are, as evolving, growing beings.

Measuring up

Human beings, like all life forms, have an innate imperative to grow. Cells divide and our bodies get larger. We have experiences and grow in wisdom and knowledge. We stretch ourselves, physically and mentally and it feels good. We get satisfaction from trying hard and succeeding. We all feel a natural rejoicing not only in what we are able to do but also in our efforts. As children, we feel pure pleasure and fascination with our development. A toddler who tirelessly works to stand alone is just as pleased with himself as is the child who, having learned how to skip, skips everywhere.

Judgment is sneaky. It slips into our thinking and robs us of our joy in just being alive. We no longer look at what is and celebrate—we look at what could be and say it's what should be, so that what we do and who we are is never enough. Judgment dooms us to failure for it says perfection is a goal that is attainable. Judgment measures us against an ever-changing and unreal standard that is based on a fantasy born of fear and hope.

Judgment promises an end to feeling vulnerable by giving us the illusion of control. "If I can just perfect myself or reach a certain standard of accomplishment or being, then I will feel safe. Bad things will not happen and life will be the way I want it to be." Self-criticism and judgment can also be our attempt to protect ourselves: "If I do not expect much in life, then I will not be disappointed."

"Measuring up" is a tool that is absolutely unnecessary in life and yet it intrudes everywhere. Everyone struggles with their inner measuring. "I'm not pretty enough, smart enough, tall enough, talented enough . . . ." "That man (or woman) is too good for me." And, once we are in a relationship, we begin to measure our Other to see if they are good enough. "My husband is not as kind as her husband." "My wife is so much more critical than his wife."

We can never measure up enough to feel at peace with ourselves, for we will never attain the ideals we can envision. Like the proverbial donkey striving for the carrot dangling in front of him, we strive unsuccessfully for accomplishments and success that will forever be out of our reach. Judgment is condemning and can never be satisfied. Judgment tells us that we do not deserve happiness or to have good things in our lives because we do not measure up and therefore do not have the right to exist just as we are.

Self-esteem and self-worth

Lack of self-worth and self-esteem is commonplace in our world of judgment. Why is that? Why would so many of us have such a low opinion of ourselves? Does a baby have poor self-esteem or think he is not worth much? Babies blissfully make all kinds of body sounds and messes, wake us up at awful hours and do practically nothing useful except, perhaps, provide some entertainment. But they do not worry about their value, and we, their doting parents, adore them just as they are.

At some point, however, we become aware of our vulnerability and begin the futile attempt to protect ourselves by engaging in the hopeless pursuit of perfection. We stop adoring each other and open ourselves to the world of judgment.

Judgment is tricky and is delivered in many styles:

- Scathing: "You are a low-life, disgusting human being."
- Helpful: "You know, if you added a scarf, that outfit wouldn't look quite that stupid."
- Righteous: "It isn't surprising to me that someone like you would have done that."
- Angry: "I'm sick of your stupid mistakes!"
- Hurt: "You never care about my feelings, only your own."
- Sweet and loving: "Bless your heart, but you're ugly."

Judgment can also come in disguise. "Self-worth" and "self-esteem" are two of those disguises. They are insidious and sneaky challenges to our basic right to exist. They seem like they are positive goals to strive for, but they are actually internalized tools of judgment that we use to measure ourselves. The right to exist is our birthright, a fact of existence just because we are alive. It must simply be recognized and accepted. Self-worth and self-esteem say that if you meet some ideal or standard, you will have the right to exist—they pose as the vehicle to achieving the right to exist. But this is a false system. You can only claim the right to exist, not earn it. Insecurity, hopelessness and despair are the only results of pursing self-worth and self-esteem.

Self-Worth/Self-Esteem	Right to Exist
I am valuable because I am handsome.	I like to look good, but it's not relevant to my value.
I am embarrassed because I don't have a better job.	I am disappointed I don't have a better job, but that has nothing to do with who I am.
I am important because I have a good job.	I am happy that I like my job.
I think a good person is patient. I am ashamed that I lost my temper.	I am sorry I lost my temper.
A good mom always puts her child first.	Today I just didn't have a lot to give.

Statements of self-worth and self-esteem are always statements of judgment. They measure us to see if we have met some nebulous standard of acceptableness. They demand the presence of an undefined amount of positive qualities in order for us to feel good about ourselves. They trick us into objectifying ourselves, making ourselves "things" to be assessed, rather than evolving beings who living as the center of our Universe. Even when we make positive statements about ourselves, we stand outside of ourselves to evaluate our worth, rather than experiencing life from inside of ourselves, as a baby does.

The concepts of self-worth and self-esteem prey on our sense of being vulnerable and echo the judgment of the world that it is unacceptable to be a fallible, growing being. Because we are trying to attain the goals of having self-esteem and self-worth by traveling down the path of judgment, we can never reach the destination of being in self-acceptance just as we are. Not realizing we are traveling down the wrong road, we mistakenly think that something is wrong with us when we never are able to feel accepting of ourselves.

We need to focus on staying on the path of self-acceptance and compassion. When we judge ourselves, we are constantly evaluating our self-esteem and self-worth. The path of compassion allows us to accept ourselves simply because we exist. Having the right to exist, we do not need to do anything to prove our value. Because we are evolving beings, we can lovingly guide ourselves to live in a way that makes us feel strong and proud of ourselves. Self-esteem and self-worth say "I can only feel good about myself if I have certain qualities and abilities." The right to exist says "I have compassion for myself and accept myself simply because I am human."

Compassion frees us from judgment

Al: Think about how odd it really is that when we make a natural and innocuous body sound, we all apologize! Take the burp, for example. Why is it considered offensive, a transgression necessitating apology? It's just a sound. In some countries, it's actually a compliment. When our son, Seth, was very young, we tried to teach him basic manners, as all parents do. One day, when he burped, we asked, "Seth, what do you say when you burp?" Not yet shamed into judgment about what is "proper" behavior and seeing a burp as just a burp, he replied to our question by obligingly replicating the sound: "A-a-a-a."

Jan: Our granddaughter really understands this. When her teacher asked her, "Paisley, what do you say when you burp?" Paisley was bewildered, and finally answered with the only thing that made sense, "You're silly!"

The alternative to living a life based on judgment is living a life based on compassion and the right to exist. We can accept that we are evolving beings with the right to be more ignorant now than we will be in the future. We can accept that we have the right to exist and the right to learn and grow. This allows us to feel the same kindness to support ourselves as we change, learn and grow that we would feel in helping a child to grow.

> *Al: Judgment would have said to Seth, "It's not nice to burp like that!" Compassionate would say to Seth, "Some people don't like to hear burps, so we say, 'Excuse me!'"*

No one responds well to being shamed and beaten. When we treat ourselves with compassion and understanding, we maximize our chances to grow. We are affirming that we already have the right to exist just as we are.

> *Jan: I used to beat myself black and blue (emotionally, that is— remember, I don't like pain!) over things that I realized, in hindsight, that I had done (or not done). I would judge every word, every tone in my voice, every act, agonizing, writhing in self-condemnation over everything that didn't meet my standard of how I wanted to be. I felt such shame at being exposed in my imperfections.*
>
> *Then, during a term in graduate school, everything changed. I was a teaching assistant, and had just been criticized by students in a class I was leading. When I told a fellow T.A. about sitting there feeling terrible about myself, knowing that I was capable of every critique leveled at me, I was stunned by her response. She said "Oh, Jan. Don't you know this isn't about you? They're just anxious!" That thought had never occurred to me!*
>
> *The next day was the beginning of a new semester, and I stood outside the classroom door, reminding myself that at some point, their anxiety would turn on me, but it wouldn't be about me. I opened the door, walked in and said, "Hi. I'm Jan. I'm the T.A." One of the class members turned slowly toward me and said, "You b#*ch." He proceeded to lay into me ferociously. I thought, "Have we met?" and sat there listening to him, so relieved to know that what he was saying had nothing to do with me! Had I not had the conversation with my friend, I would have sat there thinking self-critical thoughts: "I must have sounded arrogant when I announced I was the T.A." "Maybe I interrupted them rudely." The absurdity of that experience freed me and took me off the path of judgment and onto the path of compassion.*

Goals and ideals can give us positive direction for our life but do not need to hang over our heads, always threatening self-condemnation.

We do not have to spend our life measuring, comparing and judging ourselves. We can accept that we each grow at our own pace, in our own way, and simply congratulate ourselves for our growth and rejoice in the experience of becoming wiser and more knowledgeable, knowing that this is the human journey and that nothing is wrong with us.

We are not unusual. Whatever feelings and challenges we face are human feelings and challenges and we can refuse to punish ourselves or allow anyone else to punish us for being human. We can live our life in kindness and compassion, knowing that whatever we are going through is a natural part of being alive.

Judgment and analysis are two different tools

If the dictionary were really accurate, we would look under "human" and see the definition: "Human: An evolving being who journeys from ignorance toward knowledge of self and the world." (Notice that we did not say that we journey *to* knowledge but rather that we journey *toward* knowledge.) We are limited beings. We will never be able to become all that we can envision. The reality is that things do not always turn out as we hope or expect. We learn from hindsight—we have an experience and then have the opportunity to analyze it and refine our knowledge.

We all have things we would like to be able to do better. They might be tasks at work, being able to speak to our spouse or child without impatience or anger, or eating in a more healthy way. When we are stuck on the path of judgment, it is painful to become aware of ourselves or think about things we would like to change, for when we see a *flaw*—a part of ourselves that is not as refined or developed as we would like—we become self-critical or feel ashamed or bad about ourselves. Anytime we are revealed in our humanness, we are reminded of how "inadequate" we really are and we feel exposed. How embarrassed we become if we even sneeze vehemently! *"Excuse* me!"

There is a difference between judgment and analysis. Judgment puts everything in terms of right and wrong, good and bad. Analytical thinking makes no value judgments—it impartially and logically considers things, weighing cause, effect, price and consequence. Judgment teaches us that we are unworthy, unimportant, inferior and inadequate. Analytical thinking challenges us to grow, to expand our awareness, knowledge and abilities.

Example: Judgment: "I shouldn't have gotten angry at my husband. I am a bad person."

Analysis: "What made me angry? I guess I felt hurt and didn't know how to express it."

Judgment tears us down and is negative. Analysis educates us and is positive. Judgment punishes us for being human and ignorant. Analysis has compassion for us as evolving beings. The result of judgment is shame and paralysis. Seeing ourselves as bad and inferior, we feel frozen and stuck, knowing that it is impossible to magically transform and be different. The result of analysis is that we can have compassionate understanding for our feelings and reactions. Compassion allows us to use hindsight—analyzing an unsatisfying situation to gain greater knowledge. Analysis gives us insight into ourselves. Simply sharing what we have discovered allows us to both change ourselves and shift relationship dynamics.

Example: "I'm sorry I got angry at you. What was really going on with me was that I was feeling hurt and I didn't know what to do with that feeling or how to tell you."

Identifying and sharing our awareness of ourselves is always an act of self-acceptance and a rejection of the underlying premise of judgment that says who we are is not good enough.

Creating a Self without judgment

As soon as we are conceived, every need we have is met instantly by our mother's body. From her comes sustenance for our growth and survival. We do not need to do anything. When we are born, however, all of this changes. No longer connected physically to our mother, we must take action to get our needs met. We learn that when we cry, someone comes and attends to us. We learn that calling attention to ourselves brings response. It is not always a positive response, unfortunately, but the lesson is still there—we exist.

Paying attention to our needs is a natural act—every baby cries when in physical or emotional discomfort—but in our world where the right to exist is often conditional and threatening to others, we may face the judgment of others who have been trained out of their right to speak for themselves.

The essential task of childhood is to create a Self—a sense of *me*. Therefore, a child is, of necessity, self-involved. It is a developmental imperative. Note, for example, a baby's fascination with his fingers and toes. "Wow! Look at me! Look what I have! Look what I can do! How cool is this?"

The task to create a solid Self begins in childhood but never really ends. Throughout our life we are faced with new situations in which we must constantly be discovering and affirming our own reality. We must always be looking to find our own feelings and needs, where our toes end and the rest of the world begins. Each new situation presents a new lesson to be learned, a new challenge to expanding our awareness of who we each are. With each new situation comes the necessity to affirm our right to exist, for confronted with our separateness and the existence of someone else, we will always face the temptation to disappear into fear or self-judgment rather than risk loss.

Finding and affirming our true Self is the life-long task of human development. Because we are and will always be evolving beings, our growth from being more ignorant and inexperienced toward being more evolved, experienced and knowledgeable is an inevitable part of our life. In every new situation, we will have the opportunity and the necessity to learn or our lives will be driven and determined by our ignorance and fear.

If we can accept this reality, we can feel peace and relief, knowing that nothing is wrong with us. Whenever we feel lost or ignorant, we do not ever need to judge ourselves as inadequate or imperfect or to see if we measure up to some arbitrary standard of acceptableness. Even though we initially might be overwhelmed, we are just facing a new challenge in life. We are once again in the position of being inexperienced.

Jan: When Seth was three, frustrated at not being able to tie his shoes, he began to hit himself on his head. I was horrified. We had never modeled turning our helplessness into anger against ourselves. This incident made me realize that we must naturally fight our helplessness, and the most natural target of that fight is our own Self.

As long as we are alive, we will be presented with new challenges that require stretching ourselves and learning. We have no choice about this—it is an essential aspect of being human. We are helpless to change this reality and do not need to turn against ourselves in anger or in judgment.

And it is in our important, significant relationships that we are especially challenged by this necessity to learn and affirm our right to exist with compassion and self-acceptance.

CHAPTER 2

Why Can't You Just
Be Like Me?

I f I have the right to exist and you, also, have the right to exist—which makes sense—what on Earth do we do when we discover our differentness, when our needs, perceptions and ideas are not the same? If we love each other, why do we get so upset when we notice that differentness? Why is it such a challenge to have our own Self, our own feelings and our own needs and coexist with someone else who has their own Self, their own feelings and their own needs?

It all started with Mom

Our first experience in life, which happens as soon as conception has occurred, is being fused with our mothers. This state of *fusion*—a sense of oneness—is our only point of reference. It is inseparable from "life." We come into existence in the state of fusion—it is our foundation. We have never had any other experience. There is nothing to compare it with. It is beyond consideration or question. At the cellular level, it is our standard for all experience.

We are connected to mother and know nothing of separateness. Everything that our mother feels creates a different chemical that goes through our body as well as hers. Intertwined with our experience of life is the experience of sameness, of oneness, of literally feeling what another is feeling. Fusion is synonymous with life, itself. And "Mom" is the first of many *fusion objects* we will have during our lifetime.

At the moment of conception, we begin the process of becoming a separate individual. We grow until we can no longer remain inside of our mothers without the risk of death for both of us and so we are born. Separating is necessary for life, but the pull of fusion will always remain in us, calling us back to our origins, to that familiar and blissful state of oneness in which we first came into life and consciousness. Fusion is an instinct and is imprinted on our very cells. It will always pull at us to return "home."

> *Jan: I have a vision of myself, a single-celled amoeba in the roiling primordial seas of the newly created Earth, watching with horror as I begin to subdivide. Shrieking hideously, I clutch at myself to prevent the end to this effortless simplicity of oneness . . . . And, later, I feel myself, a contented sea creature that feels the imperative to move toward land. I hold fiercely and piteously to an undersea rock, sobbing and protesting, "I don't want legs!"*

This urge toward fusion, comfort, the familiar, the womb, toward passivity, contentment, stupor, the status quo makes us fervently and intuitively resist separating. Reinforced with the adrenaline surge accompanying change that we have learned to label "fear," this urge toward fusion can only be transcended by the one force that is more powerful—the urge toward growth. These are the two forces whose interplay shapes our lives. Every time the urge toward growth emerges, our fusion needs wage a terrible battle, no holds barred, to stay put.

Finding balance

For our whole lives, we will move along the continuum between fusion and *separateness*, or individuation—becoming an individual and having our own Self. With every experience or feeling, we will travel back and forth along this continuum. Sometimes we will enjoy the closeness and comfort of intimate fusion, while other times we will move in our own direction and experience our separate needs and wants.

Both fusion and separateness are natural parts of being alive. Each of us, however, tends to become stuck at one end of the continuum or the other. We need to learn to move fluidly and appropriately between these two states of being. Every relationship and situation we encounter after we are born is an exercise in mastering this challenge.

The journey along the fusion-separateness continuum is a challenging one for us and for our parents. The parents' ability to move appropriately is a major determinant in the development of the baby. There are three basic experiences a child can have. Each one brings its own lessons for not only the parent-child relationship, but also for future intimate relationships. See if you can tell which experience of the following experiences you had.

Healthy fusion, healthy separation

Healthy fusion is an important part of an infant's life. It is the experience of feeling comforted and safe because of the attention the mother gives him. The mother needs to fuse with her baby in order to be able to make her needs secondary and give him the care he requires to thrive. Her attention lets him know that he is important and that his needs matter. This experience of healthy fusion in infancy builds a solid foundation of Self and security that will last throughout the baby's entire life.

As the baby grows and starts to move along the continuum toward greater separateness, both mother and child experience freedom and relief, but loss, as well. The reality of being two separate people is exciting and full of possibilities and yet it sometimes stretches the heart and is painful as we have to let go of each other. Take the kindergartner who cries on being left at school and the mother who chokes back her tears until she arrives at her car.

> *Jan: Well, I have to admit that's what I did. Megan was just fine, but I was broken-hearted!*

> *Al: I cry when Jan drops me off at work.*

As much love and joy as we may experience with a child, the reality is that they are not the center of our existence—they are separate from us and are only passing through our life.

> *Jan: I remember passing a mirror as I was holding Seth, our first baby, when he was only a few weeks old. Catching our reflection, I was stopped cold, stunned by a shocking realization: "You're going to leave me! I need to keep my own life!" Even in the middle of new-mom bliss,*

I saw the reality that my time of "holding" my son would be short. He had his own destiny and would have to leave me to follow it.

As close and loving as relationships might remain between parents and children, the time always comes when children must venture out into the world to find themselves and their own paths. This is no reflection on the love between them and their parents. It is the inevitable course of human development. No matter how close to each other they live or how many values and preferences they share, separation and individuation occur—they each like different flavors of ice cream, watch different kinds of movies, and dress and decorate their bodies and hair in different styles.

The experience of separating can be an exciting and satisfying one for both parent and child if there is no misunderstanding about it. It is a cause for celebration when a child is born—a new and precious life has entered existence. The marvel and wonder of it moves many parents to tears. However, when that new and wondrous life gets a mind of its own, it is a sign of growth, not of trouble between those once teary parents and this newly opinionated being.

Jan: For two years, Al and I deliberately avoided the word "no" with Seth. We would redirect him into more appropriate or necessary behaviors, or when we could, we would take the time to sympathize with his feelings and explain our decisions. Then came the day when he went to a babysitter's house where there were some other children. He came home with a new word that clearly satisfied a huge need in him and caused him endless delight. "No!" he would exclaim when we asked him something—anything! "No!" he didn't want a cookie, as he eagerly reached for it. "No!" he didn't want to go visit his beloved Gramma as he raced to get into the car. "No! No! No!" He had his own reality, determined by his own wants and needs, not ours. He was Seth. Himself. Not-us. And was he ever thrilled with his existence.

Parents who foster healthy separateness will recognize and be prepared for their child's journey of separation. They will enjoy the closeness of the times of fusion and will still be ready to release their child to create his own separate and unique life. His process of separating will cause them no hurt, anger or confusion.

Healthy fusion, unhealthy separation

Jan: People used to cross large boulevards to see Seth, drawn by the joy that emanated from him. So when he was four, and began to separate, I was stunned and horrified by his willfulness and anger in pushing us away. I was hurt and tried everything I could think of to get back our sweet closeness. I wanted my angel back.

It is a natural thing for all living beings to seek closeness and to avoid pain, so it is common for both parents and children who have experienced positive and loving fusion to want to hold onto each other in order to avoid the heartache of separating. This makes the task of separating even harder. Pain can make both parent and child think that something is wrong with feeling separate and so they get stuck at the fusion end of the continuum.

Parents foster unhealthy separateness by remaining stuck in fusion, taking everything their children do personally and as a reflection of their children's feelings about them. These parents are not able to see that their child is on his own journey of learning and that this journey is not about or because of the parents. It is a child's developmental task to exist as a separate person. It is the parents' role to guide their children into greater consciousness and self-empowerment, but they need to allow children to have their own uniqueness. If children do not have the freedom and encouragement to be whoever they are, to explore themselves and life, even if they are different from their parents, they may get stuck in being a "good" boy or girl. A child might also react by rebelling and getting stuck in being "bad." Either way, the child will feel too much loss and fear to be able to separate and find his own true Self.

Stuck in fusion, there is no separate existence where each person has his own feelings and wants and can make his own unique choices. Stuck in fusion, no one can accept this separateness as right and natural. Children learn that their feelings are not rightfully theirs but rather determine their parents' well-being, which then affects the child's own sense of security and safety. These children feel responsible for taking care of their parents, to make sure that their parents are okay so that their parents will be able to take care of them.

> *Al: When I brought home my first report card, my father looked at my grades. I had gotten some A's, some B's and a C, and I felt pretty good about that. When I looked in his eyes, however, after he read my report card, I could see hurt and disappointment. He didn't say much, but I could tell that my performance in school had caused him pain. I knew that I had hurt him and let him down. Had he known how to be separate, he might have asked me how I felt about my grades and been happy for me that I was satisfied.*

Children want approval for just being themselves. While parents are crucial in helping to create the foundation for their child's life, children want to be released into the world with their parents' approval and encouragement to find their own way. When parents are stuck in fusion, the children are not supported in feeling that they are important just for who they are, or that their experiences in life are for themselves, not the parent. They do not receive encouragement to go out and create a life for themselves that feels right to them. They do not feel that they can explore and make their own choices without "hurting" their parents or having to pay the price of the loss of their parents' approval or love. These children become either pleasers or rebels. They cannot think about what they want or like. They are afraid of their parents' reactions. They have not had the support to know that it is normal to feel vulnerable when separating and that the parents like who their child is becoming.

Pleasers and rebels do not act for their own selves. They do not make choices based on what feels right to them. They react. Rebels react in anger against being held onto by their fusion object (parents, and later in life, friends and spouses). Pleasers react with fear about being different from their fusion objects. Both pleasers and rebels are in reaction to the parent, rather than acting from their own ideas, needs, and individuality.

Culturally common behavior and language can subtly communicate fusion without people realizing it. A parent might tell a beaming child that he is "proud" of him, but this statement reflects unhealthy separateness, for in fusion, the parent is claiming a part of whatever the child has done for himself. A statement of healthy separateness might be "I am impressed by what you did." In this statement, the parent has stepped out of his fusion, appreciating and looking at his child as a separate being, rather than claiming, through his words of fusion, a part of whatever his child did. As parents, we are witness to our children and their behavior. They are not who they are because of us—we do not have that kind of power.

> *Jan: I once explained this to a friend who regularly told her son she was proud of him. He always brushed her off with irritation. She soon had occasion to tell him she was so impressed with something he had accomplished . . . and his response was totally different. There was a long pause, and then for the first time he was able to receive what she said, saying with emotion, "Thanks, Mom."*

Without healthy separation, children cannot find their own life's purpose and may confuse feelings with obligation: "I love you, therefore I need to please you and be who you want me to be." Without healthy separation, it is impossible for children to have their own life when they are confronted by the existence and needs of someone else.

Unhealthy fusion, unhealthy separation

Some children have the experience of unhealthy fusion. They have no parent with whom to bond, experience healthy fusion and build a strong life foundation. Neither their mother nor their father may be emotionally or physically available to provide this important experience. Perhaps as babies, the parents were, themselves, without a positive fusion object to make them feel safe and wanted and so are unable to give what they did not receive. They may be stuck in narcissism, so stirred up in their own baby feelings, unresolved from their pasts, that they are unable to separate and see their own child as a current-day baby with current-day needs. Perhaps death has taken one of the parents and the other is unable to compensate for that loss, in addition to taking care of all of the other demands of life. Perhaps, in this world of single parents, the parent is just too overwhelmed with survival needs and responsibilities. Even worse, some children experience abuse or abandonment because they have parents who act out their pain in anger or violence, targeting their child. For these children, it is frightening to exist at all, let alone to be seen in their vulnerability—and they carry this fear into adult relationships.

Children who experience unhealthy fusion do not develop the right to exist. They do not learn that their needs are important and that they have the right to live for themselves. The message they receive is either that there is no room for who they are or that they are here for the benefit of their parents. These children learn that they have a place in the world not for who they are but for what they can do. Their role in life is focused around the needs of their parents and how well they can fulfill those needs: take care of their parents and make them feel good, or allow themselves to be the scapegoat for their parents' frustration and pain in life.

> *Al: When I was a young child, my mother told me, "If I have to tell you what I need from you, it's not worth it." Even as a little boy, I remember thinking that if I didn't somehow figure out what she needed without her telling me, I'd be in trouble. How could I ever do that? I made it my business to watch her carefully all the time so that I could learn how to anticipate what she needed. Her criticism and disapproval when I failed to anticipate her needs taught me that my life couldn't be focused around myself and my own needs and experiences, but that she had to be the center of my existence.*

Healthy separation cannot occur when there has been no healthy fusion. Children who have experienced unhealthy fusion may physically escape their situation, but they are unable to have the experience of healthy separation. They cannot rid themselves of the lessons that over time and with reinforcement have become part of their very cellular response system. The lessons they have lived with their parents have let them know, even without words, who they are and what to expect in a relationship. These expectations are conditioned responses—automatic, and beyond thought or awareness. These children do not have the right to exist and their purpose in life is to sublimate their needs to those of someone else. Even when these children are angry in reaction to this expectation, they are not free from it. Their task in adulthood, just as it is for all children, is to learn healthy separation.

Fusion is an instinct

All children will fuse with their parent, regardless of the parent's emotional availability. Fusion is inevitable—all animals do it. It is a survival mechanism. Baby ducks hatch and fuse with whomever or whatever is present, even if it is not a mother duck. This is not love. It is animal bonding that is a life-furthering instinct.

It can be very helpful for us to remember, as we are trying to find and accept our own Self, that we can be bonded or fused with someone and yet not like them or love them. Fusion is different than having a loving, reciprocal, emotionally intimate relationship. Someone may pull at our bonds of fusion, but we may experience anger or obligation, not love. Many of us get confused by this combination of intense connection but negative feelings toward our Other, whether a parent or anyone else with whom we have a significant relationship. Not understanding the dynamics of fusion, many people think that something is wrong with them for having their negative reactions and they feel guilty for not loving their Other. This kind of guilt is not a true feeling. It is a reaction against feeling trapped in fusion. Guilt covers up feelings of sadness, loss or anger that we may experience when we do not feel safe to separate from our Other and be our true Self.

The legacy of our fusion-separation experience

What we learned about separating in childhood directly transfers over to every significant relationship. We all internalized the messages we learned from our parents about who we are, our role in life and our right to exist. The system we grow up in with our parents determines the system we establish with our Other. We see our Other through the influence of our experiences in the past and we usually assume the same role we had with one of our parents, usually the one with whom we had the most difficult relationship. Although sometimes we take the opposite role, it is still not a centered stance of who we are but instead is a reactive position based on our past. Understanding our own experience with our parents of fusion and separating allows us to have a deeper understanding of the challenges we face in our current relationships.

Exercise

Below are questions to help you identify which fusion/separation model most closely fits your experience:

1. Healthy Fusion/ Healthy Separation
2. Healthy Fusion/ Unhealthy Separation
3. Unhealthy Fusion/ Unhealthy Separation

First, remember yourself as a young child. Pick the image or age that stands out the most to you. If you have trouble remembering, look at or think of a photo of yourself when you were young.

1. How old are you when you think of yourself as a young child?
2. What feelings do you see when you look at that child's face?

Now, ask yourself these questions:

Fusion questions:
1. Close your eyes and visualize the faces of your mom, dad or both. What feelings do you see expressed on their faces?
   * Feelings that indicate you had healthy fusion: They look happy, loving, adoring, accepting, proud, confident, peaceful, secure in themselves.
   * Feelings that indicate you had unhealthy fusion: They look disappointed, anxious, fearful, impatient, distant, overwhelmed, insecure, angry, burdened, weak, critical.
2. Do you get the feeling that they just loved you, without reservation?

Separateness questions:
"Yes" answers to these questions indicate unhealthy separateness:

1. Did I feel guilty when I asked my parents for something?
2. Did I feel responsible when my parents were disappointed, hurt, scared or insecure because of my actions or things I said?

3. Was I afraid of disappointing my parents or making them sad or angry?

4. Did I feel a haunting sense of doing something wrong to my parents when I set off to do something with a friend?

5. Did I feel responsible for taking care of my parents?

6. Did I feel responsible for their physical or emotional well-being?

7. Were either of my parents selfish?

8. Were my parents jealous of my successes or experiences?

9. Did I feel guilty when I had successes or experiences they were never able to have?

10. Were my parents angry or hurt in response to things I did or said?

"Yes" answers to these questions indicate healthy separateness:

1. Did I feel free to express my thoughts and ideas, and disagree with the opinions of my parents, throughout my childhood?

2. Did my parents support my ideas and needs even if when they felt uncomfortable?

3. Did they encourage me to try new and different things, even if they had never done them?

4. Were my parents delighted when I expressed myself?

5. Did my parents seem to respect me when I expressed opinions that were different from theirs?

6. When my parents said "No" to me, , did it seem like they were just trying to be good parents, even if I didn't agree with them?

7. Were my parents happy for me when I succeeded or was able to do things they never had the chance to do?

While you may have some mixed answers to the questions in this exercise, most likely you can see a pattern in the relationship you had with your parents. This exercise will give you an idea of the experience of fusion and separateness that you bring into all of your important relationships. Your unconscious assumptions about what to expect and how you will be treated in these relationships was established in the first few years of your life before you had the ability to realize what was happening. Becoming conscious of these expectations can help you identify and understand your reactions and feelings as you relate to people who are important to you now, whether those people are children, a spouse, friends, an employer, co-workers or strangers.

Regardless of which fusion-separateness model we had with our parents, all of us are pulled back and forth along the continuum between fusion and separateness. Fusion pulls us toward loving intimacy, both emotional and physical. Separateness pulls us toward independence—finding and expressing our true Self. Finding balance between the two, affirming our own right to exist as well as the rightness of our desire and longing for closeness is our life-long journey, one that we take with our most significant Others.

Scared of intimacy or scared to death?

As much as all of us want love in our life, the truth is that being so close to someone that they truly know who we are is scary. In fusion, there is no separate *me* and *you* to judge or even observe each other. The more we get to know each other and the more important the other person becomes, the scarier it is. People talk about "fear of intimacy." But all of us long to be close and loving with a special person and to feel accepted for our true selves. The fear is a much more primitive one—it is a fear of being vulnerable, stripped of all our usual societal protections of what we do or think and visible for who we are as a human being. We have the same animal instincts that associate "weakness" or vulnerability with death. So we hide the truth of ourselves, afraid we will be "killed" by the person we love and with whom we long to be intimate. We fear being rejected or judged, or that we will have to "disappear," since only one of us is able to exist.

This push-pull may feel confusing as we find ourselves trying to be as close as possible without scaring ourselves too much or without losing our freedom—ceasing to exist. If we are not aware of these primitive fears, we will do a fine balancing act—trying to maximize our closeness at the same time that we minimize our feelings of vulnerability, or danger. That is where the sudden need for space comes from. That is the source of our unexpected anger and blame when we want to do something different from what our Other wants us to do. Those angry feelings are our attempts to protect ourselves, to help us stay hidden and not expose our differentness. Like guilt, they are a response to feeling trapped in fusion, unable to separate.

The power of understanding the pull of fusion and the necessity for separateness is that we do not have to be reactive and fearful when feelings of anger or blame come up. We can support ourselves and each other in claiming our right to exist, and comfort each other through the scared and vulnerable feelings that are a natural part of being in a relationship.

Selfish or separate?

There seems to be an unwritten code of behavior in our culture that says, "I won't talk about my needs, and you won't talk about your needs, either." We make an unspoken and unconscious pact with our Other that neither of us will fully exist so that we will not have to feel separate or risk losing each other. If someone breaks that code, their Other often reacts in judgment and anger because they have been denying their own needs—how dare their Other speak up! "You think you're tired? What about me! I've been up since dawn, working my fingers to the bone." In other words, speak up at your own risk! Any need you can have, they can have bigger! Any suffering you have had, they have had, too! (Think that would make a good song?) It is easier to go along with and accept the belief system of our culture or our family—that speaking up in separateness is bad—than to risk being called selfish.

Our survival as a species depends on cooperation. There is a difference, however, between coming together as a group for a common goal and unnecessarily sacrificing our individuality out of the fear of being judged or abandoned. The instinct to blend in is a natural one, but it can make us become stuck in fusion. Standing out from the crowd and being noticed creates vulnerability. We are herd or group beings. What happens in a herd to those who straggle outside the group or who try to find their own way? They are much more vulnerable to being attacked from those outside the group or to be attacked from members of the group who are threatened by their differentness. We sacrifice being connected to ourselves in order to feel a part of our relationship, group or society. We are unconsciously acting on an instinctive impulse that has its place in being helpful for our physical survival but also contributes to our emotional self-betrayal.

While wanting to fit in, feeling frightened of being different and feeling safe when we are the same as those around us are natural instincts, it is also natural and right for us to be separate from our group, sometimes. When someone says what he wants, everyone becomes aware of their own separateness. Our instinctive desire to fuse makes this an uncomfortable experience and the easiest thing to do is try to keep the other person from triggering our discomfort by accusing him of being selfish. In other words, "You are not doing what I want you to do, so you are selfish." The truth is, "You are doing what you want to do and that makes me feel separate. I don't want to have to speak up for myself because that would make me feel vulnerable."

The term *selfish* is used as an attempt to control our Other without having to be vulnerable in declaring ourselves. Although people who do this seem controlling and judgmental and even may appear angry and rejecting, their behavior is most likely their reaction to feeling too frightened and vulnerable to simply speak for themselves.

We seem to have to choose between the safety of fusion and belonging and the chance to be more separate and whole. No one wants to be isolated and criticized for being seen as selfish, so we tend to hide our true Self and try to blend in, even if it means giving up what we truly want or believe.

> *Al: The first Christmas I spent with Jan and her family, her brother, Bruce, presented me with a Christmas wish list, after I had asked him what he might like for Christmas. It was a twenty item list, starting with a new stereo system and going down, pricewise, to a pair of socks. I couldn't believe how extremely selfish he was, and I told Jan that. I was an eighteen-year-old student and could afford almost nothing on that list. Jan encouraged me to just get him whatever I would like, whatever I could afford. I was embarrassed and uncomfortable about giving him something modest, with all the extravagant things on the list, for I thought he was being greedy and selfish.*
>
> *What actually happened was that he was thrilled with my gift, very happy that he got the pair of socks he wanted. It was my first experience of seeing that when a person expresses what he wants, he is not necessarily being selfish. Bruce told me later that just thinking about what he wanted and making the list had been a game and was so much fun for him. Getting the socks had been a bonus.*

In an important relationship, when one person speaks up about what they want, and the other does not feel like they have the right to do the same, they will feel trapped and suffocated. Just as it is impossible to stay underwater too long without bursting up to the surface to catch our breath so we can survive, so we cannot repress our existence without, at some point, bursting out of the cramped state of fusion.

When we do not have permission to separate and exist in the fullness of who we are, we minimize ourselves and may use the tool of manipulation to try to eke out a bit of existence for ourselves. In the absence of feeling supported and accepted in our right to exist and our separateness, we may use indirect means to try to get our Other to do what we want.

When we are unable to directly speak for ourselves, we turn to the use of fear and its variations, invoking shame, guilt and judgment. We tell people what they should do, rather than asking for what we are wanting. We tell them that a good person—someone who is not selfish—does the right thing (in other words, what we want them to do) rather than simply asking them to do something from our own right to exist. A parent may tell a child they are "good" when they say "Thank you" instead of helping their child understand about being in a relationship and why it feels good to people to be appreciated. When we use judgment to control our Other's behavior, we shift responsibility for our want to a higher realm—a rule or higher power—in an attempt to avoid the vulnerability of asking *as if we were important* in our own right and our feelings mattered.

We each have a Self. This Self is our beginning point, our home for this lifetime, the source of all of our awareness and needs. Our Self needs air, food, comfort, love—all "self-ish" needs. Everything we do comes from a need our Self has. It is impossible to not be "self-ish." If we were to anonymously give a million dollars to charity, it would be for self-ish reasons—something in us would be satisfied by what we did. A truly self-ish person will need their Other to be happy, too, for it would be painful to them if their Other were not. True self-ishness—connectedness to our own Self—will seek everyone's well-being.

We are concerned that if we say, "I deserve good things" what others will hear is "I am the *only* one who deserves good things." Who wants to hear, "What makes you think you're so special?" But there is a difference between saying "I exist"—a statement of Self—and "I am the *only* one who exists"—a statement of narcissism.

A statement of Self is the beginning of an exploration of everyone's needs, not an ultimatum that one person's needs are the *only* ones that are important. An awareness that "I want dessert!" is only self-involved or narcissistic if there is no willingness for anyone else to need something different. "I want dessert!" is just a statement of desire that may precede an the question, "What would you like?"

It is impossible to have a successful relationship if we do not have the right to exist and to be separate. We may be frightened that we will not be wanted for who we are, but it is only by taking this risk that we have the chance to establish an emotionally intimate relationship that supports the well-being of both people. Separateness is a condition of being alive. When we separate, we can clearly feel our own Self and all our self-ish needs, including our love and desire to be close to our Other and our need for our Other to live as a whole and complete being with their own right to exist.

CHAPTER 3

Understanding Gender Differences Helps Us Separate

We want to start this discussion with a disclaimer. As we discuss gender differences, we want to acknowledge that there can be no absolute statements or generalities. All physical phenomena fall on a continuum, not in fixed or discrete boxes. There are exceptions and individual differences that do not fall into the general descriptions we are making, reflecting an overlap on the continuum between the extremes of gender differentiation. Some men share more characteristics commonly considered to be female. Some women share more characteristics commonly considered to be male. This is normal and inevitable.

That being said, there are some basic differences between men and women. Studies of the brains of men and women have shown that the differences we notice about how we react and handle our emotions have biological as well as cultural and psychological causes. The actual structure of our brains is different. Testosterone creates anatomical differences in the male brain in the womb and a lack of testosterone results in the feminization of the brain.

Language and emotions

There is a biological reason for women's often noted superiority in language: two areas in the brain related to language (the frontal and temporal lobes) are significantly larger in women. In addition, it easier for women to talk about their feelings because they have more speech centers in their brains than men do. Women also have more activity in the centers of the brain dedicated to verbal communication and emotion. Men usually have more activity in the mechanical centers of their brains so it is easy and natural for them to focus on mechanical activities. Such activities actually stimulate men's brains, so they may find it easier to talk about their feelings when they are engaged in a physical activity.

Because their emotional thinking center is closer to their speech center, women can verbalize their emotions more effortlessly than men can.

Processing information and emotions

There is a part of the brain (the orbitofrontal cortex) that is involved in regulating emotions. Another part of the brain (the amygdala) is involved in producing emotional reactions. In women, the regulator is larger than the producer, so women tend to be more capable of controlling their emotional reactions. (*Al: This may explain why sometimes men don't even know that women are upset until there is an explosion, long after something has happened.*)

Another part of the brain (the deep limbic system) is much larger in women. This gives women the advantage of being more in touch with and better able to express their feelings than men are.

> *Jan: In a very funny television commercial, a couple is showing off their new home to friends. When the woman brings the other women to her huge walk-in closet, they all start screaming and clutching each other in excitement. After a moment, there is an outbreak of screaming from their husband. Bewildered, the women follow the sound. They find the men expressing their excitement in exactly the same way the women did, except over a huge walk-in refrigerator filled with beer. The humor of the ad is based on the difference in the deep limbic systems of men and women! We are just not used to seeing men express their emotions as exuberantly as women do, except while watching sports.*

While men tend to be larger and have the advantage of physical strength, women have the ability to use language—especially discussion and persuasion—to their advantage. They have an increased ability to bond and be connected to others, while men, with their less complex limbic system, more naturally express their emotions through action.

Differences in thinking

Sometimes women move so fast emotionally and verbally that men, regardless of how intelligent they are, get overwhelmed. There is a biological reason for this. Men have more than six times as much gray matter (where the information-processing centers of the brain are located) as women, but women have nearly ten times as much white matter (which provides the connections between these processing centers). This means that a woman is able to "connect the dots" (transfer data between the right and left brain hemispheres) faster than a man can. Having greater ability to access information in both sides of her brain, the left side and the right (which is involved in more holistic and intuitive thinking), she is able to integrate and assimilate information more quickly.

The greater number of connections between the two sides of the female brain explains the biological basis for a woman's ability to multi-task. When scientists observed the brain functions of men and women who were involved in a task, more centers in the women's brains were activated than were in the men's brains, which have more specialized areas.

> *Al: Okay, men! Let's go to a shopping mall with our Other and spend two-and-a-half hours while she finds a dress she likes. Or would you rather put both your eyes out with a stick? Why do we, as a whole, hate shopping? Shopping involves collecting, integrating and assimilating information, and then comparing between choices. So Jan says to me, "Do you like the cut of this neckline more than the one in the other store? Which shade of blue is best?" (She is asking my brain to find something that isn't there.) And so I say, "I like this neckline and that color blue. Let's buy it and go." (Anything to get me out of here!)*
>
> *Okay, men! We need pants. We know exactly where they are. We look for the right waist and length. We buy them. End of story.*

The hypothalamus is a small area in the center of the brain that is responsible for aggression, among other things. It can grow to be up to four times larger in men than in women, resulting in a man's tendency toward more dominant and goal-oriented behavior. When men are faced with a problem, they tend to more quickly come to a decision, act and move on than women do. Women tend to discuss and explore the situation and move toward a decision through consensus. A woman's process typically takes more time, as she considers more aspects of the situation than does a man, who tends to observe more broad and obvious clues as he processes information in coming to his conclusions.

Men tend to think in a linear fashion. They focus on a single task and do not like to be disturbed in the middle of it. Men want to fix things. Men tend to be more left- brained, which is the side of the brain involved in logical and analytical functions. If there is a problem, they focus on coming up with a solution. This has historically made them quite handy in the continuation of culture. They are quick to respond to a crisis, bringing their singular focus and physical strength. They are able to see a direct link between problem and solution.

We were in the produce section of a market when we overheard this interaction between a man and his son, who looked like he was about five years old:

Father: "Okay, potatoes are next on the list. Oh, no. She didn't say how many to get!"

Boy: "I know, Dad! How about five?"

In fusion, a woman expects a man to know what she is thinking or have the same understanding of a situation that she does. This woman expected her husband to have the same "feeling" or thought about how many potatoes to buy. For a man, a project such as buying potatoes is a math problem: how many? In his fusion, this husband expected his list to be linear and logically specific, which is the way he thinks. The son, not having a startled reaction to broken fusion, assessed the situation and quickly came up with a solution that satisfied him, with no further need to explore alternatives or possibilities.

Al: In an intricate problem-solving situation, as shopping or decorating a house, I either want to take control or I want Jan to be in control. If we try to collaborate and if I try to think about things the way Jan does, there is nothing there—my brain can't find preference. Jan does something she calls "feeling into" the situation, which she describes as "opening up" to allow information (feelings or other factors to consider) to "come" to her. What? I become frustrated or anxious, and I feel like just giving up and letting her make the decision. I can see subtle differences in what we are considering, but I don't care. (Think of it like this: There is a herd of mammoth. I need mammoth! Jan would ask, "Which is the best one—which one has a prettier hide for our winter coats? Which one is the right age so we don't separate it from its mother too soon? Which one looks less grizzled and tough?" I don't care! I just want to hunt a mammoth—any mammoth will do! I don't want to marry it!)

Jan: The words Al most hates to hear are, "Which one do you like best?" I will hold up two really cute coffee mugs, for example, and he looks for a wall to bash his head against. Or he will tell me to buy them both, just to put an end to his agony. (Plus, it's less expensive than a trip to the ER to fix his head.)

The impact of biology on personal communication

When women consider things, they tend to see possibilities. When men consider things, they tend to see solutions. It is not accidental that during the hunting and gathering phase of human history, men, with their linear brains, were the hunters. Their singular focus and intent, undistracted by the delicious berries or the beautiful flowers they might pass, helped them organize and efficiently accomplish their goals while maintaining their safety. Women had a different task and their brains supported their ability to focus on alternatives and choice. Their job was to explore the food of their environment, taste and compare what they found, note the subtleties of the effects of plants that they determined to be of medicinal value, while at the same time, they watched and taught the children and created a communicative community of women who could establish compromise and consensus, with the needs of everyone being considered so that everyone was happy. Whew! (*Al: Let's review: Men—hunt. Women—do everything else!*)

Though the tasks of daily life are different today, our brain functions are not, and we approach life and relationship issues with those same biological differences influencing our interactions and responses. By bringing these differences into our consciousness, we can learn to watch ourselves and our reactions, and become better able to understand and work out issues within our significant relationships.

> *Al: I asked Jan if she knew where a particular street was located, so I could find a business I needed to go to. She said that she didn't, but that she was free the next morning to call and get directions for me. I immediately felt confused and irritated. I was expecting either "No, I don't," or "Yes, here's where it is." Jan was talking about how she could help find the directions. That was a whole separate step that I hadn't been prepared to take yet, so it took me off guard. I hadn't thought about what I wanted to do if she didn't know, so I felt rushed and overwhelmed by her moving on so quickly. I was working with a simple, single idea: did Jan know where a street was? I hadn't found my way to the next step, yet. Her response was jarring (my response to separateness) and annoying (my brain was locked into and wanted a concrete, linear answer).*

Men typically see parts. Women typically see things as a whole. When men open up an issue with a linear question or comment, women do not think to limit their response to the narrow range of his remark. Without hesitation or thought, women jump into the creative process.

> *Jan: I was working with a whole picture of how to get Al to that street. But more importantly, I knew what he ultimately wanted—to be able to find the business. My mind saw the whole picture, although he had only initiated the first small step—musing about the possibility that I knew where the street was. With my white matter facilitating my grasp of the whole concept of what Al was after, I was seamlessly on my way to the next step. I had already resolved the whole issue before he could even take in that I didn't know the answer to his initial inquiry.*

> *Al: I would have found my way to that next step, but I was not there as quickly as Jan was. And her leaping way ahead of me to something I hadn't considered yet was very jarring to me.*

When the male brain is asked to do something it cannot do—move too quickly or out of sequence—or when men are interrupted in the middle of a task they are involved in, anger or frustration may be the result. A typical male brain cannot keep up with sudden changes—his brain moves in a very specific, concrete direction. With sudden changes, his experience is one of being startled and overwhelmed. A typical female brain is not only able to multi-task but is typically is always surveying a bigger picture and looking for options.

> *Al: There's a woman at Costco who really likes Jan, always serving Jan a huge portion of the samples she gives out. One day, it was roasted nuts. She loaded an enormous amount into a napkin and put it in Jan's hand. Jan immediately put them into her pocket, not wanting the woman to get in trouble for her generosity. Later, in the car, Jan pulled them out of her pocket and offered them to me. "Do you want a nut?" she asked.*
>
> *I froze. I sat there for a long time, immobilized, unable to move or speak, looking at those nuts. I hadn't asked for any nuts. I was not connected to a need for nuts. My mind desperately searched for clarity. Why was she was offering me nuts? Was I supposed to want some nuts? Did she have plans for the nuts? What was the correct answer? I didn't know what to say. My brain was so startled that I couldn't respond.*
>
> *I finally managed to choke out, "What do you mean?" Jan looked at me like I was crazy. She was just offering me something that might make me happy. All she wanted was for me to check in with myself, see if I felt in the mood for nuts, and say a simple "yes" or "no." Doing that never occurred to me.*

Because we are each involved in our own thoughts and experience, we frequently say something that takes our Other by surprise, for they are involved in their own thoughts and experience. If you were suddenly pushed backward, you would be startled, but before you could even formulate what you might like to say to the person who pushed you, your focus would be on the physically struggle to maintain or regain your balance. A similar thing happens emotionally when we hear a response or question that we are not expecting. When taken by surprise, both men and women may try to get oriented by asking questions that are not a direct or linear response to what the other person said, for they are attempting to get their bearings. This can be the source of questions that seem either unnecessary or that bewilderingly require a repetition of what has already been said. When we separate, we will know that our Other is not questioning or doubting us—they are just trying to catch up.

Additionally, a man's brain does not identify a specific emotion as quickly as does a woman's. His deep limbic system is not as large as a woman's, so he is not in touch with and expressive of his feelings as quickly as is a woman. There is nothing more vulnerable and disorienting than to be disconnected from your Self—the source of all information about your reactions, needs and preferences for the action to be taken. For this reason, when a woman initiates conversation or responds in a way that a man does not expect, his response might immediately be defensive, a reaction coming from feeling disoriented.

How do we coordinate life when our brains are so different?

> Al: I told Jan I wanted to stop by a market, on our way home to pick up some sushi for lunch the next day. She immediately offered to go get it for me in the morning and drop it off to me at our office. I felt annoyed. I was in the process of scratching things off my list. I wanted to buy sushi and we were driving right by the store that had it. I couldn't even understand why she was looking for an alternative to the plan I had when I was happy with my plan just the way it was!
> Jan: The last time Al bought sushi, he complained about how stale and unpleasant it had been the next day and that from then on he was only going to buy it the day he wanted to eat it. I knew I had time in the morning to get it for him, and I would have been happy to do it.

Men just want to have a solution that works well enough, so they often feel challenged when women want them to consider possibilities. Even when a man has a preference, entering into a detailed discussion about all the millions of possible variations that each have their distinct advantages and disadvantages usually does not feel worth it. (*Al: Just reading that last sentence could make a man want to shoot himself!*) Women tend to compare, contrast, refine and explore, opening their minds to be creative and to allow intuition to guide and inspire them. Men typically just want to make a decision and keep going. The possibilities might make sense, but men do not want to be engaged in the process of thinking about them. Their idea felt good enough.

We often see that women make choices and decisions while men passively sit by.

> *Al: The next time you go to a store, take note of how many men are following their women around, looking spiritless and bored. We once watched an older English couple wander around a store, the man numbly pushing the cart behind her. The woman stopped to pick up a basket filled with teas and cookies, and literally cooed with pleasure! "Oh, Edward! Don't you think Beatrice would be positively thrilled with this?" "Yes, dear," the man replied woodenly, "Absolutely thrilled."*

Sometimes a man truly has no preference and a discussion is simply not worth the time and effort, but more often it is because the process of making a decision feels like a war—someone will win and someone will lose. Someone else's idea or need is a challenge to their own.

If a man were to say his idea or preference, it is highly likely that the woman would respond in the way she is predisposed to do—by exploring ways to refine or build on the idea, integrating the needs of both of them in the creation of a new solution. This can make a man feel frustrated or defeated—what is the point of bringing up what he wants if his idea, once again, is not good enough, just as it is.

For a woman in fusion, anything a man says is an invitation for a conversation and exploration—it is not just a statement. Having had many experiences in which he has been asked his opinion only to have the woman not simply accept it (which to a man means "act on it") the man is very likely to think, "What's the point?" and just acquiesce to whatever the woman wants. For a man, it is just not worth it. It is uncomfortable to tolerate a lack of resolution in order to consider possibilities. Something would have to be awfully important to make him willing to mobilize for war.

If, in addition to brain overwhelm, a man had unhealthy fusion, his right to exist issues might be triggered—he cannot even have a small want without it being questioned. Although a man who has experienced healthy fusion knows he has the right to exist and that his ideas are perfectly fine, he may feel like she is trying to control or criticize him. The woman may be considering alternatives that will please both of them or be trying to make his idea even better to please him even more, but the man may still feel like he is with an adversary. His tightness feels like fight alert. "Why is she always messing with my ideas? 'If it ain't broke, don't fix it!'"

We are constantly operating in fusion and do not realize it. It is an indicator of how unseparate we are that men do not expect women to talk in possibilities and women expect men to enter into consideration or discussions about possibilities with the same enthusiasm they feel.

In this way, we are like the caricature of the American tourist who goes to another country and expects everyone to speak his language. If the natives he meets do not speak English, he just speaks louder. It is a challenge to be separate and to constantly be aware that we are not talking to someone who is just like us. Fusion causes us to automatically and unconsciously expect our Other to not be an Other but to be an extension of "me." We do not remember who we are talking to.

Al: My fusion with Jan in the Sushi Incident caused me to be annoyed that she was interfering with my plan for me to get my sushi. When I was able to separate, I could see that she was being thoughtful about what I had told her before about wanting to have fresh sushi. Jan isn't me. She always thinks in terms of possibilities about how things could be better - and better for me, because she loves me.

Jan: My fusion with Al, as revealed in the Sushi Incident, causes me to never, ever remember that he isn't necessarily looking for help. I don't do him any favors when I offer help without asking if he would like some. Had I been separate, I might have just reminded him of his unhappiness about stale sushi and let him catch up with my thinking so he could find his feelings about the sushi. At that point, instead of him having a plan he was happy with (buying the sushi right then) and feeling as though I were interfering, he might have found that he had a plan he wasn't happy with. I could have then asked if he would like any help. When I already have the solution in place before he even thinks that he has a problem, he is overwhelmed and confused.

There are two things men can do to help themselves when they feel disoriented. They need to separate and remember that women tend to move faster and like to look for options. Women have a different brain and are different from men. They are engaged in their own natural brain processes. They are not necessarily being controlling or critical. Their brains are considering multiple factors, not just the single aspect of the situation that a man might be thinking about. They are looking at the whole picture for resolution.

Because things move quickly in relationships, feelings are triggered. *Broken fusion is signaled by the irritation or hurt that each person might experience.* We can use the presence of those feelings to remember, "Oh! We must be having a *different* experience, right now" and to ask "What is going on for you?" or "What are you thinking I'm doing?" instead of personalizing it—"Why is she so controlling?" or "Why is he attacking me for helping?"

The male brain understands fusion more than separateness. Women are as susceptible to fusing as men are, but with brains better designed to consider possibilities, they can understand and work with the concept of separateness more easily. When men and women realize that they have each had a reaction to being separate, it may be easier for a woman to acknowledge that they were just feeling fused and more quickly release the feelings from the incident. A man may struggle more to internalize the realization and take longer to release the intense feelings that were stirred up.

Jan: Women! Listen up. I know it's incredibly difficult to believe or remember, but this is important and it's true. It's really painful for a man if he has difficulty finding alternatives that will make him feel okay. Often, men have the experience of being locked into a brain that does not automatically move to consider alternatives and possibilities. It's so common for most women to go into that mode that it is really, really hard to comprehend that men don't necessarily think the way most women do. Their brains do not notice the things we notice or remember what we think should be remembered. (Think toilet seats: when a man is off hunting mammoths, he doesn't think about putting them down.)

Many women have the experience of looking at men and thinking, "Why are they so rigid? So angry? Are they just stupid?" without realizing that they might be having a totally different experience than we are at the physiological level. This is not necessarily something they are choosing to do. Because of their biology, they may be stuck in a narrower, more linear approach to situations. They notice what they notice, not all the subtleties and variations that we pay attention to. It's not that they don't care about us or our needs, though that may certainly be true of some men. Their brains are just occupied by and attentive to different details of life.

Men have a different thought process than we have. When they lock down and seem unreasonable or childlike, we can remember that their brain is operating in a different manner than ours does. We can know that they are working with a different brain function, not just being obstinate. If we find ourselves jumping into hurt, anger, judgment, frustration or irritation ("He's such a baby." "He's so controlling / angry / stupid." "If he really loved me then he would . . . .") we need to remember that we must be in a state of fusion with them or we would not be having those reactions. It is our job to separate. Then we can use our reaction as a signal to ask them any question that will both help us learn what is really going on with them, as well as help them get oriented and connected to themselves. "Am I being confusing?" "Are you overwhelmed right now?" "I'm not sure I'm explaining this very well." "What are you thinking?" "Do you need some time to think about this?" If we forget to do this, we will remain reactive and competitive and into an either/or kind of thinking. We will experience the feeling that men struggle with of being at war, where only one of us can exist.

Al: Men! What we have to remember is to appreciate and understand how our brains work. There is a lot of power in being able to cut through details and see the essence of a situation. We also need to have compassion for the fact that because of the way our brains operate, a conversation with a woman may be overwhelming because it's not a linear experience. But if a woman said to a man that she felt really sad and that she would love it if he would go to the store and buy her some ice cream, he would be thrilled! Something to do to please her and solve the problem? Great!

But, no, that isn't how a woman usually thinks. Instead, she is more likely to talk about her feelings without asking for a solution, just wanting us to care about her feelings and hang out with her while she has them . . . which is frustrating for us because we do care about them and want to fix their unhappiness. We can get very agitated because everything in us designed to find a solution, and yet none is apparent. (Our engines are revving but her foot is on the brake!) We tend to keep forgetting, despite the fact that it happens again and again, that they just want acknowledgement. Hmmm . . . and we say we are logical and it is women who are illogical! Why do we continue to forget this simple difference despite the clear evidence that it exists?

If we do not acknowledge our differentness in how we approach a situation, we can get frustrated. Women often misunderstand why we are frustrated. They may think we are controlling or angry people, not realizing that our behavior is a reaction to feeling helpless and uncomfortable when we are being asked to do something that is often difficult for us.

If we accept and acknowledge how hard it is for us to engage in a complicated, nonlinear process, then we can actually change the process (slow it down so we can catch up and participate) to make it easier for both of us. "I'm not following what you're saying." "This is too fast or too complicated." "Can you tell me what you want from me in bringing this up?" We need to let her know what is going on for us and try to understand what she is trying to do and why. Remember, women have the ability to switch modes quickly if they understand what is happening and they naturally seek to find alternatives so everyone will be okay.

This is a process that requires us to have humility. But it's also important to remember that although our world is increasingly complex and intricate, our linear thinking still has valuable applications and contributions to make. For example, when Jan and I make plans to travel, she is excellent at researching and finding great possibilities for us, but often, if not always, she becomes overwhelmed by them. I call *this "Preference Hell." Jan and I have developed an approach that uses the strengths of both of our brains. She researches all the options she knows we will both like, and then, once she is at the brink of entering Preference Hell, I come in and save her by my ability to see and suggest a linear plan.*

It is difficult to experience the discrepancy between the workings of a man's brain and a woman's brain without being in judgment of our Self or of our Other. Understanding how our brains function allows us to accept our differences and the vulnerability that results for each of us. This information can help us to be separate, instead of being fused and struggling in shock over the fact that we are not the same and are not reacting as our Other expected. Otherwise, we are left comparing and feeling inferior or superior, and definitely lonely.

If we each do our part, this will be an easier process to go through. We each need to accept the fact that our brains work differently. Men often look at women in bewilderment and frustration because it seems as though women change their minds all the time, whereas what is happening for women is that they are opening to possibilities, weighing their choices, noticing subtle differences and often struggling to find the "right" alternative. Women look at men, who struggle to keep up with them, and wonder what is wrong with them, not realizing that a man's brain does not have as much white matter to enable them to assimilate data as quickly. In those moments of frustration or bewilderment, women may not be remembering that unencumbered by all that white matter, men are more capable of more easily coming up with quick, simple and effective decisions.

It is tempting for both men and women to judge the difference between their brains and come to the conclusion that men are limited or inferior, for they are very visible in their disorientation, or that women are inferior because they are "too" sensitive and emotional and may struggle to make decisions. A man often feels angry and resentful when he thinks that a woman is pushing him to communicate differently (the way she does) and does not accept him for who he is. A woman can feel frustrated and hurt that a man does not value her emotions or communicate in a way similar to her style. Global creative thinking— the strong point of a woman's brain functioning—is highly valued and necessary in today's world but so is the ability to quickly make clear and definitive decisions. As in the example given above of planning travel, both brains have their limitations and resulting consequences: a woman can face Preference Hell, and a man has the pain of struggling to find his equilibrium and feelings and to come up with alternatives. Working together, we will create a powerful and complementary balance *if we remember and honor, not judge, our differences.*

Freedom and clarity come with separateness

We automatically fuse with our Other in a significant relationship. From that place of fusion, we become confused, bewildered, hurt, angry or frightened when our Other acts in ways that are different from what we expect. When we are able to separate and remember that each of us has our own reality, our own historical issues, our own approach to or style of handling life, as well as very different brain functions if our Other is a different gender (husband-wife, mother-son, father-daughter, co-worker) we will be able to make sense of our different reactions and behaviors. These differences need not be a problem.

We need to remember *to whom* we are talking, and not assume that they are just like we are. Being prepared with this understanding allows us to slow down the interactions and speak *to each other* rather than talk as though we are musing aloud and that *of course* our Other is right there with us in a similar process, thinking the same thoughts, having the same understandings that we are having, seeing the same aspects of reality and approaching reality in the same way.

Separating allows us to see each other. Separateness allows us to understand how we each see the world. Separateness allows us to find language that we both understand. Separateness frees us from confusion, hurt, anger and blame.

Dude! Really? (A Rant by Jan)

"Maybe something is wrong with his mind!" I thought in sudden terror. "No, no," I quickly remind myself, comfortingly, "He's just a man." (Now, men, please keep reading. I will get mine, in the end!)

I am sorry to have to admit this—I wish I were a more enlightened and liberated and compassionate person—but . . . the things Al does make my jaw drop . . . constantly. I am *constantly* coming across evidence of his ... well ... male brain at ... shall I say work ... and being shocked by what I see.

He hung his dripping wet swimsuit on the curved shower curtain rod that jutted past the bathtub and over the floor, instead of putting it in the tub where there was a convenient rack. I realized this right after coming into the bathroom and slipping on the sopping wet floor. Dude! Really?

I took out a knife to cut some vegetables, got them out of the fridge, only to find he had already washed and put away my knife. Dude! Really?

I gave him the task of returning an item to a store and he came back with the credit having been put onto a credit card we don't even own. Dude! Really?

I find the dental floss lying on the floor next to the bathroom trash-can. Well, at least he remembered to extend his arm somewhat in its vicinity before releasing ... but, Dude! Really?

I hear it from friends, as well. Like the time my friend came home to find her husband and little son curled up on the couch watching a television show together. How sweet! Then she noticed the inch deep water flooding the kitchen floor. "I was going to take care of it after the show." he explained. Dude! Really?

I mean, *seriously?*

Now, I know that there is a wide range of individual differences among both men and women, but generally this seems to be how it is. This doesn't mean that men aren't really wonderful human beings. Al is as sweet and thoughtful and vulnerable as they come. He is just trapped between awareness and physiology. He doesn't take refuge behind the traditional male unconsciousness and bravado, but he also isn't in possession of a more fluid female brain. Excruciatingly aware of the fact that he has to navigate life with a male brain, he feels pain and exhaustion from trying to focus and manage it. He doesn't *like* being trapped with a male brain. Every day, he can see how it limits him.

But this has always been the reality of our physiology, so what is going on here that women get so upset and shocked?

It has only just recently occurred to me how much the Women's Liberation Movement of the 1960s and '70s has impacted our culture. Although women still struggle to break through glass ceilings and redefine old stereotypes, before the advent of Women's Lib, women were trained by example, custom and culture that we were the inferior sex. Men were stronger, had better judgment and should therefore be dominant. We were taught to submerge our ideas and our strength in deference to theirs, even when we truly believed ours were better. This led to an underground culture among many women of ostensible submission but secret derision toward men that was shared in jokes, stories, eye-rolling and a sense of covert superiority as we deigned to tolerate them.

Women in the Women's Liberation Movement worked to establish the equality of the sexes—women and men are equal and should be treated equally. But I am realizing that this is only partially true. We are equal in terms of value and worth as human beings, but we are simply *not* the same, and the assumption that we are managed to creep into our thinking, even though it might never have been explicitly expressed. As women worked to prove that they had many of the abilities formerly ascribed only to men, that women were as competent and intelligent, they also began to expect men to have the same abilities we have. While we can match men in intelligence and the value of our abilities, the physiological difference in our brain structure results in the essential difference in functioning in crucial ways (processing emotions and in the ability to multi-task) we have focused on in this chapter. A woman's brain is far more equipped to handle the multi-faceted nature of modern life than is a man's. It is not his fault. It is physiology.

If a man is interrupted in the middle of a project, he can get thrown off course, often responding with either confusion or anger. (Remember stalking the mammoth, eyes and body focused intently on the kill. Enter the woman: "Oh, my *God!* Look at those incredible blackberries over there on that bush! They are the biggest I've ever seen! We *have* to stop by here, on the way back, and pick some!")

Now, to a woman, who can be cooking, cleaning, dealing with children, balancing the checkbook and talking to her friend on the phone all at the same time, a man's response to being interrupted is a bewildering phenomenon that makes us question our sanity. How could we not have realized, before we married him, what a moron our husband was. But, he can't help it! It is his physiological response.

I am suddenly having a new understanding and interpretation of some old historical customs and stereotypes.

There's the image of men coming back from the hunt, gathering around to talk or whatever men coming back from a hunt would gather around to do, while the women would take care of everything else. Or women serving men their food, then retiring into another room to eat their own. Or women going to a women's hut during that time of the month. *Clearly* subservience and oppression, I had always thought with indignation . . . . But I'm not so sure, anymore.

"No, really, Honey. Just relax! I'll take care of it. After all, you did all the hard work of killing the mammoth and dragging it home. And it was so heavy! I'll handle the other things around the cave/castle." (Because it is sooooooooooo much easier than giving you the microscopic instructions you would need to "help" me out with these tasks that are [to me] so self-evident in the simplest and most efficient way to do them!)

"No, really, Honey. Just sit and enjoy your dinner. Let me know if you want anything else and I will bring it! Don't bother getting up! You've worked so hard! I will just sit in the other room with the other wives and let you rest." (Because it is sooooooooooo much more peaceful and we understand each other so easily.)

"No, really, Honey. It will be much better if I don't get my nasty old cooties all over everything here at home. I will just take a vacation over there with my girlfriends . . . . I mean I'll remove my bad spirits and go with the other contaminated women. We don't want to risk jinxing anything, now, do we?"

When Al and I researched brain differences for this chapter, we were both stunned and amazed by what we learned. I was shocked to learn that the brains work so differently. Al was relieved, for he always felt that his brain was inferior to mine. Our cultural interpretations of sexual differences were blown away by the information about how differences in physiology led to (or were intensified) by differential task assignments for each gender.

After writing the explanation of brain physiology, we wanted to discuss the advantages of the functioning of each brain and how we can all benefit from having men and women work together. I wrote up the section on the advantages of the female brain fairly quickly, then made the heading for the section on the advantages of the male brain . . . and was totally stumped. I couldn't think of a single one!

"Oh, no!" I thought in horror. "This is really bad!" Well, after a brief moment of panic, I was able to think of the advantages. (Now, women, before you read this chapter, I know you would have been sitting there, scratching your head, struggling to come up with any advantages, thinking that I was lying and really couldn't find any, and was just saying that to be nice!) I truly had never realized that with their linear, single-minded clarity, men have the ability to cut through the astounding number of alternatives that inundate a woman's brain, sometimes totally overwhelming us and leaving us floundering in indecision, looking for the "right" or "perfect" choice. Their incisive simplification is like a welcome lifeline in a stormy sea.

Women have had centuries to develop their awareness of emotional and communication nuances. Men have not. While women may struggle with their ignorance of how to communicate from a place of empowerment, not victimhood, men usually don't even care about those nuances. They just don't want to be beaten up because of who they are, or asked to do something that pits them against their brain, which is designed differently than a woman's brain.

My daughter started to share an experience she had running but had gotten no further than literally three sentences, when Al broke in with "Get to the point, already!" My son-in-law burst into laughter, admitting that he had been feeling like he was suffocating, as she spoke! Dude! Really? As a woman, I was just beginning to journey along with my daughter, starting to feel into her emotional experience as she described her run. They couldn't bear the suspense, even with such an inconsequential event.

A man doesn't like possibilities *in every decision*. I hold up two coffee mugs, asking Al which he likes best, and he just wants to beat his head against the wall. Or I ask, "Do you like the neckline on this dress better than the neckline on that one?" And he thinks, "There's a place for the head to go through. Works for me." He can't differentiate and *doesn't care about* the unique differences between them. He just wants a mug and thinks any dress is as good as another.

A woman explores dinner possibilities with another woman, evolving a plan that pleases both of them. A man says to another, "Wanna eat?" "Yea." "Pizza okay?" "Great." There's a reason that a well-known comedian has a huge following of men, as he endlessly intones, "Git 'er done!"

Because of our physiology, women are allocated certain tasks. Of course, we must bear the children and our brains are more than well equipped to multi-task in the management of the home and balancing raising those children with our other needs. But maybe, just maybe, we have another task, as well.

At this time in human history, it seems that women must reclaim their abandoned power and that men must work to connect with and own their unexplored or forbidden vulnerability. Because of brain physiology, women are the more likely ones to be the emotional leaders in the relationship. The structure of our brains allows us to notice, process and communicate nuances of emotion and relationship dynamics more quickly than the structure of a man's brain can. But we must stop expecting men to be just like us and we must slow down so we can encourage them to find and express their feelings—even if that expression is different than we would expect from another woman.

But most importantly, we must look to our own behavior to make sure we are being the people we can respect being. (I find for myself, I am that person when I speak to people as if they were children. Now, I'm not holding myself above anybody! I'm the biggest baby I know! It's just that when I talk with children, I don't have expectations or judgment — I'm able to explore what they are feeling and why they do or say what they do. I like who I am when I talk to kids. So, if I'm aware of something Al isn't aware of, instead of beating him over the head in irritation, I want to invite him, in the same way I would with a child, to share my vision of the situation. And when I react with irritation or roll my eyes in disbelief, I can't help but ask myself, now, "Jan! Really? Is this who I want to be?" I'm still expecting my husband to process things the way I do? I'm still shocked at our differentness?)

All of us have a physiological response of shock when we are startled by the behavior of another person.   Whether our ability is to multi-task or to incisively cut the Gordian Knot of Possibility, when someone we are close to responds in a manner that is completely different from what we would expect, our adrenaline surges and, at an animal level, we are put on the alert. Some of us experience this surge as anger, while others of us experience it as hurt. Same adrenaline, different individual response style. But the task for each of us is to be in charge of our adrenalized response, not non-reflexively at its mercy.

Men and women must all recognize and accept our physiological differences. And all of us must work to communicate, even though it is *much* harder than any of us think it should be. Giving up, becoming angry, hurt, withdrawing, feeling victimized or abused are all responses that do not acknowledge this basic human task of becoming an adult we can each feel proud of being. Maybe God or the Fates just had a perverse sense of humor that we were made a mating kind of species. But however that came to be, most of us long to develop and nurture love and emotional intimacy and tend to seek out someone to make a home with. So this task of "growing up" is unavoidable and essential to creating the life we each long for.

Men and women may have differences in how our brains operate, but our longing to come together for acceptance and closeness is the same. And, the tasks are the same for each of us. Be patient with our Self and the other person. Slow down our adrenalized response. Speak our truth and ask our questions with curiosity and compassion. Only then will we be that adult we can respect. That is not only our job and our responsibility, but it is also all we can ask of ourselves. And, it is enough.

CHAPTER 4

Healthy Separateness: The Key to Successful Relationships

Everyone struggles to establish healthy separateness in their significant relationships, regardless of their experiences as a child. This is a developmentally normal continuation of the task we began at birth. We are usually unaware that our childhood patterns of dealing with our separateness are set in motion as soon as we are drawn into a relationship and our Other becomes important to us.

Childhood patterns overlay new relationships

While children who have had the experience of healthy fusion may feel important and wanted, if healthy separateness does not follow, their ability to establish an emotionally intimate relationship will be affected. They will not have learned how to create and live in relationships where people co-exist.

People who had healthy fusion but unhealthy separateness have relationships that are based on the idea that only one person gets to exist. A man who had this experience is threatened when his needs are not the most important ones in the relationship. A woman who had this experience generally knows that her needs are important but is more likely to make them secondary to the goal of keeping her Other from feeling threatened. She cannot see how her own needs are going to be met in the relationship, but at least she can keep the relationship.

A man who has experienced unhealthy fusion and unhealthy separateness has the belief that if his Other has a need, he has to make her okay or fix the problem, even if he does not want to. Soon after the initial excitement of a relationship ends, a man may start to feel overwhelmed or suffocated and may feel that things are moving too fast. He may resist making a commitment because that will mean he will be trapped in a role he does not want. Because he did not have the experience of the successful coexistence of two separate individuals, his relationship seems to present him with a choice: which one of us gets to exist? His choice is to give himself up (acquiesce and take care of the woman) or become controlling so that he is the one who gets to exist. His response of being controlling comes from his fear of being vulnerable and disappearing into nonexistence. He does not want to be forced to give up who he is or what he wants.

If a man experienced healthy fusion, but not healthy separateness, he is likely to have the illusion that life is all about him. For him, fusion in a relationship is when both people have the same needs—his. Separating can come as a shock, but even more profoundly, as a threat. When the needs are different, it is likely that the man would think, "She thinks something is wrong with what I need" (a statement of fusion—"It's all about me") rather than "She has different needs" (a statement of separateness). Because his brain does not naturally expand to seek and work with possibilities, he will tend to immediately feel controlled and trapped when he becomes aware of his separateness. This awareness can be precipitated by such a simple thing as the woman expressing an idea that he does not agree with or a need that he does not have in that moment.

> Al: A couple we know has been happily dating for three months. When she brought up the idea of them exclusively dating each other, he immediately responded by criticizing her for being too possessive and said that maybe they should just be friends. He panicked and "ran." It didn't occur to him to suggest they think about it or talk about it, or to even declare himself that he wasn't ready or that this was sudden and he didn't know how he felt about it.

Separateness is experienced as a threat in a linear brain because the man does not automatically move to create alternatives. A woman may think she is initiating a discussion but the man may experience this as being cornered with an ultimatum. He thinks he must say yes or no to her proposal. The possibility of exploring alternatives for both people getting their separate needs met within the relationship does not occur to him. The very existence of his Other threatens his independence because he cannot imagine a win-win scenario. He fears being swallowed up and losing control, his freedom and his identity. The only way he can imagine separateness is to be physically separate. Not knowing how to establish emotional separateness, he needs to go away in order to be who he really is.

Although it may seem sudden, bewildering and artificial, creating a physical separation is a simple solution for someone who has no concept of how to be in a relationship and still be emotionally separate. "Maybe I should keep my own place." "Maybe we should date other people." "Maybe we should separate or get a divorce." "Maybe we should get a divorce but still date each other." "Maybe we should get a divorce but still live together." The options do not seem logical, given that the man often does not want to end the relationship, until we remember that these options are the result of a linear brain struggling with the issue of separateness.

Many men have an enormous fear of being dependent and losing control over their lives. They may have no understanding of their emotional responses or the reasons behind their inability to negotiate, compromise, discuss alternatives and create new plans. They only know that they feel exhausted and it feels easier to just give up whenever their Other wants something. They see other men who allow their wives to make decisions and characterize them as "wimps" or "whipped," secretly fearing that something is also very wrong with themselves.

A man who experienced unhealthy fusion has no right to exist, and so does not feel as threatened by separateness as a man who experienced healthy fusion does. He is used to it. It is familiar, as his childhood taught him that he cannot have his own Self, but instead must take care of his parents' needs in order to feel safe. A man who experienced unhealthy fusion enters a relationship with a woman hoping she might be the "good mom" who finally wants him and approves of him. Hoping that if he is "good" enough that he will finally get the right to exist, he is even less likely to reveal who he is and jeopardize the possibility of being accepted.

A woman who experienced unhealthy fusion is more similar to a man who experienced unhealthy fusion than she is to a woman who experienced healthy fusion. She also feels that she does not have the right to exist and that her role is to meet the needs of her Other. As with a man who experienced unhealthy fusion, her hope is that, in this way, she will get some of her needs met and although she still might not have the right to exist, she will have a reason to exist, which is better than nothing.

Our childhood experiences of fusion and separating automatically determine the type of relationship we establish with our Other. Even if we deliberately try to choose someone very different from our parents, our internalized lessons and patterns are still there and are innocently and unconsciously set in motion. As the new relationship deepens and our awareness of separateness triggers and illuminates these lessons and patterns, we have the opportunity to begin a new level of growth.

The overlay of the past

Each of us had a foundation laid in our childhood that taught us what to expect in life and how to handle the challenges and situations we face. As soon as we are drawn to be with someone in a relationship, this foundation influences our reactions and our behavior. This does not occur consciously and so is even more powerful in its effect on us, for we automatically and unquestioningly interpret what we are seeing and experiencing through the teachings of our past and assume that we are correct.

We are all startled when we experience any movement along the fusion-separateness continuum. The experience we had in childhood with fusing and separating, however, creates enormously different reactions and abilities to cope with this movement.

Jan: Whenever Al and I had different opinions or needs, I used to become frantic. Thinking back, it seems as if I chased him all over the house, trying to talk about whatever the topic was so we could reach some sort of resolution and I wouldn't have to feel my separateness. It finally dawned on me that on every issue, we always came to a satisfying conclusion and that I didn't have to get so upset. I learned to allow him time to get centered and think about his needs. I remember deliberately sitting in another room, trying to calm down, telling myself to just breathe, forcing myself to leave him alone until he could figure out his feelings and thoughts and felt ready to talk.

People who experienced both healthy fusion and healthy separateness are as startled as anyone when they become aware of being separate in their significant relationship, but they tend to feel optimistic. Their experience has taught them to just hold on—the shock will end and a healthy separateness will be reached. Because they accept the validity of the different needs and feelings of each person, these people believe that if we just bring our real selves to each other, we will create a healthy system of co-existence. Even though the moment of separation can still be extremely shocking, they have a positive expectation about the outcome.

People who experienced both unhealthy fusion and unhealthy separateness can be optimistic about the possibility of establishing close and loving relationships but they do so by not revealing who they really are. Not having been supported in their separateness as children, they are pessimistic about the possibility that they will be accepted and loved for their real selves. The only way they know to maintain their relationship is to take on the responsibility to make their Other feel safe in their fusion by hiding their differentness.

Al: When I met Jan, I thought she was the coolest, prettiest, funniest person I had ever met. I immediately went into the fear that is the legacy of my unhealthy experience of separateness. I began my unconscious process of trying to figure out what pleased her and what threatened her. She talked about her politically active family and so I focused on my own political activism. She told me that she was afraid of anger—and I made an entry into my internal computer: "Don't get angry!" Having long ago established my process of how to deal with fusion, I gently shaped myself to fit into her world. Similarly, when I discovered ways we were different, I realized they might make her feel threatened and so didn't tell her about those thoughts. Like everyone, I longed for closeness, and this was the only way I knew to get it.

When people who experienced both unhealthy fusion and unhealthy separateness become aware of separateness in their important adult relationships, their experience is one of fear. They focus on being who their Other wants them to be and hide their own feelings and needs. They do not dare to live in the reality of their true Self, so they acquiesce to their Other's needs. While there may be loving closeness in the relationship, it is conditional. They believe it is based on them not threatening the fusion of their Other. The expectation of the outcome is positive, but dependent on them hiding the true extent of their differentness.

People who experienced both unhealthy fusion and unhealthy separateness fear exposing the truth of themselves. They may feel frustrated in their relationships because while they have the longing for the closeness of healthy fusion, they also have the sadness of never feeling truly seen and accepted. They often choose to leave a relationship because it is too painful to not have their own existence and it is too frightening to reveal themselves and risk rejection.

Knowing that all of us have struggles when our separateness issues get triggered, we can be prepared for some discomfort in our relationship and we do not have to worry when it occurs. We are stretching ourselves to grow. *Feelings will get stirred up as we enter this new territory of learning how to separate in an adult relationship, but we do not need to be concerned that something is "wrong."*

Separateness always makes us feel vulnerable

Although with time and experience we develop other dimensions of ourselves—experienced, knowledgeable, capable, mature, adult—we will always have a core of vulnerability. In this core, we will always be as innocent and as sensitive as we were when we were babies. When startled out of our fusion and into separateness, we become frightened, threatened, surprised or hurt, and we tend to react to protect that vulnerable part of ourselves. Although we may experience it or express it in different ways, this is how we all react. Whereas a baby would probably cry, an adult is more likely to get angry or withdraw, depending the person's history and nature.

Jan: One time, when Al and I were first married, he came home from work with some Chinese food for himself for dinner. I had been waiting to talk about what we would eat, but he was so tired and hungry that all he could think of was getting food. He hadn't even called me to see if I wanted anything. Although he hadn't intentionally been thoughtless or mean, I was very startled that I hadn't even been in his thoughts. Now, when startled into an awareness of my separateness, I tend to get angry (as you might have already realized from reading my thoughts in The Beginning!) Poor Al withdrew, as he does when he's startled. He was very hurt that I saw him as uncaring, although he could also totally understand my feeling of being left out.

The concept that we react from fusion is crucial to understanding our relationships with others. The more emotionally intimate a relationship is, the more vulnerable we are. When the relationship is an important one, we are more sensitive and more reactive than we are with people who do not hold a central place in our lives. With our Other, we tend to rest closer to the fusion end of the fusion-separateness continuum. Instead of being able to simply shift along the continuum, step back and separate, and wonder or ask what had happened for our Other, in our fusion we personalize their behavior or words and we feel as if we were attacked, abandoned or criticized. That would be the same thing as seeing your Other vomiting, running over to stand beneath the flow, and then feeling hurt and asking, "Why are you throwing up on me!?!" The illness is something that is happening in them not to us, unless we get in the way.

Jan: If we had understood that we had only been startled out of our fusion, the whole interaction would have been different. I would have understood that Al was too tired and hungry to think clearly, and that his choice to buy Chinese food had nothing to do with me. He was just in a very separate place, and was only trying to take care of his needs. If he had been able to be separate, he would have been able to give me comfort and reassurance without having to feel bad or protective of himself. If neither of us had been fused, I would not have gotten angry and Al would not have withdrawn.

We do not usually think of ourselves as being this vulnerable, so it can be very surprising, not only to our Other, but to ourselves, as well, when we have such strong reactions. Understanding the source of our emotional reactions will give us the ability to deal with them in different ways.

> *Jan: One time when Al hurt my feelings, I was so proud, because even though I yelled at him, I was able to say, "I know I sound angry, but I'm really feeling hurt." I wasn't where I wanted to be, someday, but I had stopped the automatic and unconscious cycle of anger that had been my survival mode.*

Our reactions in our significant relationships are usually so radically different than they are in every other relationship in our lives that we often think something is very wrong with our Self, with our Other or with our relationship. We may think our Other just wants to be unhappy, because we know our innocent intent and are very aware of the efforts we are making to please them. We do not understand why they have the reactions they do. If we do not understand the concept that fusion inevitably occurs in every significant relationship necessitating that we continue to grow, we will misinterpret the fact that it is so easy with everyone else. We will think that someone has to be at fault when issues come up. After all, our Other does not respond to us the way other people (who are not fused with us) do! The reality is that we also do not respond to our Other the way we do to people with whom we are not fused! (We may forget that part, though!)

Relationships are the school for personal freedom

Every important relationship will bring out our unfinished issues, places where we are still ignorant and reacting in emotional panic. When hard times occur with people who are not central in our lives, we can easily walk away. But when these hard times happen in emotionally intimate relationships, we are then in a dilemma. Leaving is hard, for we are fused, or bonded, with our Other. Staying is hard, too, for we must take a look at the emotions and reactions that get stirred up in us. But staying gives us the possibility to grow and to create the relationship we long for.

The stage where we left off in our process of separating from our parents is where we continue our growing "up" in our significant relationship. We do not necessarily pick someone who is like one of our parents. Without even realizing it, we each pick someone with whom we can continue our learning, picking up exactly from the point we left off in our relationship with our parents. (Just like when we start second grade, we pick up just where we left off at the end of first grade.)

> *Jan: While I had healthy fusion and separation with my Mom, my experience of being young and vulnerable with my biological father was a frightening one. I was scared of men and knew it. Al was the sweetest and kindest man I had ever known. He made me laugh and could diffuse any tense situation between us. I knew he would rather stick a knife in his heart than ever threaten or hurt me. He was smart, but never pushed his thoughts or needs with me. I felt safe with him.*

Even if we have had the most positive experiences in fusing and separating with our parents, when we begin a significant adult relationship, we once again must return to these lessons. There is no avoiding this. Separating is a life-long process.

> *Jan: I felt safe with Al or I never could have married him. But inside me was a terror that came from my early childhood that I could not simply choose to ignore. Even though I logically knew there was no danger, whenever Al and I had a disagreement, I felt that at the end of it, one of us would be lying on the floor, dying. I used to walk around our house, looking at him out of the corner of my eye, trying to take down into my heart that I was safe. I would tell myself, repeatedly, "He's not my father. He's not my father."*

If we understand the potential for working through our old issues into a new sense of peace and freedom, we can use the reactions that come up for us in our relationship to strengthen ourselves.

> *Jan: I knew I had picked wisely when I picked Al, but I still had to grow through my fears into my current reality of not only being safe with him, but also of having an adult "me" who could take care of myself. I was no longer a helpless little baby who was trapped with an angry man. And more importantly, whatever happened, this adult me could handle it.*

Role models for each other

People often wonder why we are attracted to opposites and why we do not seek out replicas of ourselves when we look for our Other. We are drawn by an innate desire for completeness. We are drawn to people who complement and balance us and challenge us to continue to grow. People who are timid, for example, may pick a fiery Other, drawn by their right to exist, whereas that fiery Other may be drawn to their Other's vulnerability. We innately strive to become what we are missing in ourselves, learning and getting permission from the qualities of our Other to become bigger than we were.

The strengths we each have are the qualities that draw us to each other. We each occupy one end of a continuum, for example—the continuums of logic and emotion, of awareness of others and awareness of Self, of self-containment and outgoingness. Two people choose each other usually because together they create a balance. The task they each face, then, without losing who they are and their own strength, is to also become the strength of their Other. In this way, we each become more complete.

> Jan: In the beginning of my relationship with Al, I needed his vulnerability and gentleness in order to feel safe. Having found my safety in being a fighter, I was afraid to be vulnerable, myself, but I loved his acceptance and vulnerability. As I became more secure and trusting, though, something changed for me. I began to feel lonely and frustrated, for he didn't express his needs or share his feelings much. I realized that although I had picked him specifically for that unobtrusive and quiet quality of his, I had outgrown my need for him to "go away." I had developed the ability to trust in myself.

At some point, most of us have a negative reaction to the very qualities that may first have attracted us to our Other. We forget that those qualities served an important purpose for us. The balance that once existed when we first came together shifts as we get used to the benefits of those qualities we needed. We begin to feel critical when we become aware of our differentness.

> Jan: It wasn't a problem nor was it a reason to leave the relationship. We had just progressed to a new phase. Now I knew that it was my

turn to support him in growing into his strength and his right to exist, the same way that he had allowed me to work through my fears until I felt safe to be vulnerable in our relationship.

Many people take the statement "And the two shall become one" as meaning that we should become fused with each other and create an undifferentiated whole where no conflict or differentness exist. Another way to look at that thought, however, is that we can each grow into the strengths our Other brings into the relationship, claiming a missing or undeveloped part of our own Self at the same time that we support our Other in doing the same.

Jan: Neither Al nor I have lost anything of ourselves as a result of being together. Instead, in addition to his gentle vulnerability, he increasingly claims his power and his right to exist. And, in addition to my sense of who I am and that I deserve to be here, I increasingly am becoming the vulnerability I see and love in him.

Healthy separateness:
The key to successful relationships

Separating is a mandate of human development and the growth of consciousness is a lifelong process. Marriage is one of the most important relationships in life and is where we have the opportunity to continue our learning and deepen our ability to move fluidly along the fusion-separateness continuum. It is with our Other that we undertake the journey to come to a deeper understanding of ourselves and to practice separating in a healthy way.

Falling in love or finding our "soul-mate" does not change this developmental imperative or make us suddenly more wise or mature. The magical experience of falling in love is an experience of fusion. It sets the stage for continuing the process of separating and individuating—developing our true Self.

In the initial stages of this falling-in-love fusion, we recreate the inseparable closeness of the mother-child relationship—we cannot bear being apart. But just as in the case of the baby needing to be born, to separate or be suffocated, and the mother needing to let go, to give birth or die, in our significant relationship we must also create healthy separation. Our ability to grow and change and yet stay loving and close will determine the success of any important relationship. All the struggles we experienced as children as we worked to separate from our parents will reemerge in adult versions. We will find ourselves in situations where we must learn how to deal with the feelings that come up as we recognize our differentness. We must learn how to create a life together as two separate people.

We bond, or fuse, with someone who has the potential to grow with us and yet who presents us with the triggers that are catalysts for our unfinished work. This fusion creates the next opportunity for our growth.

> *Al: I was looking at my appointment book one afternoon, as I stood in the kitchen. Jan came up behind me and looked at it from over my shoulder. Without thinking, I turned away so she couldn't see it as well. She silently left the room. I immediately thought, "Jan was just curious about what my day was going to be like. She wasn't trying to be invasive." In the other room, Jan was thinking, "Al just wanted a private moment for his thoughts. He wasn't pulling away in order to hurt me." We sought each other out and shared our thoughts. It felt good to have been able to separate instead of getting upset.*

Inevitably, natural differences and needs arise in every relationship. No one is exactly the same as anyone else. If we forget this, when we are startled into an awareness of our differentness, we can easily become self-critical or critical of our Other. Not understanding the true cause of our sudden differentness, we latch on to various explanations that only add to our hurt and confusion. We mistakenly think that superficial differences—addictive behaviors (alcohol use, shopping, overeating, watching sports or soap operas endlessly), an unsatisfying sex life, differences in politics or habits, or in emotional makeup (for example, quiet versus talkative)—are the cause of the problems in our relationships.

Most of the struggles we have in our important relationships, however, are symptoms of a greater issue. They are the result of ignorance about how to accomplish healthy separateness—how to coexist as two different people with two different sets of needs and styles of approaching life.

The Last Frontier of Childhood

It is in the relationship with our Other that we are faced with the necessity to continue our work to not only have an intellectual understanding of what being separate is but to internalize that understanding—to *become* it—so that we are able to move easily and appropriately along the continuum of fusion and separateness. Only in this way can we claim our full right to exist and establish true intimacy.

None of us will ever become a perfectly evolved or "grown-up" person who never has issues or non-logical reactions (reactions that we do not yet understand, that are not of the world of logic but are of the world of emotion). The last frontier of childhood is to grow into balanced and healthy separateness, learning to accept and be at peace with being different from our Other. It is in our significant adult relationships that we continue this challenge.

CHAPTER 5

Relationships— A Mirror Into Our Self

Jan: Al and I had been together for about six months, and I had had enough! In high melodrama, I had my hand on the doorknob about to walk out into the dark night and end our relationship! Suddenly it hit me—this was the third relationship that had ended in the same pattern . . . it couldn't just be him! I must have had something to do with it going wrong, as well! I hated that thought. I much preferred the role of innocent victim!

Our nature as human beings seems to destine us for a lifetime, committed relationship. We are a mating kind of animal. We long for closeness and intimacy and to be seen and accepted for who we are. Even when a relationship is not successful and we move on, it usually is not long before we find ourselves being attracted to another person . . . . and the whole cycle starts all over again.

It is in these relationships that we have the opportunity to learn more about our own Self. We have observed the marriages of other people, especially our parents, and we have all learned from books and movies what marriage is theoretically supposed to be like, but our own direct experience of being married ourselves does not yet exist.

We are all beginners in knowing how to create and develop a successful, committed relationship. Not realizing that we bring the experiences we had of fusion and separateness with us into every significant relationship, we ignorantly hope that all will be well and that "all you need is love."

Falling in Love 1: Head over heels in chemicals

Whether or not we experienced healthy or unhealthy fusion in our childhood, everyone yearns for and loves the feeling of being in love. This feeling is the result of both a physiological and an emotional reality. Scientists have proven that there is a unique chemical released in our brain that corresponds to each emotion we feel. The chemicals released during the first ecstatic phase of a relationship are part of our animal mating response. We are driven by our hormones (chemistry)—swept away by passionate attraction. And, these chemicals are very addictive. They are the same ones released by substances like cocaine and nicotine. Before we even know much about the object of our love, these chemicals have become the trigger for a wonderful experience that happens *inside* of us. We may be focused on the object of our desires—the catalyst for the release of the chemicals—but we are loving our own inner chemically induced experience of being "in love."

The initial period of attraction serves to bring two people together and helps them identify a good potential match, but the excitement of this stage always fades. The chemicals continue to be released for up to eighteen months of a new relationship. The fire has then served its purpose: we have discovered and bonded to each other and are ready to move on to the next stage—deepening our relationship and our knowledge of our Self.

When the chemicals stop being produced by our body as this first phase ends, we often think that something is wrong with our relationship, for while we may love (feel bonded to) the other person, we no longer feel "in love." We may mistake the natural process of a relationship evolving from the first phase of attraction to the next phase of emotional intimacy as a sign that we need to find another relationship.

The difficulty with this is, of course, that "in love" feelings do not last. People who do not understand this will mistakenly seek an experience that can only be attained by continually starting new relationships. They mistake a chemical "high" for love.

Falling in Love 2: Head over heels in fusion

What can compare with the discovery of a kindred spirit, someone with whom we can talk for hours and never run out of things to say, someone who shares our feelings and thoughts and seems to even use the same words we use? How wondrous is the feeling of "Me, too!" as we share our histories, fears and dreams. Our culture speaks of soul-mates and we all long to find ours—the one and only other half of our soul, whom we are destined to marry and with whom we will experience feelings of deep and natural affinity or ease. No struggle, always in agreement, every need met instantly. (Isn't this a perfect description of the fusion an unborn infant feels? Mother—our original and only soul mate.) And, in the first ecstatic phase of our relationship, it may seem that we are among the lucky few who actually have succeeded in that quest. People who experienced healthy fusion in their childhoods will once again find themselves feeling loving and close with their new fusion object.

For people whose childhood experience of fusion was unhealthy, this first phase of creating a relationship is very different. The chemical high they experience is also automatic and addictive and they feel the same excitement in the possibility that they might be able to create real closeness with someone—but for them, the process of establishing an emotional connection is filled with danger. Not having had the experience of being valued and wanted for who they really are, they experience fear of being known and seen as their true Self even when there is no real reason to not be forthright.

> *Al: Early in our relationship, especially when we were first together, I would always focus on what Jan wanted or needed. I remember one time she was sitting on the floor of our first apartment, trying to get me to tell her what I would like to have for dinner. I didn't care and told her so, but she persisted. "If I weren't here, what would you have?" she asked me. "Pizza, I guess." I responded, without much enthusiasm. With excitement, she pounced. "That's a want!" she said triumphantly. And we had pizza for dinner that night. As simple as that might sound, it was terrifying for me to say what I wanted for it left me visible in my needs, instead of being there to take care of hers.*

For people who experienced unhealthy fusion safety depends, as it did in childhood, on them being hyper vigilant, remaining as acutely aware of the moods and needs of their new fusion object as they once were with the needs of their parents. They fear revealing their true feelings and thoughts and hide their inadequacies and imperfections, fearing judgment and rejection.

People who experienced healthy fusion in their childhood fuse and feel oneness. People who experienced unhealthy fusion, however, work hard to create a sense of *sameness* with the person with whom they have bonded. Although there might be warning signals of trouble, we often overlook them in the hope that perseverance, love and endurance will create and sustain a successful relationship. That sense of oneness or sameness may even be maintained until the day we get married or move in together, but typically disappears shortly after. And, most often, it is much more short-lived. What happens?

We bring ourselves wherever we go!

Every time we begin a new relationship, we bring our whole Self along—our self-image, our fears and hopes, our childhood fusion-separateness experiences and the adaptations we have learned in order to try to manage the challenges of the world. Think of it this way—imagine an intimate evening with a hot date, just the two of you . . . And surrounding you are your parents, your past boyfriends or girlfriends, yourself as a child and a teenager and a young adult—all bending close to interpret to you what is being said, advising you as to what things mean and what you should do and say. *There is no such thing as a fresh start!*

When two people first meet, they are totally ignorant of each other and totally new to each other. While this is an obvious fact, what is important about it is that any unlearned lessons we each have (and everybody has them!) are right there, ready to be activated. Just like Pavlovian trained dogs with their reaction to a ringing bell, each of us has catalysts that unconsciously trigger us to do what we have been trained to do.

Because we are new to each other, we are not tangled up in each other's issues yet, but we still bring our own issues to the relationship.

Al: I discovered teasing when I was an adolescent. In retrospect, I think it was my way of laughing at myself and the other person and of talking about issues in a lighthearted way that wouldn't be threatening. I grew up with so much self-criticism that this was a way to interact without being in judgment of myself or of the other person. If I was teasing Jan, for example, I didn't want her to feel judged, but I was trying to bring up something I needed to deal with.

Jan: Whenever Al teased me, I felt skewered by his words. I didn't know why he was after me, but his teasing felt like criticism and anger. Because his communication was in the form of teasing, I felt as though there was no way I could respond to it or resolve anything. He would laugh and play around, and I would feel increasingly hurt and helpless, not knowing how to reach him so he would just talk to me. Sometimes, these interactions ended with me feeling desperate and either trying to tickle him (which for him was pure torture) or I would punch him in the arm.

Not only do we act according to our old patterns of adaptation, but to make life even more challenging, we are usually operating on automatic and are not even aware of our own feelings in the moment or of the issues that we carry with us. We may be self-conscious but we are typically not conscious of our Self.

Al: When Jan teased me, I got her point. I knew what she was doing—she was making a statement and providing me with the opportunity to laugh at myself. It wasn't the same when I teased her and it never occurred to me to ask her why she got upset. I just thought I wasn't doing a good job of making my point and so kept trying harder. I certainly wasn't trying to make her feel bad. When I was teasing her, I was not aware of her sensitivity and vulnerability about feeling attacked.

Jan: Al's teasing was smart and relentless as well as very funny. But I was so frightened of being attacked that I didn't know how to handle it. It also never occurred to me to ask him why he was teasing me or to just tell him how awful it felt to me and how vulnerable I felt.

I don't even think I thought in those terms. I just wanted it to stop. Even when it did stop, it didn't occur to me to revisit it and explore what had been going on in him that caused him to tease me. Because we were in fusion (Jan: "How could you think that was funny?" Al: "How could you think I was attacking you?") *neither of us talked about our own experience and intentions, nor did we think to ask about each other's experience and intentions. Neither of us could talk from a separate place, because we didn't know about separating, at that time. We were unconsciously fused.*

Fusion in the first phase of a relationship

A woman who experienced healthy fusion in her childhood will approach a relationship with optimism, seeing the potential of who they can be together. She will see all the positive promise of the traits she and her newfound love are each working to become. For her, in that first stage of newness and wonder of a relationship, it is as though the clouds part and the mountaintop appears in all its glory. She experiences joy, excitement, wonder, longing and always thinks that this brief vision (of what could be and what will be if they each go through their work of learning) is a vision of what already is now that she has found the right person.

Since a woman's brain more easily sees possibilities, she is biologically set to see the potential for the relationship, but because of the influence of her culture's romantic illusions and her natural urge to fuse, she does not realize that she is seeing the promise of where they could *go*, not the reality of where they *are*. It might be very inspiring to catch a glimpse of the mountaintop, but we still have to take each laborious step on the path that leads up to it.

A man who had the childhood experience of healthy fusion is first chemically attracted to a woman, and then finds himself more deeply interested in her if she has similar values and interests. He approaches the relationship with excitement and optimism, unconsciously seeing the potential of having another loving woman in his life who will focus on his needs. He is happy with having met someone who meets his fusion criteria, especially if she is loving and accepting of him as he is, showing no signs of wanting to change him or anything in the relation-ship. Because of the way his brain works, his feeling is "Mission accomplished!" He has completed his project of finding a mate. He is ready to settle in and enjoy his new relationship, especially if his physical needs are being met and his interests and values are shared.. Nothing needs to change. All is well just as it is.

Both men and women who had unhealthy fusion experiences tend to approach a new relationship with hope but also with fear. Their goal is to be someone the other will want. They carefully watch the other person to determine that person's needs and monitor their own behavior to gain the approval of the other person. They also see the potential for a relationship in which they might finally be able to be themselves. Just like those with healthy fusion, they are oblivious to the overlay of their childhood issues.

The time of establishing and enjoying fusion is fleeting for people of all fusion experiences but it is a necessary and important phase in the development of a relationship. As we get to know, spend time with and become important to each other, we begin the inevitable process of getting our issues intertwined. We are setting the stage for the next phase of deepening our ability to separate. Our unfinished lessons from childhood are being set in place for us in this current relationship.

In this phase of a relationship, we become bonded to each other. We begin to matter to each other so much that when we are finally shocked into awareness of our differences, we cannot simply just walk away. Our human nature has snared us into a situation in which we will either be forced to learn or we will have to experience the heartache of breaking up. We have become fused with our beloved.

We do not even have a clue that we are fused

We are in relationship with someone else from the moment of conception. We do not exist as a separate being. Our thoughts and language reflect this. We define ourselves in terms of others: "I am her daughter, his son, his wife, her husband, their friend." Even if we were to say that we are single, we are defining ourselves in terms of a relationship—"I have no Other."

All of us expect that our Other will see reality the same way we do. We expect that we will both interpret and feel the same way about things. Conceived in oneness and literally having shared the emotional life of our mother before we were born, our standard of relationship is *oneness*. Used to feeling each emotion our mother experienced as the chemicals accompanying her feelings flowed through her body into ours, we do not think to question our fusion with our new fusion object, our Other. All of us either move naturally to meet our Other in their reality, to respond to them as though we shared that reality, or to demand that they meet us in our reality.

Sometimes this feeling of oneness is just perfect. We enjoy the intimacy of fusion without a negative price. This shared reality is comfortable and easy. We feel at home and with our fusion object, we find refuge from the world. We become more important to each other and bond more deeply. Our experience of fusion is undisturbed in these times and we are able to feel a sense of ease and oneness similar to our first experience of life. Everything seems to be as it should be and the world feels very, very familiar.

As infants, we observed the world and came to conclusions about how it works and our place in it. As the center of our own experience, we constructed a worldview or paradigm of reality without even being aware of what we were doing. This worldview was formed long before we had mature or sophisticated reasoning and analytic powers, and so it is inevitable that it contains many misinterpretations and misunderstandings. We each formed a deep conviction about who we are, our value, how relationships work and what our role is in life. We were not conscious of ourselves, so we did not realize that this was happening.

Fusion always ends

When we reach adulthood, we do not even think to question ourselves about such a thing as what our assumptions about reality might be, and it never occurs to us that someone we love might have different assumptions. As we do not question ourselves, we do not question anyone else, either. In our fusion, we simply assume that everyone thinks and believes as we do. We have no reason to think otherwise. We can explain away the differences between ourselves and our parents, because what do they know, anyway?! They're . . . like, totally out of it and *old*! As proven by how all of our friends agree with us! But when we fall in love and then our beloved does not think the way we do . . . Something is very wrong! ("With them!" thinks healthy fusion. "With me!" thinks unhealthy fusion.)

Where once we felt the bliss of oneness or the safety and closeness of sameness, we are now horrified by this new experience, for we are totally unprepared to deal with anything but fusion. When we suddenly become aware of being different—or separate—from our Other, we experience a physical as well as an emotional shock. Jolted out of the fusion we thought would last forever, we feel deeply alone and threatened. The aloneness can induce the same state of panic that an infant might feel if their mother suddenly disappeared. Unlike a baby, however, when startled into an awareness of our separateness, we personalize our sudden sense of aloneness or separateness.

> Jan: I met Al when we both worked for the YMCA. He was the most popular director in the day camp. Wherever he went, kids would follow him as though he were the Pied Piper—literally hanging off his back and each of his arms, and swarming all around him. He was the shining star—the funniest, the most creative, the most thoughtful, the most dynamic and energetic person in camp. He helped everyone with everything and always made everyone laugh and feel good.
>
> We weren't together too long before another side of him became apparent. He would become very quiet and withdrawn. I didn't understand it. I felt lost and confused and very alone. What happened? Where did he go?

People who had healthy fusion as children experience separateness as abandonment or betrayal by our fusion object. We instantly realize that something is wrong . . . with our Other who did something bad to us—and we don't like it! People who had healthy childhood fusion wonder who this stranger is that we married! How could we have been so deceived, so blind? We set out on a course of action to get our bliss back—by changing our beloved back into their true Self (doesn't this sound like the theme of many fairy tales?) or the Self we want them to be. We pursue them, trying to change or correct their thinking or behavior. (Read: arguing, criticizing and reacting in anger, hurt, withdrawal or blame.)

> Al: I certainly was that charismatic YMCA leader, because I felt safe with the kids. But my experience with my mother taught me that I

didn't have the right to exist, that my feelings and needs didn't matter. When I was with Jan, I was very quiet and withdrawn, studying her to figure out how to anticipate and meet her needs so I would feel safe. It didn't work because Jan felt abandoned when I was quiet or withdrawn. I felt guilty and responsible and afraid that I would lose her, but also frightened to reveal who I really was.

People who had unhealthy fusion in their childhoods also know that something is wrong but think that they are the ones who are at fault and that their Other is reacting to their inadequacy. These people feel panicked about losing their Other, and so desperately work to apologize for having made them upset (aware of their separateness).

When we are in a state of fusion, we do not experience our vulnerability. We feel at one with the world. Jolted out of that fusion, it is easy to think that something is wrong either with us or with our Other. We do not think that we are just different, and we do not think to ask questions about what happened. In order to be aware of and acknowledge the fact that we are different, we must feel at peace with our separateness, which is a difficult thing to do, for the pull of fusion is so strong.

From happiness to heartbreak

Jan: I was listening to a song on the radio. The singer, in the saddest of voices, was asking his girlfriend what had happened to their love. He sang that not knowing if they would break up was "killing" him and begged her not to leave until they could "see" if they were "in love."

Love and relationship is, for most of us, something that happens to us. We are the passive recipients of good fortune when it comes and as long as it lasts, and the passive victims of heartbreak when the love mysteriously disappears. We delight in the first stages of attraction and discovery of each other but do not know what to do beyond that. So we explain our experience with the idea that we fall "in" and "out" of love, which leads to serial monogamy: "I love you! . . . Oops! My mistake! You're the wrong one. He's the one . . . . Oops! You're the wrong one, too! I think he's the one!" And on and on. We do not realize that all relationships, even good ones, go through different stages, each with its lessons and challenges.

Innocent and ignorant, we do not have the tools to actively take charge of developing and nurturing separateness, nor do we even have the understanding that we all need to do this. We therefore see the issues that come up in our relationship as problems rather than exercises in separating. People who experienced healthy fusion tend to hold on, hoping that the problems will go away or resolve themselves, that our Other will change, that circumstances will relieve the situation and we will be free to love each other (be fused) again. Some men who have had healthy fusion but unhealthy separateness just flee, moving on to look for a woman who will confirm that they are the center of the Universe. Their inability to feel separate coupled with their linear brains give them no indication that anything other than looking for a new relationship is possible.

We hope and wait, feel helpless and lonely, swallow our anger and frustration or vent it without being able to make the changes we long for. We endure faithfully, adapt around each other, waiting for something to shift between us that will magically bring back that feeling of contentment or happiness that was too fleeting. And worst of all, we simply do not understand what has happened.

We each may feel that our heart is innocent, our intentions are good and that we are patiently putting up with a difficult situation. To women who had healthy fusion experiences, it usually looks as though the other person is obliviously and selfishly thinking only of their own needs and feelings. The woman may hint, suggest, ask, cry, criticize or rage, but somehow nothing seems to work. It just seems as if her Other has changed, does not care or love her anymore or is just being obstinate. People who had unhealthy fusion think that their strategies to make their Other feel safe in their fusion have failed and they too try to change the situation. They try to please their Other, taking on more responsibility, hoping that they can find a way to make their Other feel safe again.

If we try to stay exclusively in fusion in our relationship, we will fail. If we believe that only a fused relationship is a successful relationship, we doom ourselves to disappointment and heartbreak. Only when we understand that moving from fusion to separateness in a relationship is inevitable and not a problem can we avoid the heartbreak that comes with misunderstanding this natural progression.

Marriage is a project

Most of us think of a relationship as being about fulfillment, not growth. As long as we look at the negative feelings and conflicts that inevitably come up in our relationship as problems, we will be frightened and our fear will make it more difficult for us to find our way. We will fear that our having different opinions or needs means that we are incompatible. The romantic notion in our culture that "two shall become one" is born of our longing for fusion, but is a setup for failure.

> *Jan: I once worked with a couple that owned a huge fish tank. The man always wanted his wife to sit with him and watch the fish. But it wasn't enough that they were cuddling together, enjoying the beautiful colors and movements of the fish. He wanted her to watch the exact same fish he was watching.*

While we do join together to journey through life, it is physically and emotionally impossible to join our two selves into one Self, even if the thought of doing so gives us the illusion of safety. If we think that only when we are in a state of fusion are we having a successful marriage, we will panic when we become aware of our differences.

> *Jan: As we walked out of a movie I couldn't stand, Al commented that he liked it a lot. I was immediately furious. (Remember, anger is my signal that I feel separate.) "How could you like that horrible movie?!" I exclaimed in shock. But my reaction was so ridiculous that even I noticed it immediately. What difference did it make if we liked different movies? The movie wasn't important. I was being presented with another opportunity to see how much I automatically live in a place of fusion.*

We will desperately try to reestablish fusion, even if the issue is a minor or unimportant one. We not only fear losing our relationship, but we also have an instinctive panic reaction to suddenly experiencing our separateness. In response to both of these reactions, people who experienced healthy fusion try to get their Other to change their minds. People who experienced unhealthy fusion tend to give up their right to exist in their own individuality, just to eliminate their fear of being rejected when their Other feels separate. To all of us, the experience of separateness is shocking and threatening.

Marriage is an ongoing project. Nothing that comes up is a problem. Everything that causes us to be startled (however we each react to separateness—hurt, anger or any of the other emotions that come from the sudden awareness of our differentness) signals another opportunity for us to work on the endless project of coming to peace with our vulnerability and helplessness, our separateness and our right to exist. Through the interaction in our relationship, we can become aware of areas in which we have the potential to grow. We must always remember that it is in significant relationships that we continue our growing "up" where we left off with our parents.

Nothing in our life has prepared us for the work involved in developing and enriching our marriage. We are all subject to the "happily ever after" illusion. Contrary to the popular mythology of our culture, falling in love is where the work begins, not ends. We do not find a true love and live happily ever after. We find someone with whom to deepen our initial attraction so we can create a lasting and meaningful human relationship.

> Jan: I used to read fairy tales to my daughter, Megan, when she was young. I always ended them with, "And then they (for example, Cinderella and the Prince) got married and went to live in his castle. They learned how to talk about their feelings and problems, and they had a good life together."

We all need to learn to slow ourselves down so we are not simply reacting in a panic to stop the uncomfortable feeling of separateness. Slowing down allows us to identify our own feelings and issues so we can understand our triggers, instead of interpreting our reaction as a response to being attacked or abandoned by our Other. We each have the task of understanding not only our individual issues but also how they are intertwined with those of our Other.

While marriage is not an easy project—it demands infinite compassion and forgiveness for ourselves and our Other, as well as requiring endless time and practice—we can remember that this is what marriage is for all of us. Nothing is wrong with us or with our relationship when issues come up. We do not need to worry or feel afraid that we are not a good match. We just need to remember to go off to *our* castle, and learn how to talk about *our* feelings and problems, so *we* can have a good life together!

Emotional alarms

It is in a marriage that we become aware of reactions that signal our opportunity to grow. When a smoke alarm goes off, we do not panic (hopefully!) We know what it means and know the appropriate action to take. When an *emotional alarm* goes off—any negative or tight feeling—we are just being alerted to separate and get in learning mode. While it is definitely startling, there is nothing to be afraid of or worried about. We are just reacting to a movement along the fusion-separateness continuum. An emotional alarm does not indicate that anything is wrong with us or with our relationship. An opportunity to learn, grow and have increased freedom and peace is just presenting itself.

Marriage is the mirror that enables us to catch a glimpse of ourselves. Our emotional alarms alert us to the areas where we have yet to gain more personal wisdom and to take another step toward the potential as a couple and as the individuals that we saw when we first began our relationship. We cannot stress this enough—fusion is so seductively wonderful and the primitive pull of fusion is so strong that it is easy to mistake this movement on the continuum as a problem. But it is not. It is a challenge and an opportunity to learn and grow. It is necessary and unavoidable. None of us are fully developed beings.

> *Jan: When one of these _____ (insert curse word) "opportunities" for growth occurs, I now tell myself, "I'm so theoretically happy. I'm experientially miserable, but I'm theoretically happy!" It helps me to remember! Nothing is wrong. Al and I will become happier and closer as the result of going through this experience!*

Emotional alarms go off all the time during the course of a day. They interrupt the peace we might be feeling. Adrenaline is released into our bodies and creates the physical sensation of tightness. We call this tightness by various names: hurt, sadness, anger, frustration, shock, fear—but physiologically, we are simply being flooded with fuel (adrenaline) to enable us to take action to meet a challenge. The sudden energizing of our body calls us to attention. We can no longer proceed in peace without assessing what is going on and coming to a deeper understanding of our Self and our Other.

Although the emotions we feel seem instantaneous, they are not. In the split second between the physical experience of tightness and our emotional reaction, we have interpreted what our fusion object is feeling or has done. The fact that we interpret is the result of fusion— we assume that we know what our Other is feeling and intending. The nature and content of the interpretation is based on our past experiences or fears. All of us look at the world through glasses of our past. Our histories of pain and happiness and our unfinished development issues color what we see. All experiences in our lives are perceived and interpreted through these glasses, especially the experiences in which we feel vulnerable or that trigger memories, conscious or not, of times in the past when we were vulnerable.

The content of our interpretation of what is going on with the other person is not the point. The very awareness that we are making an assumption or interpretation is a call to action, the signal to pay attention, letting us know that the time of fusion is over. *Tightness is the signal that we have moved away from the fusion end of the fusion-separateness continuum and need to pay attention.* If we accept the need to separate, we will be able to take steps to understand ourselves and our Other more deeply.

It is easy to misinterpret emotional alarms and think that they signify danger. We tend to react like threatened animals by either pulling back and protecting ourselves or by attacking. That is as logical as when a fire alarm goes off, either cowering in a corner or ripping the alarm from the ceiling and jumping on it. The alarm itself is not the point. What it signifies, however, can be life furthering. Every emotional alarm lets us know that we have encountered a situation where we have the opportunity to become more conscious and aware of ourselves and our Other.

If we accept this call to learn, when we have upset reactions, we can explore together what got triggered in each of us. If we were talking and a fire alarm went off, we would not get hurt or angry at each other or at the alarm. We would stop, analyze the situation and act based on our analysis. An emotional alarm is no different from an external alarm. It signals us that action is needed to further our well-being.

Reach for each other

If we were with our Other in a plane and suddenly heard an engine explode, we would most likely reach for each other and hold tight. Whatever we might have to face, we would rather face it holding onto the person we love. If we approach every situation in life in this way, rather than turning on each other in fear, anger or hurt, we will remember that we are life allies, exploring and learning together. We will remember that it is the very purpose of a relationship to facilitate our becoming more conscious beings. When an alarm goes off, we can remember that it is the recess bell calling us into class because there is something for us to learn. We each have the opportunity to become wiser and more free from our automatic survival reactions.

When an emotional alarm goes off, we are being signaled to take a step back from the close and easy openness we were sharing with our fusion object in order to do two things. We need to recognize that we no longer know what is going on in our Other. They have not trans-formed magically and suddenly into a monster. *We are just disconnected* from them and do not understand their reality in this moment.

Secondly, we must ask ourselves what is going on in ourselves, as well. What are our feelings, our thoughts? In that moment of not knowing, we are disconnected from both our own Self and our Other. We are ignorant of what they are feeling or experiencing and of what got triggered in us. We are in an adrenaline reaction.

Marriage, as is true for every significant relationship, serves as a powerful mirror to our own Self. Bonded with our Other, we must understand the reactions we have to our Other that occur nowhere else in our lives. This is where our work begins.

CHAPTER 6

Lost in Fusion

Women lost in fusion: Princess or victim— A note from Jan

I grew up around strong women. My mother didn't put up with unconscious men and so divorced both of the ones she married. I watched my other female relatives verbally flay their husbands. My aunts, great-aunts and grandmother easily dispatched my seemingly helpless and long-suffering uncles, great-uncles and grandfather. Most of the other adult women I encountered did the same with their husbands. They were often really funny and witty as they did so, but they were clearly in charge. They expected to have their way without question and they could be brutal. Everyone would laugh, men included—although they also rolled their eyes a lot—but no one took on these matriarchs about how they handled what they were feeling. Cousins and second cousins avoided their sharp tongues and when they could, moved away. The men just stayed till they died.

These women were smart and funny, their eyes sparkled as they laughed at themselves, and I grew up loving them for their strength and for the sense of community they gave me. I belonged to them and with them. I would get to grow up to be strong, just like them. But it was always very clear who I was—I was a member of the ruling class. There was no question that we each wanted a man—they were very nice to have around—but there was also no question about who was supposed to be in charge. I was born to be a princess.

Some women have a totally different experience in childhood. They come from a family culture where the men were dominant and sometimes even verbally or physically abusive. They were taught that only the needs and feelings of men were important and that the woman would only be wanted if she served those needs. A man was not to be questioned or challenged. If the woman were to get any of her needs met, it would be either surreptitiously or by supplicating and pleasing the man. And, some women are born into a family where although their mother was a princess, she did not entitle her daughter to be one, too. These women were also taught that their needs are not important. Whether it is the mother or the father who makes no room for the needs of their daughter, these women are born to be victims.

Both princesses and victims are taught fusion, not separateness. Both learn to be either dominant or weak, but not to be their true Self. Neither are taught how to be in a true, connected relationship.

Stuck in fusion

While the surface experience and sense of entitlement or importance of the princess and the victim are quite different, essentially, their lesson about fusion and separateness is exactly the same. Neither princess nor victim has a separate Self. Both are fused to the Other in their lives and both pay an enormous price for this fusion. They live in fused reaction and are at war or in competition in their relationships, for only one person will have the right to exist. For a princess, it has to be her. For a victim, it can never be her.

A princess knows she is right and becomes angry or indignant if her Other questions her or has different ideas than she does. Her way is better—end of story. If her Other does not cheerfully acquiesce to her desires, then something is wrong with him. She calls him a victim or says he is pouting or controlling. A victim knows that what she wants has to be secondary to the needs of her Other. If her Other asserts himself, she fearfully or resentfully (or both) sublimates her needs. She calls him controlling or selfish or calls herself unworthy.

A princess is the boss. If she can fit in her Other's needs without sacrificing any of her own, then she will graciously do so, but only if it is convenient. A victim is the servant. If she can satisfy all of her Other's needs, she might get some of her own taken care of—as long as it is not an inconvenience to her Other.

Both princess and victim have distorted views of the power or intelligence of their Other. Women often see men, for example, as stupid, helpless and incompetent or as tyrants. Even a woman who feels victim to a man may still feel superior to him, just too intimidated and with too little right to exist to assert herself.

Often, women alternate between the roles of princess and victim, sometimes feeling helpless to their Other, sometimes feeling superior and powerful. Both roles are attempts to protect themselves from the experience of vulnerability. Caught in the role of either princess or victim, they do not think to insist on the exploration of their relationship in a separate and scientific manner. They have trapped themselves and their Other in roles and do not even realize it. Neither has learned healthy separateness and both are living their demand that they should not have to feel separate.

Both are dependent on their Other. The princess depends on her Other to have just the same needs as she does so she does not have to feel separate. The victim waits for her Other to finally grant her the right to exist so she does not ever have to step out of fusion to be a separate adult.

Both princess and victim often see their Other as being a child without recognizing that in their own dependency, they are also being childlike. Stuck in fusion, they cannot experience their true strength. Neither of them have a sense of how to create a connection through separateness or how to work with the reality of each person so they both have the right to exist.

Fused and personalizing

Al was watching a basketball game. I had just read a very funny anecdote in a magazine and wanted to tell him. Realizing that multitasking is not a male strength (see—I'm learning!) I asked if he wanted to hear while he was watching or wait till the game was over. He said he wanted to wait but he never came back to me and asked to hear it. My first reaction, out of fusion, was to feel hurt and think that he really wasn't interested in me or in what I had to share. I played with that for a while and then decided that he was just involved in his own thoughts. I need to remember that and not make it about me. I again asked if he wanted to hear the anecdote and he was happy that I had reminded him.

The examples, for all of us, go on and on. If we pay attention, we will find that the tiniest little interaction will startle us out of our fusion and we will feel some version of hurt or irritation.

Another time, Al asked me to read him a list so he could write it down more quickly. I had only gotten a couple of items out when he interrupted to ask if some particular item was included. I immediately felt jarred. "Give me a chance to finish!" I snapped. That item had been next. The easy fusion I slipped into of us being a team and thinking together had been broken and I was startled—which I expressed in annoyance. But a thought had come into his mind that he wanted to check out. He wasn't trying to control or correct me, even though that was my immediate interpretation. In separateness, I would have only replied, "That's exactly what's next." Only in fusion would I expect him to not have his own needs or thoughts.

It takes work to step back, contain myself and separate. It is much easier to just demand that he is me! And punish him (with irritation or worse!) if he isn't. Hel-lo-o! I am a princess, in case you have forgotten!

Fusion can also be smothering!

We have two dogs, Cassie and Maya. Although they are crazy about Al, for some reason, they have primarily attached themselves to me. They wait patiently by my bedside for me to get up in the morning, moving from room to room with me as I get ready for the day. As soon as I put on my shoes, they know it is almost time for our morning walk and they start making excited little puppy sounds. They will accompany me as I get the items I take with me on my walk and prepare to go. I cannot move or turn around without their excited breathing, panting, barking, licking and whining surrounding me. I feel like Disney's Cinderella! Good thing I'm not! I think I would go crazy with all those bunnies and birds and deer and mice scurrying around me every time I made a move, chirping and scampering and singing. I can barely stand it with our two dogs.

As much as I have princess inclinations, the reality is that it would drive me nuts to have Al live totally focused on me. I need him to be the center of his own life, to have his own needs and thoughts, even if sometimes his expressing them makes me feel jarred. And if he were too focused on me, as indeed he once was, I would feel so lonely, for the uniqueness that is Al would not be there. While fusion seems as if it offers closeness and comfort, it is an experience of oneness and can be suffocating and lonely. Only in separateness can we experience coming together in emotional intimacy and sharing who we each are so we can have the real comfort of knowing someone deeply and not being alone.

Separate and equally valid

One day Al and I took Seth and Megan to a community event at a park. When lunchtime came, Al wanted to get them hot dogs and lemonades. I thought, "Yuck! Hot dogs." But there wasn't anything else nearby and the kids were excited, so I agreed, only making the slight suggestion that at least we let them drink water so lunch wouldn't be completely junky. But Al wanted to buy them lemonades. He wanted them to have the experience of being at a fair and eating fair food. He said they eat healthy food all the time and it wouldn't hurt. I looked at my nutrition-ally superior idea and at his legitimate experiential and cultural idea and realized that there could be no comparison of them. His idea was as good as mine. Just different.

A diamond has many facets, each one important to the integrity and the beauty of the gem. In our lives, we are each focus on a different facet of development and experience, the one that is important and necessary to our becoming whole. One facet is no more important than another. They are just different. In our relationship, we will most likely focus on different aspects of reality than our Other does and come up with ideas, needs or feelings reflecting the aspect of reality we are paying attention to. All aspects of reality have their own validity—and unless it is a life or death situation, there is really no *better* idea, feeling or need. Just different ones. It is not a competition that the most logical idea wins. Logic is only one dimension of reality. Each idea has its own validity.

If we are in fusion, we will think that the facet of life we are attending to is the most important one. And it may be—to us. Being separate, however, means recognizing that our Other is most likely focusing on another aspect of reality that is equally valid and important to them.

The good news

I just want to report that it really is possible to make the changes we are talking about in this book. And, it is interesting to me that a lot of change has happened for Al and for me as a result of working on this book. We have known about the tools for a long time but writing the book has forced us to take a step back from the intensity of our immediate reactions and look at how things work in our relationship with that scientific curiosity we have been talking about. This stuff really works! But it takes commitment to ourselves and to *doing* the work. *Knowing* is not enough. As with any activity or skill, theory only gets you so far. We have to jump in and practice taking what is in our minds down into our bodies so we can *become* our knowledge.

Having worked on my right to exist and being the adult to take care of my own vulnerability, I have come to a place where it is no longer so frightening to feel separate from Al. Once I would have done anything to have appeared innocent, for I feared the vulnerability of being exposed in my human fallibility. Even though it made no sense to me in any logical way, I believed and felt that if I admitted to being anything less than perfect, I would somehow be destroyed. Literally. But I do not have that reaction anymore. Now, if I get triggered and he says something about it, it is no big deal. A confrontation is not a threat anymore. It is more like I erupt and then ask myself "What was that all about?"

I know what I am working on in my development—all that separateness stuff—so when things come up, it is almost like watching someone else. I am not threatened. It is really no big deal anymore! I just notice and take my separateness deeper into my consciousness. And, I am saying this as someone who used to fight visciously for what felt like my very survival.

I certainly have been exhausted from things I have been grappling with in myself in these last months but I know this is just a process of transformation. I am being reworked inside and changed. And that change has always, always led me to greater peace and happiness and a closer connection with Al.

So, what I want to say to you, women, is: Take hope and take heart! It *really* is possible to do this project we call marriage.

Men lost in fusion—Independent or scared? A note from Al

Men struggle with how to have an intimate emotional relationship and still maintain their separate sense of just being who they are. In this way, they are no different than women. But there are three major differences:

1. Men have not been encouraged to have emotional awareness or expressiveness and so they lag behind women in confidence that they know what they are feeling and how to express those feelings effectively.
2. Men's brains do not move as quickly or multidimensionally as women's brains do, so as a rule, if the conversation is emotional, they are not able to keep up and can easily feel overwhelmed.
3. Men place an enormous importance on freedom because they are not confident that they can collaborate with women without becoming overwhelmed and losing themselves.

In addition to these three factors is the effect of fusion, which we all experience. Generally, men think in fused terms—everything is about them (self-centeredness) or because of them (a false responsibility for causing the problem as well as for fixing it). If a woman has a need, she is really making a statement about the man. In his mind, she does not exist as a separate, independent entity. He never thinks that the woman has a different set of needs.

Men characterize women from a non-separate position—the woman is trying to control him and criticize him so she can have power over him. And since men generally feel that they are fine just the way they are, if a woman notices or informs a man about something about him that could be different, he is likely to be startled, hearing what she says as criticism of him. The idea that the woman might have a separate need or that she hopes he wants to learn or grow as a person is usually not the way a man interprets her message.

Example: A man thoughtfully puts up rice to cook in the rice cooker. His wife informs him that the steam from the rice cooker is also cooking the cabinet above it, so they both need to remember to pull the rice cooker out away from the cabinet. The man hears her saying, "You didn't do it right."

Example: A man is driving and his wife observes, "I think it's a lot faster to go down this street." The man hears her saying, "You're not driving right." The woman may be collaborating or co-driving, but the man wants the freedom to be the only driver. Not feeling the need for a co-driver or collaborator, he hears what she says as criticism.

Example: A woman says, "Will you go shopping with me? I want to buy a dress for that party." A man says, "Why can't you go by yourself? You know I hate shopping." He thinks that she is trying to force him to do something he does not want to do, not that she has a need for company or help. It probably never occurs to him to think, "She knows I don't like to go shopping. I wonder why it's important to her for me to come?"

Example: A woman tells a man when he comes home from work, "I need a break from the kids. Would you watch them? I'm exhausted from being with them all day." The man hears "You're responsible for everything." The man is only aware of his own experience—he may be tired, he just walked in the door and she already has demands. He will interpret the situation from his fears and will feel put upon—he has been at work all day and now he has to watch the kids. He has to do everything.

When women share their needs or observations, in their fusion, men perceive that they are being criticized, controlled and judged to be inadequate. Women often approach situations with a collaborative feeling. Men look at situations and think in terms of tasks being assigned.

This difference in approach to a situation can easily be seen in sports. Male athletes collaborate to win, but in order to do this, each player has a role—the quarterback, the tight end, the defensive back—that he alone is responsible for. Although it is a team game, each player feels an intense responsibility to fulfill his role or he feels like he "let the team down."

A man's brain becomes overwhelmed with the unsolicited new information coming from a woman. His explanation for his need to be independent comes from feeling scared that he does not have the awareness, the desire or the capacity to be separate and negotiate in the relationship for what he needs. Men talk about valuing their freedom as though they are in a position of strength and centeredness. They are critical and self-righteous about how women mistreat them. The need for this artificial separateness, or physical separation, is really a substitute for feeling confident and comfortable in being able to figure out how to be separate emotionally.

Usually when the weekend comes, I have a mental list of things I would like to get done. When Jan talks about what she is interested in doing, I immediately panic. I instantly get overwhelmed with all the alternatives and get scared that I am not going to be able to get my list done. What I forget is that Jan is very good at looking at my needs and her needs and coming up with a plan to organize our time. What I also forget is that I can ask for help and that I don't need to be good at organizing our two lists. I just need to have faith that I won't abandon my needs and that we will create a good plan. I am an excellent organizer and executor of plans when I am either alone or in charge. I don't have the same confidence in myself as a collaborator.

Misinterpretations that come from being fused

1. *She is trying to take away my independence.* Often, a man is afraid of losing his independence. If he does not see that the woman is just expressing her needs so that they can have a conversation about how to address the needs they both have, then of course he will misinterpret her.

Content in what he is doing, a man can be immediately threatened by the sudden presentation of a new set of needs—the woman's. Slow to identify choices, men operate in a win-lose system and fear having to give up what they want. Two sets of needs means someone is not going to get what they want and someone else is. It is a competition. Like women, men, too, do not conceive of separateness as an alternative explanation of what is going on.

2. *What I have to say is never right.* Example. Woman: "I was talking to my friend today and really felt like she was trying to make me feel guilty for not calling her more often." Man: "Maybe you shouldn't be her friend anymore."

A man does not necessarily understand that the woman may be asking for him to be responsive, not responsible. A responsive answer is compassionate and caring, acknowledging her feelings without having to do anything about them. It is fairly effortless. A responsive answer does not take on the problem with the responsibility of having to be the one who not only solves the problem but also is responsible for how it all turns out. No wonder men do not want to make a commitment!

Too much pressure and too many opportunities to feel like a failure! For men who cannot differentiate between being responsible and being responsive, a relationship is like taking on a bad second job.

In fusion, if the woman is struggling with something, it is hard for the man to step back and allow her to have her feelings. In addition to caring about her happiness, he also wants to stop her struggle so he is not affected by it. He interprets his wanting to stop an uncomfortable feeling from getting stirred up in him as the woman wanting him to be responsible for fixing the problem so that there is no uncomfortable feeling in her.

> 3. *I am not ready to make a commitment.* This statement is the result of a man being in a state of fusion with his Other. He is focused only on his own needs, unless her needs are nonthreatening and convenient to consider. (This is somewhat like the "princess" feelings Jan described earlier in this chapter.)

The need to be free is a given for a man. Any threat to this freedom—in other words, the separate existence of someone else—is experienced as danger. In fusion, loss of freedom is defined as having to consider the existence of someone else and the possibility of needing to give up something—feeling trapped or responsible for fixing the problems of his Other. It is therefore never something a man would want. His experience of separateness is that he is being controlled, asked to be someone that he is not, endlessly being asked to change and being told that what he offers in the relationship is never enough.

Given this view of reality, why commit—*ever?* Pulled between the fear of losing his freedom and the desire for a close relationship, a man might not realize that being committed does not mean being in prison or in a mental hospital!

For all people, feeling free is one of the most important needs in a relationship. Separateness and mutual respect are necessary for true freedom—where both people support each other to be who they really are. In true separateness, where both people have the right to exist and where they are responsive *to* each other—not responsible *for* each other—the obligation, pressure and loss of Self that men fear will not become a reality.

Vulnerability as power

Men sometimes claim that they have too much pride to be the one to break a power struggle with their Other, to share their true feelings or to come with curiosity and ask what can be done to reconnect and find a satisfying resolution. They refuse to acknowledge or talk about what issues got triggered in them. They do not want to feel as if they are defeated, weak or less-than their Other. They react in judgment of themselves or in fear of being judged and humiliated by their Other.

What might lie behind this pride is a deep sense that they are emotionally ill equipped to be vulnerable. They are like animals whose security lies in their physical strength. Vulnerability is instinctively linked with a primitive sense of weakness and danger.

During a fight that Jan and I had early in our relationship, I made the decision to stop fighting and just feel what I was feeling. While I felt the pain of her words, what was more powerful for me was that I had confronted an internal bully who had controlled me my whole life—a bully who said I couldn't feel what was going on in me or show my vulnerability to anyone else. It was one of the first times in my life where I felt absolutely fearless and completely strong.

The illusion is that vulnerability is a weakness when actually the acceptance of it allows us to be powerful in a way that is unshakeable. When we accept our vulnerability, nothing can be done or said to us that can shake us out of being at peace with who we really are. This acceptance also allows us to communicate from a separate place because it frees us from the need to be fused. We can step out of a reactive stance, free to be our true Self.

There is nothing about us to judge or hide or be ashamed of. There is no need to feel defensive in response to what a woman says, or to impotently fight for independence, or to project that she is being critical, when in fact, all along, we were the ones who were afraid and self-critical of our own vulnerability. In acknowledging our vulnerability, we can claim a truer power. We can accept our humanness and reject, absolutely and forever, any judgment of ourselves.

When we step out of fusion and into separateness, we feel our vulnerability much more. Most of us have an internalized cultural judgment that we are not men if we are vulnerable—we do not measure up to the societal standards of what a man should be like. As emotional awareness is neither supported or developed in boys nor encouraged in men, we simply are not used to being emotionally connected to ourselves. Not knowing how we feel gives us the sense of being out of control, yet feeling our emotions brings up the fear that we will be overwhelmed. But this is not an inevitable state or fate that we are condemned, by either physiology or culture, to live. With loving support for who we really are and education about how to live as vulnerable and emotional beings, we can change the role that has historically been given us.

One Christmas, when our son, Seth, was two and a half years old, Jan's grandmother gave her mother, Bette, a family heirloom that was very meaningful to her. As Bette sat there, tears running down her face, Seth stopped playing with his gifts and quietly came over to her. He stood by her side for many minutes, silently stroking her cheek.

We do not have to teach our children that they are responsible to fix anyone's feelings or problems. Seth was not trained to hide his feelings or fear showing tenderness. He loved his grandmother and just wanted to be with her while she was having her feelings. Neither his vulnerability nor his grandmother's were threatening or overwhelming. There was no discomfort or judgment associated with the emotion or the vulnerability. When we allow children to feel the natural empathy and caring that come from their hearts, they will be comfortable with vulnerability.

And then there is little John, three years old. Since he and his twin were born, Jan has been making house calls to their family in order to make life a bit easier for his busy parents. So, for his entire life, John has been hearing the words of true feelings and has been exposed to the tools of separateness.

One day, his father, Steve, took John and his sister, Ellen, to meet Annie, their mom, at her office. On the way, Annie called and asked that they meet at a nearby restaurant instead. When Steve announced the change to the children, John immediately and calmly said, "That not okay with John. That make John sad. John want to see Mommy, now. John want to go to Mommy's office, not restaurant." Steve was stunned and thrilled that his son was able to process his feelings and communicate them so clearly. "Thank you for telling me how you feel, John!" he said. "Your feelings are very important to me. Let's go to Mommy's office right now!"

Because John is growing up in a family where vulnerable feelings are valued and self-awareness and direct communication are encouraged, he knows he has the right to exist and that his needs are important. He was able to identify and express his true feelings, select the alternative that he wanted and advocate for what he needed. He was not overwhelmed with helplessness and emotions for which he had no words and that might have led to a tantrum, as he faced a change of plans that upset him. If he were growing up in a different family culture, he might have grown into a man who would have adult versions of tantrums when he felt startled. He would have only known that he did not like what was going on but would have had no support to pay attention to his emotions or to develop the ability to come up with alternatives that would address them.

In an era when men are being asked by their women to be more vulnerable, we men have opportunity as well as the task of learning to access and accept ourselves as emotional beings who are just as sensitive as women are. And, we can give this opportunity to our children.

Let's settle something once and for all

Men, we need to be honest with ourselves—are we independent or are we scared? Do any of these situations feel familiar to you? And what do they really mean?

1. *Sometimes I feel comfortable and relaxed, but then I suddenly want to have space*—translates to: My Other has expressed a desire or asked a question and I immediately feel trapped or responsible for coming up with a good answer or solution, so I want to get away.

2. *Sometimes I get angry when she wants something from me*—translates to: I feel overwhelmed, burdened and do not know how to make room for my needs. I feel trapped and obligated to do what she wants me to do. My anger is a way to push back at her so I can have room for myself.

3. *Sometimes I find myself making up reasons to blame her for getting angry or for my needing space*—translates to: I never feel this way when I am by myself or with my friends. It must be her. She is just too demanding.

4. *Sometimes I need to get away someplace where I can just be myself—*
translates to: I might be able to maintain a relationship with her
if I have a place to get away and be safe when I feel overwhelmed.
I don't know how to make room for myself except by physical
separation.

These are typical responses that men have to interactions with women.
Essentially, what men want in each of these situations is to hold onto
themselves. They do not want to feel responsible for anyone else and ignore their own wants and needs. As long as they are trapped in fusion,
they have no recourse but to create physical separation or to make a
case for their independence.

Separateness is the key that allows both of us to exist

When we learn to separate, we learn to take responsibility for ourselves,
increasing our awareness of our feelings and our ability to talk about
our emotions and needs in a collaborative way.

The gift of separateness is that we will be free to have emotional
intimacy, rather than the burden of responsibility for someone else. It
will be enough for us to be who we really are, present in our needs and
thoughts and responsive and caring with our Other.

The task of our era for all of us

In fusion, we focus on our Other. We "re-act" to our Other rather than
act *for* ourselves. We demand that our Other be adult and judge or fear
them when they are not. But the truth is that they are innocent and
ignorant—if they knew how to deal with their feelings and do their life
better, they would. The same truth applies to us—if we knew how to
deal with our feelings and do our life better, we would, too.

Although we all have so much to learn, we are all adults. When
we blame, accuse, criticize, get impatient or are hurt by the actions of
our Other, we are not claiming our own adult power. We are putting
ourselves in the position that our well-being is dependent on someone
else (who is just as ignorant, vulnerable and fearful as we are) being
separate and adult.

The fear we all have of claiming our right to exist and separating is that we will feel our vulnerability more. Only when we are at peace with our vulnerability—our lack of control over each other and our helplessness about outcomes—can we truly separate and focus on our own truth. Our Other will either turn out to be a good match for us or they will not. We do not have control over that. We only have control over revealing ourselves as completely as possible, so that we will more easily be able to see if we are a good match.

We will pay an enormous price if we do not ask ourselves to claim our right to exist and learn to separate. We will live frightened and on the defensive, always ready for conflict and never at peace with who we are. We will never be able to have the joy of a truly close emotional relationship.

The task of this era is for women to claim their power and for men to claim their vulnerability. Both have the opportunity to exist as more complete beings. Women are powerful and do not need to hide it by submitting to the "strength" of a man or overcompensating for their fear and vulnerability by being domineering or angry. Men are as vulnerable as women and have the right to be unashamed of their sensitivity and not hide or overcompensate for their fear and vulnerability by being passive, domineering or angry.

All living beings fear being vulnerable. The style we each have to deal with this fear varies but the core fear is the same, as is the core task of coming to peace with the simple reality that all we can do is live our truth, be the people we respect being and release the illusion that we have ultimate power over outcomes.

It is an ironic paradox that by separating and releasing the illusion of control, we have the best chance possible of creating, in the truth of who we each are, a good relationship with our Other. Holding on to our relationship in fusion creates a distorted dynamic that eventually becomes too painful to continue. By being *willing*—though not *wanting*—to lose our relationship, we have the best chance of keeping it, for we bring our true selves to each other.

At this point in the development of human consciousness, we can overcome the historical and traditional roles and limits on who we were allowed to be and claim our right to be our whole selves. With a deeper understanding of ourselves and with tools to break down old patterns and replace them with new ones, we can create a new vision of what it means to be in an emotionally intimate relationship.

CHAPTER 7

Building Conscious Connection

We each have two distinct aspects of ourselves. We are animals, driven by our hormones and by our survival needs. Equally powerful is the fact that we are humans, driven by our natural imperative to grow, to find satisfaction and meaning in life and to create meaningful connection with other people. Studies have shown that when a woman is in the fertile part of her cycle, she is drawn to the more stereotypic masculine type of man, instinctively seeking a healthy and strong mate and provider. Those same studies show that when a woman is in the part of her cycle when she is not driven by hormones—when she is incapable of conceiving a child—she is drawn to more sensitive and communicative men, seeking satisfaction for the human need of a meaningful connection with her mate.

We can enter a relationship from either aspect of ourselves. Our animal nature will drive us into a relationship with our hormones—we will be swept away. Because the initial surge of hormonal arousal is so powerful and pleasant when we feel passion for someone, we have confused it with love. Our culture has played a big part in this confusion, primarily focusing on relationships that revolve around this hormonal arousal. People see each other and "fall in love." They feel alive and energetic, surging with vitality, aware of their senses and of their maleness or femaleness. In our culture, this is presented as being enough. Truly this is a wonderful feeling and if we wanted only to mate and then go on our way, it probably would be enough.

Our human nature will cause us to choose to be with someone with whom we experience emotional closeness. An animal is responsive to the presence of another animal. A human can actively choose their life companion. We need more than animals do. We have a human consciousness, in addition to our animal needs. Passion can only take up so much of our time. If we try to develop a rich and meaningful human connection in a relationship based on passion but cannot because the communication is not good, there will be trouble, for passion or love is simply not enough. Such a passion cannot last—misunderstandings will result in hurt and anger and the passion will eventually be destroyed.

When we understand this, it is not troubling when the fire grows dim or other feelings surface. These are just the signals that we are ready to begin deepening our communication and learning more about each other and ourselves. When we use these signals to look for and discuss with scientific and (even!) loving curiosity those often ignored small issues that we have not bothered to explore before, our feelings begin to grow in a different way. We may not necessarily have that hot excitement, but we will have a richer, deeper experience of closeness and love. Instead of intensity and aliveness being the results of our passive animal chemical reaction to each other, our deliberate choice to expand our human consciousness and engage in emotionally intimate interaction does an amazing thing—it creates those same chemicals that make us feel alive and loving. The more we choose to relate to each other in this way, the more those chemicals will flow. This might even cause good friends to be romantically drawn to each other, their emotional intimacy having created the chemicals of love.

Good communication creates the foundation that allows two people to be best friends, to feel safe and loving with each other and to find a deeper kind of passion—one that will not be driven to extinction by the lack of an emotionally intimate relationship.

There has to be a "me" before there can be an "us"

Jan: I remember being with my first boyfriend. One day, seemingly out of the blue, he asked me if I were angry. Feeling just fine, I responded "NO!!!" in the loudest, most angry voice imaginable! He was startled—

but I was dumbfounded. I literally had absolutely no awareness of being in the slightest bit angry, and yet the intensity of my response was undeniable. I was shocked that I was so disconnected from myself.

Before we can begin to establish good communication with someone else, we must have a good connection with ourselves. Just as an emotional alarm in a relationship signals that we have shifted along the fusion-separateness continuum, we also have emotional alarms of tightness that let us know that we are not connected to our own Self.

Jan: Whenever I get tight inside, I always ask myself: "Am I feeling helpless and vulnerable, separate, or that I don't have the right to exist?" It never fails that whatever is going on boils down to one of these basic issues or some combination of them.

Helplessness: I don't feel critical of myself or of other people anymore. Ever. So, if I do find myself having a critical thought, I look to what issue is getting triggered. It is always that I am feeling sad for someone or about something and am helpless to do anything about it. When I recognize this, the critical thought always goes away and I just allow the helpless and sad feelings to be there.

Separateness: Sometimes I can hear irritation in my voice when I am talking with Al. Often, it's when he is withdrawn (my experience) or quiet (his experience). I am aware that there is nothing wrong with him being quiet or with my wanting to know what is going on with him. We are just having different needs. I feel disconnected from him and don't want to be. When I recognize and accept this, I can change from being irritated to being able to calmly ask him what he is thinking or feeling.

Right to exist, Al: Sometimes at dinnertime, Jan will say she doesn't care what we have to eat. I often go immediately to feeling that I shouldn't care, either—but I do. I have to work to give myself permission to acknowledge that I have wants instead of succumbing to my old pattern of fusing to be just like whomever I'm with.

We all need to learn about ourselves—our reactions, our triggers and how to correctly understand what we are feeling. Without this knowledge, we are stuck in reactiveness, disconnected from ourselves and driven by our unconsciousness. If we cannot understand what we are feeling, we will never be able to learn how to take care of ourselves in ways that are satisfying or to talk about our feelings with our Other. If we are not connected to our own Self, there will be no one there to connect with our Other!

Permission to be yourself

There is something inside each of us that hesitates to feel vulnerable and identify what we are really feeling. Over time, we can become disconnected from ourselves and forget who we are or why we are feeling what we feel. We may lose trust in ourselves and feel lost.

Deep inside each of us, however, is a guiding wisdom. We each have a Self that knows exactly what we want and what is right for us. We know exactly how much salt to put on our popcorn and what our favorite color is. We know what movie we are in the mood for and when we are tired and want to sleep. We do not need anyone else to tell us. This information can come right up from deep inside of us if we are at peace with the three basic human issues—our right to exist, our separateness, and our helplessness with its resulting vulnerability. None of us, however, are perfectly at peace with all three and so we tend to get disconnected from ourselves.

Our knowing Self watches in amazement and despair as we act in ways that defy common sense and logic. We can often look back and see that we may have known how we felt or what we wanted but for some reason did not act on that knowledge.

Exercise

Have you ever asked yourself any of the following questions?

- Why do I do things when I know they are not good for me?
- What is wrong with me?
- Why do I doubt myself?
- Why don't I like myself?
- Am I crazy?!?
- Why don't I listen to myself?
- Why don't I even know what I want?

We all tend to question and doubt ourselves when one of our three basic human issues is stirred up. These questions reflect how difficult it is to be different from other people and to have permission to be our own unique and separate Self. When we accept and trust ourselves, we are saying to ourselves and to others that what we think and feel is important. Instead of being stuck in feelings of self-judgment and doubt and feeling bad about ourselves, we can use any negative self-assessment as a valuable signal that simply alerts us to reconnect with ourselves.

Look at the questions above through the lenses of the three basic human issues.

"Why do I do things when I know they are not good for me?" becomes "I am feeling vulnerable and don't know what to do with those feelings. It is easy to do things even when I know they are not in my best interests to numb or cover up those vulnerable feelings" or "Sometimes I do those things so I don't have to feel different (separate) from other people because it is hard to feel like I have the right to exist as who I am."

"What is wrong with me?" becomes "I don't feel that it's okay to be who I am. I push myself to be someone else because I don't feel as though I have the right to exist as me. I compare myself to someone or some standard of what I think I should be like, rather than learn how to exist as who I am" or "I can't stand feeling helpless, so I would rather blame myself than accept reality" or "It's hard for me to separate and feel different from other people."

"Why do I doubt myself?" becomes "It's hard for me to feel different (separate) from someone else" or "I don't want to be vulnerable and be wrong (and risk being judged or attacked)" or "It's hard to feel that I am important and that my ideas and needs are right for me (because I have the right to exist) even if they aren't right for someone else."

"Why don't I like myself?" becomes "I feel as though something is wrong with me (I don't have the right to exist) and that makes me feel so different and so alone (separate). If only I were different, maybe I wouldn't feel this way" or "If I were only a better person, then I wouldn't feel helpless."

"Am I crazy?!?" becomes "When I know what I feel or want, I feel vulnerable because I feel so different from everyone else (separate)" or "It's easier to question myself and feel judgmental than it is to feel as though it's okay to be who I am (for me to have the right to exist)."

"Why don't I listen to myself?" becomes "It's too hard for me to stand up to someone else and do something I do not think they would like or understand (separateness, helplessness and the right to exist)."

"Why don't I even know what I want?" becomes "I'm afraid to see what I really feel and want because that makes me feel vulnerable and exposed (separate)" or "Maybe something bad would happen (vulnerable), or I would be wrong (separate)" or "Someone might be angry or critical of me (and my right to exist and to be separate)."

We may never have been encouraged to listen to our inner voice of wisdom, but it is there, waiting. We may ignore that voice of wisdom but it never disappears. It waits for us to come find it.

Exercise: *Do any questions about yourself haunt you?*
* What behaviors or secret feelings do you have judgments about
* Which of the three basic human issues lie beneath those behaviors or secret feelings?

Al: Haunting questions: Having grown up in a family where I didn't learn anything about how to be in a relationship, I am regularly haunted by the question of whether or not I am capable of being in a marriage. Sometimes when I forget to communicate something that is important for Jan to know and she feels upset that I didn't tell her, I think I might be more suited to living by myself and not having to be sensitive or aware of another person's needs. I feel vulnerable because I don't feel confident about dealing with relationship issues when they come up.

Judging my behaviors: I regularly feel critical of how I respond when plans change in our daily live. For example, if a dinner plan is changed, it's hard for me to change gears and let go of my disappointment. I contain myself, but inside I feel like having a tantrum or flying into a rage. I turn against myself instead of allowing myself to have the right to exist and simply be disappointed.

Secret feelings: I immediately feel defeated when I struggle to accomplish a task or repeat the same childlike behavior that I have been working on for years. I don't want anyone to know (except for the millions of people who are reading this book!)

We all have questions that we puzzle over at some time or another. It cannot just be that we are stupid (although all of us certainly feel that way at times). When we feel bewildered by our behavior, it is easy to judge or feel bad about ourselves. We do not think to lovingly explore what emotions, fears or reactions have been triggered in us. We have not (until now!) been taught to think in terms of our right to exist, our separateness and our vulnerability and helplessness, so we have not known how to comfort and handle those feelings when they come up. The right to exist gives each of us permission to accept ourselves exactly as we are, even as we strive to become increasingly free from old patterns.

Look to the rightness of what you are feeling

Whenever we experience pain, we automatically look for what is wrong. At the physical level, that is usually the most appropriate response, but even here, the assumption of wrongness has its limitations. Nothing is wrong when a woman experiences pain in childbirth. Similarly, nothing is wrong with us when we have emotional reactions and feelings, regardless of what they are. We tend to judge some feelings as "good" and some as "bad." It is "good" to feel kind, compassionate, loving, generous and happy, but "bad" to feel anger, hate, jealousy or greed.

We have all done or said things we do not feel good about, things that mystify us and bring us shame. It is hard to admit them to ourselves, let alone to someone else, so if we do talk about those actions, we tend to talk with judgment, condemning ourselves before anyone else can. If, however, we look to the rightness of our feelings, not the wrongness of our behavior or reactions, we will gain a deeper understanding of what is really going on. Deeper issues and feelings always lie beneath all the reactions we label "bad." Judgment is simply the alarm that lets us know to look more closely so we can understand ourselves.

> *Jan: Once I was so angry that I wrestled my 175-pound son down to the ground and sat on him so that he would listen to me—and then I thought, "I could have hurt him! I could have gotten hurt!" I was shocked, as I sat there, at the intensity and violence of my feelings.*
>
> *If I had stopped at this awareness, it would have been very easy to be in judgment of myself. How immature! But I knew to look to the rightness of my feelings. What was going on in me that I, who am very tenderhearted, would do such a thing? The answer was easy*

to find—I was caught in fusion with my son and was fighting my helplessness. I was extremely hurt and desperate to have him listen to and understand my feelings so I wouldn't have to feel separate.

When I didn't judge myself, I was able to understand what was really going on and take steps to act in a way that was more reflective of my deepest truth. Instead of going to judgment and shame, I was able to compassionately support myself, caring about my hurt feelings and choosing to deal with them in a way that I felt better about.

Our emotions are informational signals that alert us to the fact that something is happening that we need to pay attention to. Emotions come from the same source—our body—that informs us of physiological realities that need our attention. Hunger tells us to eat, shivering tells us to seek warmth, drowsiness tells us to sleep. The only difference between physiological and emotional signals is that we have generally been taught how to understand and respond to physical signals, while emotions are still a matter of mystery and ignorance. Like many things we do not understand, our emotions are examined and interpreted through judgment.

The concept of "co-dependency" is another example of looking to the wrongness of our feelings. The label of "co-dependent" has a very negative meaning, and people feel great shame about the possibility that they are "co-dependent."

"I'm co-dependent!" moan our clients in horror. "That's what we call *fusion*," we respond.

If we look at the attributes of someone who is "co-dependent," we find the same struggles we all face as we try to deal with the basic human issues: a person who is stuck at the fusion end of the fusion-separateness continuum, who does not have the right to exist with their own feelings and needs and who does not want to feel helpless in their significant relationships.

We all have these three basic human issues *just because we are alive*, so it is inevitable that we will see in ourselves attributes of co-dependency and every other label a human being could be given. It is crucial that we not get stuck on any label, for that will only cause us to feel bad about ourselves and make us try to control or hide our "bad" behavior.

Judgment is simply not useful. It interferes with our being able to understand the feelings and issues that are behind our actions and reactions. It does not help us create the kind of life we want to have. Imagine life totally free of judgment. Imagine having the same attitude toward judgment that you have toward heroin. "I don't do heroin, and I don't do judgment. Neither of them will take me where I want to go in life."

Only by looking to the rightness of every feeling we have do we have the opportunity to understand the real issues behind our reactions—always some form of vulnerability—and to take the appropriate steps to support ourselves in our growth.

Connecting with yourself

We will always be triggered by people and events. When we are triggered, it will always be by some form of these three basic human issues: the right to exist, separateness and helplessness with its accompanying vulnerability.

Exercise

Whenever we are triggered, we can take direct action to identify what is really going on. Here is a process to use when something has happened and you know you are triggered.

1. Take some time alone, or if someone is there, tell them you just want to be quiet for a moment to see what is going on inside you.
2. Tell yourself that there is absolutely nothing wrong with what you are feeling.
3. Ask yourself which of the three basic issues is stirred up in you. "Am I feeling helpless or vulnerable right now?" "Do I feel like it's not okay to be who I am or to feel what I feel right now?" "Am I having a hard time feeling different or separate from the person I'm talking to or thinking about right now? Am I feeling either critical of either them or of myself?"
4. Once you have identified what got triggered in you, let the tightness fade away as you stay in your awareness of what is really going on. (Try breathing deeply into that tightness and imagine scooping it up on your breath and exhaling it.)
5. Imagine telling your Other about what you discovered in this exercise.

If we try to talk with our Other without being connected to ourselves, we will be reacting to them, not identifying our own inner experience and expressing it. Whenever we feel tight and take the time to identify what issues got triggered in us and what we are feeling, then we are able to share *with* our Other, instead of reacting *to* our Other. "What just happened for you? Here's what happened for me." We can have an exchange to reveal what we discover about ourselves instead of focusing on what our Other did or should have done (so that we do not have to feel separate).

Separateness invites disclosure and mutual exploration. We can each explore what happens in us and how our issues get tangled up in our relationship. Rather than thinking of these interactions as problems, we can value them as opportunities to explore ourselves and our relationship dynamics. Emotional intimacy and closeness are deepened by sharing ourselves. These exchanges are not about changing or blaming each other or ourselves. When we accept the fact that our relationship is a project and that we are learning partners, we can feel compassion for our Self and our Other, and safe to reveal ourselves in an interaction that supports our personal growth as well as the development of greater emotional intimacy and communication in our relationship.

Being there for ourselves

People who experienced unhealthy fusion, whether abuse made it dangerous and impossible or passive neglect left them feeling alone and unworthy, have never had a sense of anyone being a loving presence that would allow them to feel supported and safe. They learned adaptive behaviors that made their survival possible and learned early in their lives that the only person who would be there for them was themselves.

It is inevitable that even those of us who had childhoods of healthy fusion would have a moment when our fusion was shattered and we became aware of being separate and vulnerable in a world that could surprise and scare us and make us "Self" conscious. Perhaps it was something as simple as walking in fused oblivion into the house, unknowingly tracking mud onto a clean floor. Our parent might startle us with a tone reflecting surprise or dismay, asking us to wait a minute so they could clean our feet. We would have been pierced with a sharp physical sensation of surprise, fear or distress. As innocuous as such an experience would have been, it would still have marked the end of our unconscious fusion and would be like a bullet lodged in our body. We would continue to grow, but that traumatic event would still be in us.

We believe that adulthood begins when we take on the job of parenting ourselves where our parents left off. With their own ignorance, histories and pain, our parents were only able to take us as far as they could. Regardless of how much our parents may have loved us and done their best as parents, all of us have more growing to do. If we remember that we will always have a vulnerable Self who needs love and guidance through the endless challenges of life, we will have the ability to be the good parent for ourselves, giving ourselves what they did not know to give us, so we can continue to grow.

Exercise

(In order to get as much oxygen as possible, inhale slowly through your mouth and feel your chest fill up until it is fully expanded. Relax your shoulders and neck. Hold that breath, resting. When you are ready, slowly exhale through your mouth and allow yourself to relax before repeating. When you can do this comfortably, move on to the exercise.)

1. Close your eyes and picture yourself as young as you can remember yourself.
2. Look at the expression on your face. What do you see? Are you happy, eager, excited? Are you sad, scared, withdrawn?
3. What does your adult Self feel when you look at that little face?
4. Breathe deeply into your heart and tell that child, "Once no one realized what you were feeling, and you did the best you could, all by yourself. But, I am here now, to take care of you and listen to your feelings. You will never again be all alone." With repetition, this support will begin to sink more deeply into your heart and over time your body will be increasingly able to relax and accept it.

When we realize that we need to connect with ourselves, when we know that we need to identify which of our feelings and issues are triggered, we are then prepared to participate in a relationship from a position of awareness and knowledge. We will always have issues and feelings that we are still learning how to take care of, but when the alarms go off, we will recognize them and know what to do. Being there for ourselves allows us to be there with someone else.

Exercise

Continue the breathing and connection to your Self that you made in the previous exercise. When you are back with that feeling, allow an image of your Other to come into your mind. What feelings do you have when you see your Other from this place of separateness?

In fusion, it feels like our Other's behavior is directed at us. When we separate, we can see that our Other is just as vulnerable as we are and we know that our Other is dealing with their own feelings and issues. Only with the perspective that comes from separating is it possible to look at our Other with compassion, curiosity and understanding.

If a child is left unattended, they will desperately attach to any adult who comes along. Likewise, if we are not taking charge of our own vulnerable Self, we will turn to anyone who is there, especially if we are bonded or fused to them, as we are with our Other, and turn ourselves over to them.

When we are not taking care of ourselves, we are operating on survival mode. We can never truly feel safe, for somewhere deep inside of us is the awareness that our Other is not our parent. Fearful of being abandoned, we either conform to their needs or try to control them. Only when we take charge of our own Self and are at peace with the three basic human issues of our right to exist, our separateness and our helplessness with its resulting vulnerability is it possible to avoid getting lost in triggered feelings and living in reaction. From this place of calm, it is possible to see the truth of our Other, in all of their vulnerability.

IMPORTANT ANNOUNCEMENT!
We interrupt this book for a special note from the authors:
"THIS STUFF IS HARD TO DO!!!" (Details below!)

The concepts we are working with in this book are fairly simple and easy to understand with our intelligent left brains. Applying them, however, is a whole different story! If we were thrown a lifeline as we clung to a capsized and sinking boat, struggling in a stormy sea, the concept of what to do is, again, fairly simple—hold onto that line, let go of the boat and keep our head above water until we're pulled in. The experience of being in that water, however, is very difficult, with the huge waves, sharks, cold, (*Al: No Thai food!*), fear of casting off from the boat into the vastness and the temptation to just give up, let go and end our suffering.

The stormy sea of relationship has its challenges, too. Waves of emotion sweep over us, threatening to overwhelm and drown us. We feel assaulted by the behavior of our Other and shocked by the cold chill of unexpected separateness. We are desperate to try to hold on to the fusion we cannot have. It is so tempting to just say, "We weren't meant to be together" and let go of the relationship.

> *Jan: I am working with a woman whose boyfriend, a medical student, recently broke up with her, saying that they just weren't soul-mates and that it shouldn't be so hard. Does the fact that he needs to study to learn how to fulfill his professional goal mean that something is wrong with him and that he isn't supposed to be a doctor? We somehow assume that we shouldn't have to learn how to have a relationship. The only time in our life when we do not have to work at a relationship is when we are fused with our mother before our birth. That's it.*

It is impossible to know these concepts and apply them without lots of patience and practice. It does not come naturally as we all wish it did. Our longing for fusion is so great that the fact that a relationship is a project and takes work makes many of us think that something is wrong.

Jan: I tried to read Steven Hawking's book, A Brief History of Time. *It was a fascinating book. By "it," I mean the introduction. I started the first chapter and got through his opening remarks. Suddenly, it was as if he had switched to a different language. I could pick out an "and" and "the" here and there, but the rest was unintelligible to me! It was an amazing experience. I had literally run into the limit of my experience, training, and intelligence.*

Emotional intelligence is like that, too. We'll be going along, talking with someone, when suddenly something will happen and—bam! We're absolutely floundering, unable to understand or follow what they are saying. We are totally lost and don't know what to do or say. In the panic of hitting that wall of ignorance, we react.

Years ago, research on emotional intelligence was published. It showed that there is a difference between emotional and intellectual intelligence, and that emotional intelligence is far more predictive of a person's success and happiness. But how are we to become emotionally intelligent? It obviously does not come naturally, or it would fall into the same category as intellectual intelligence, IQ, that we are born with. We have to learn emotional intelligence somehow.

Now, imagine that instead of being a physician, Sigmund Freud had been a teacher. Evidently, people felt comfortable confiding in him so his students probably would have talked with him about their feelings. "Professor, why do I always feel like throwing up before I take a test?" "Why do I have to go to the bathroom ten times before I give a presentation?" Being the thoughtful and curious man he must have been, he might have wanted to explore these mysteries and offer a class on psychology—the study of human emotions. Then, instead of psychology being a part of the medical system that assesses our mental health or illness, it would be just another subject in the field of education and would address our emotional *awareness* or *ignorance*.

Since psychology is a part of the medical system, however, we assume that, like physical health, we should just *have* this knowledge and the lack of it means something is wrong with us. We feel embarrassed or blame ourselves or our Other when we run into situations in which our ignorance defeats our intentions. We are released from judgment when we accept the fact that none of us received an education that taught us how to accurately understand and appropriately act on what we feel. We are simply left with the task of learning, *now*. Accepting this fact is challenging, for in addition to our natural ignorance, our culture judges ignorance as being our fault. We all have done our best to survive and in the process of doing so have developed ineffective patterns that are deeply entrenched in us.

We are all capable of changing those patterns. The tools of self-understanding and the ability to separate equip us to approach our important relationships in a new way. When we accept our humanness, knowing that despite our ignorance we are each doing the best we can, then we can have infinite compassion, patience and acceptance for our Self and our Other for just being human as we gain knowledge and new tools. It may be hard, but it is not too hard.

WE NOW RETURN YOU TO YOUR BOOK

Connection through separateness

We experience and have satisfaction in our separateness during our childhood. A toddler delights in saying "No!" and adolescents derisively declare, "You're so annoying and controlling!" By a trick of physiology, our eyes face outward, and we notice what is going on "out there" before we even think to question and search for what is going on inside of us. We experience our self-definition by negatives and complaints that arise from noticing anything that does not fit with an uninterrupted state of fusion: "I don't like this. I don't want that." If we were all fused and agreed on everything and if our environment took care of our needs as once happened before we were born, we would have the illusion of safety and of being in control. We would not have to separate and feel vulnerable. But separating is a life imperative—we have no choice.

Separateness opens us to the experience of vulnerability but also allows us the possibility of our full existence. When we are separate and know that we have the right to exist, we can transform a complaint into a positive action, a statement of Self: "I *do* like this. I *do* want that." We have the right to be our own Self, not someone else, even if they are important to us.

Having permission to be separate allows us to be different from our Other and acknowledges their right to exist, too. We no longer have to be fused in order to be together. Separateness allows us to have true emotional intimacy with the freedom to be who we really are in all of our uniqueness.

Emotional intimacy cannot exist without two people being able to connect with each other, and connection cannot exist without separateness. (It takes being separate to be able to come together in a hug, for example.) It is paradoxical that it takes strength to tolerate our separateness and the resulting feeling of aloneness, but when we do so, we are able to trade the experience of fusion for true emotional closeness and intimacy.

It is absolutely impossible to create an emotionally intimate and connected relationship without having a really, really good system of communication. All of us are far too sensitive to be without one. In our fusion, we do not realize when we are lacking such a system and valiantly, hoping for a breakthrough, struggle on in its absence—with very poor results.

A relationship can have all the potential in the world but that potential will be totally useless unless we figure out how to check in with each other and ask questions in order to learn about each other's reality. If we do not do the work to create a good system of communication, we each may have excellent perspectives and understandable feelings but we will lack the ability to communicate them to each other, making each of us feel misunderstood and hurt. The key word here is "misunderstood." Of course we will be misunderstood without a system in place to provide for a way of understanding each other. It is impossible—*impossible!*—to automatically understand each other. That is an expectation based in fusion. We each have our own experience of reality that our Other cannot know without our describing it to them. We must laboriously explain ourselves so that our Other can know our reality. (*Jan: I hate that, too, but it's true.*)

In order to be understood, we not only need a system of communication that is based in separateness but must also use words of separateness.

Words of separateness (true feelings) versus words of fusion (false feelings)

We have identified three basic human issues that underlie all other issues and reactions: our right to exist, our separateness and our help-lessness with its resulting vulnerability. Similarly, there are basic human feelings that underlie all other feeling experiences: happy, sad, peaceful, lonely, scared, startled, proud, loving, vulnerable and helpless. (Vulner-ability and helplessness are both feelings and conditions of being alive.) Most of us identify variations of these feelings (for example, happy: joyful, delighted, content, pleased, glad, blissful, exultant, ecstatic) but these variations still fall into the category of the basic human feeling of happiness. When we use these words, we are identifying our own feelings and talking about ourselves, not about the other person. These words express our separateness. They are not hidden statements, criti-cisms of the other person or emotional alarms.

We also have other feeling experiences that do not fall into the cate-gory of words of separateness. We call them *false* feelings because they are expressions of fusion. They alert us to the presence of unidentified basic feelings that are expressions of a separate Self. Among these are:

ANGER

1. A reaction to being startled out of a state of fusion. Anger is a signal (like an alarm) to pay attention to what our true feelings are. It is a call to action because something is not the way we want it to be. The rush of anger is the adrenaline that is released by our body to give us the energy to take action. We often experience it when we are feel trapped and helpless, like a cornered animal. That animal may look and sound ferocious and be growling and snarling, but is it really angry? Or is it feeling vulnerable because its existence is threatened? If we step back, we may know logi-cally that our physical existence is not threatened, but we might feel that our emotional safety is at stake.

   Example: "Why is the checkbook overdrawn again!?" translates to:
   * reaction: "I get startled when I see that the checkbook isn't balanced."

* signal: "I feel vulnerable because our money situation seems out of control."
* call to action: "Can we work out a system where we watch the balance more carefully so it's not so scary for me?"

Example: "Why do you have to always drive so close to the car ahead of you?" translates to:
* reaction: "I feel startled that we drive so differently."
* signal: "I get frightened that we won't be able to stop in time if we need to."
* call to action: "Can you drive farther back so I don't feel so vulnerable?"

Example: "I hate these idiot drivers—they're all going so slowly!" translates to:
* reaction: "I feel trapped and helpless when I get in traffic."
* signal: "I feel vulnerable when I don't have any options and can't move freely."
* call to action: "I need to prepare myself to stay peaceful when I'm driving by expecting to have traffic."

Example: "I was waiting for a parking space and that jerk slipped in and took it!" translates to:
* reaction: "I felt startled that he acted like I didn't even exist!"
* signal: "I felt so sad and helpless, like I'm not even important."
* call to action: "I'll feel more peace and compassion if I keep reminding myself that when people act "badly," they're not happy."

Variations of anger are: frustrated, annoyed, irritated, enraged, resentful, furious, exasperated.

GUILT

2. A social construct rather than an emotion. It masks sadness. It is often a reaction to being helpless or to being afraid to separate and feel or express our real feeling or need. It can reflect a false

responsibility that similarly arises from the fear of separating.

Example: "I feel guilty that I didn't call my mother" translates to "I'm sad that my mother always tries to make me feel bad when I don't do what she wants me to do" or "I didn't want to call my mother and I'm scared she'll be angry or critical of me" or "I didn't want to call my mother and it's hard for me to have the right to my separate needs."

Example: "I feel guilty that I wasn't a better mother and that my child has so many problems" translates to "I feel sad and helpless that my child is struggling so much."

Example: "I feel guilty that we lost money in the stock market" translates to "I feel sad and helpless that we lost money. I tried to do the best I could, and I didn't do anything wrong—it's just unfortunate."

If you want to find the true feeling hidden behind your "guilt" ask yourself "What would I be feeling if I couldn't use the word 'guilty'?"

Variations of guilt are feeling: at fault, to blame, remorseful, ashamed and embarrassed.

DISAPPOINTMENT

3. Sadness with an overlay of expectation due to fusion. It could also be an unwillingness to feel helpless.

Example: "I'm disappointed that you didn't like that movie." translates to "I'm sad that we didn't have the same experience."

Example: "I'm disappointed our friends had to cancel our dinner date" translates to "I'm sad and also helpless because there's nothing that can be done about it."

Example: "I'm disappointed in you that you started smoking again" translates to "I feel helpless and scared and sad that you're smoking again."

Variations of disappointment are: feeling let down, disillusioned, regretful and dissatisfied.

CONFUSION

4. A label for a particular thought process. We are not able to make sense of a thought because we were startled out of fusion or do not understand or identify with the experience that someone else had.

   Example: "How could you like that?" translates to "I don't like it, and I can't understand how you could have a different feeling." (Separateness)
   Although confusion is an intellectual experience, if we look more deeply into ourselves, we may find that we also have a basic feeling in response to being confused.

   Example: "I was confused by A Brief History of Time." translates to "I cannot make any sense of it—it is beyond my knowledge and experience" and possibly, "I feel sad that I don't understand it, because it seems so fascinating." Confusion can also hide a judgment: "I feel inadequate or unworthy because I don't understand it."

   Example: "I'm confused about why you just started to cry" translates to "I don't know what just happened for you" and, most likely, "I feel startled and sad that you're crying" or "I'm frightened that you're blaming me for making you cry."

Variations of being confused are: being uncertain, bewildered, puzzled, mystified and perplexed.

JUDGMENT

5. A thought used as a desperate and controlling tool to try to get someone to agree with you because you do not like the experience of separateness. It is response to suddenly feeling vulnerable or helpless. Self-judgment is also a reaction to not liking the experience of separateness and fearing that we do not have the right to exist exactly as we are at this moment in time.

Example: "That's a stupid way to do things" translates to "I'm startled when we see things so differently."

Example: "You're so critical. Whatever I say or do is never enough for you" translates to "It's painful for me when I don't know what you're feeling and all I hear is judgment of me."

Example: "I never do anything right" translates to "It's painful for me to accept my limitations (my right to exist as a fallible human being). I'm scared you will judge me and not want me" or "It's so hard for me to feel helpless when things don't work out."

Variations of judgment are: criticism and disapproval. Variations of self-judgment include: shame and embarrassment.

HURT

6. Sadness mixed with fusion. "Hurt" implies that something was done *to* me, as opposed to something happened *in* you. We can be startled or sad without becoming the victim of someone having done something to us. We would be startled and feel physical pain if we grabbed a hot frying pan and would quickly separate from it, but we would not get our feelings hurt by the pan. The pan did not do anything to us because of us—it was just hot. Similarly, when something happens, we need to separate emotionally to be able to understand what is going on in the other person.

Example: "You hurt my feelings when you forgot my birthday" translates to "I was sad not to hear from you on my birthday because hearing from you would have made me feel happy. I don't know why you didn't call" or "I was sad not to hear from you because birthdays are important to me. I forgot that they're not a big deal for you."

Example: "You hurt my feelings when you yelled at me" translates to "I felt startled and sad when you got angry" or "I felt startled when you yelled, and I don't know what was going on for you."

The false feelings we have identified occur in all of us as instantaneously and powerfully as true feelings do. They are different from true feelings in two major ways. When we examine them closely, we find that they are composed of basic feelings and experiences. True feelings, like primary colors, cannot be divided into component parts.

False feelings always reflect a lack of separateness. They reveal that we are personalizing what the other person has said or done. When we are fused, we interpret everything that our Other does or says as being a statement about us—their behavior is because of us and directed at us. We do not separate from them and realize that something is going on in them that has nothing to do with us, even if we are the catalyst for their reaction.

> *Jan: In our first year or so together, Al and I were having a fight. We were yelling and accusing each other when suddenly, something very strange happened. Al just stopped. He couldn't do it, anymore. He began to cry from the pain of it. I was stunned. I hadn't wanted to hurt him—I was just "fighting." But I couldn't continue our fight anymore, either, once I saw the effect of my anger and the truth of him—how vulnerable he was.*

When we speak and act from a place of separateness, using true feelings, we reveal our inner Self to our Other and something wonderful happens—a bridge is magically created between our hearts. Rather than trying to effect each other (change our Other) we affect each other (move and touch our Other's heart by allowing them to see our own). It may actually be a relief, as it was for Al, to feel the vulnerability that we fear will expose and endanger us. Our vulnerability can create empathy and caring in the other person and a true connection between us. (Jan: Al's courageous vulnerability affected me so deeply that I could never again get angry at him.)

When we separate, we will not get fooled by how our Other expresses themselves. We will look for what is really going on in each of us and speak to each other in the language of true feelings about our basic human issues. Connection serves as a bridge between two separate individuals, each with their own needs, feelings and experiences. Language is the tool to build that bridge.

"IT'S ALL YOUR FAULT!"—The tools of fusion make connection impossible

Jan: Early in our relationship, Al and I banished the words "you always" and "you never" from our vocabulary. Whenever one of them was said, the other would pop out as well and we would be lost in hurt and anger, both of us feeling accused, unseen and unappreciated. Whatever issue we had been trying to discuss would disappear as we desperately reacted to feeling misunderstood. We would attack each other all the more in our desperation to be seen.

Aware of our own hopes and good intentions, it is easy to suddenly feel shocked—which we may experience as hurt or anger—when our Other does not think the way we think, feel the way we feel or want what we want. Some people, not having their own right to exist, feel frightened to speak for themselves and be vulnerable. They feel helpless and trapped when their Other voices an opinion or need. Their experience is often one of feeling controlled by their Other. They do not realize that it is their own lack of permission to separate and speak for what they want that results in them feeling controlled and unempowered.

People who have the right to exist may still feel trapped when their Other is different from them and they are "forced" to feel separate. Their whole sense of safety and order has been shattered—they feel vulnerable and out of control. And their Other is "responsible" (the catalyst) for these feelings.

Words of accusation come from being stuck in fusion, having no right to exist and feeling out of control and vulnerable. We all tend to scramble to regain our state of fusion and equilibrium. There are many tools we automatically use in our desperate attempt to not have to feel separate from our Other, to get them back where they belong—back in fusion with us!

The following statements are all attempts to avoid feeling separate, vulnerable or helpless and out of control with our Other:

1. "You" statements: We try to get our Other to think, feel and interpret things the same way we do by accusing them of being wrong. These statements point out our Other's error, wrongness

or misbehavior and our innocence. We try to convince them of how evil and horrible they were and we tell them what they were actually thinking and intending by their behavior that brought us such grief. From our state of fusion, we interpret what our Other thinks or feels, projecting our fears onto their behavior and words. When we are startled out of our fusion, we make assumptions and interpretations based on our fears, not on our hopes.

Example: "You came home late and you didn't even care if I was worried" or "He's late because he's having an affair" not "I'll bet he stopped to buy me flowers."

2. "I feel that you are . . ." statements: These are similar to "you" statements, except that the speaker is trying to apply the concept that speaking about our own feelings is more authentic and will lead to better results. These statements are judgments, assumptions, interpretations and projections, reflecting that the speaker is in a state of fusion, unable to find himself.

Examples:

* "I feel that you are insensitive." (Judgment) The translation might be "I need to tell you what I'm feeling so you can understand."
* "I feel like you are not listening." (Assumption) The translation might be "I can't tell by your response if you're hearing me or what you're feeling."
* "I feel like you are not an equal partner in this relationship." (Interpretation) The translation might be "I need your help with something."
* "I feel like you are too tired to have this conversation right now." (Projection or Assumption) The translation might be "I don't know about you, but I need to talk about this tomorrow because I'm too tired."

3. **Rules:** We identify behaviors that are familiar to us and make us feel safe, then insist that these are the correct ways of being

in the world. We attempt to criticize or bully our Other into fusion—adopting our rules as their own.

Example: "It's not polite to burp" or "You should squeeze the toothpaste from the bottom of the tube" or "This is how a towel should be folded."

4. Criticism, complaints and blame (responses to feeling separate, helpless and vulnerable): These three weapons attempt to take the focus off of our Self and put it onto the other person.

Criticism: It is easy to find things to criticize—we need only look at what does not fit into our structure of how things should really be. Criticism is a weapon because it is an attack on our Other's character. It attempts to create a sense of the speaker's innocence and their Other's guilt. It establishes right and wrong, and good or bad, indicting their Other, leaving them no defense or credibility. Rather than take the responsibility to speak up for what we want, we criticize, indicting our Other as negligent, at fault and responsible.

Example: "You're the most insensitive and lazy person I've ever met." Instead of the speaker expressing their own needs, their Other is charged and convicted of being a bad, uncaring person with severe character flaws.

Sometimes we get into a relationship with someone who is an externalization of our internal critical voice. Their judgments reflect our own deep fears about ourselves. The illusion of fusion then becomes the idea that if we please them, we will be of value as a person. We feel valuable if they are attracted to us and we try to get them to love us to prove our internal critical voices wrong. This is an attempt to avoid having to separate and grant ourselves the right to exist. It is a denial of the reality that we are already good enough.

Complaint: Complaining is another tool of the unempowered. Not wanting to experience their vulnerability and too scared to take action or to separate from their Other and reveal their own ideas or feelings, people who complain sit back passively in misery or anger, commenting on what is not right in their world. They would also have to face their helplessness if they spoke or acted and were unsuccessful in getting what they wanted. Like fused children, they may hope that their Other takes action and saves them from having to experience their separateness, helplessness and vulnerability.

Example: "I feel like my feelings are never important." This is a demand that their Other be fused with them and know not only what they want, but also the degree of importance their want has for them. Their Other is made out to be clearly wrong and uncaring, as well as responsible for their unhappiness.

Example: "I'm hungry." Rather than separate and take action to address their own needs, they wait, like an unempowered infant, for their Other to be responsible for them.

Blame: Blame is another response to feeling helpless and out of control. When things happen that we do not like, people who are not at peace with their helplessness and vulnerability in the world blame someone or something else so they do not have to face the reality of their lack of control. If someone else is at fault, the blamer can deny the issue of their human helplessness and instead maintain the illusion that "if only" something had been done differently, they would not have had to feel vulnerable or sad when things are not the way they hoped. The use of blame also reveals that the speaker does not have the right to exist and so cannot simply ask for what they want or be at peace when they are not successful. They are trapped, hoping their Other does the right thing so they will get their needs met.

Example: "You should have checked to make sure our plane was leaving on time so we wouldn't be stuck at the airport for hours." The speaker is innocent and their Other is wrong and responsible for the situation. In a situation where something unexpected happened or in which no one took preventive action, the speaker preempts the role of innocent victim, turning the attention onto their Other and making them feel at fault. We create some illusion of control, denying our helplessness, by attempting to make our Other feel responsible and at fault for our unhappiness or for things not having gone the way we wanted.

"It's all my fault!" Some people use these tools against themselves because they do not feel that they have the right to exist as ignorant and fallible beings. Instead, they get angry and attack themselves for not having done something right.

- ❀ Criticism: "I can't do anything right."
- ❀ Complaint: "No matter how hard I try, I'm never good enough."
- ❀ Blame: "It's my fault that we're stuck at the airport for hours. I should have checked to see if our plane was leaving on time."

Self-blame is also an attempt to not feel helpless and to avoid having to face the reality of our lack of control in the world.

Using the tools of criticism, complaint and blame is like trying to do life with chopsticks. Instead of just getting in there and picking up whatever it is we want, we must try to manipulate someone else to take care of us.

People who use these tools are too frightened to separate and speak for themselves. Their anger is a response to feeling threatened, for if their Other had only been able to know what they wanted, they would not have had to be vulnerable and ask for what they want or take action, themselves. They do not want to feel their limited control in the world and so focus on their Other, hoping to avoid feeling their own vulnerability.

5. **Trust:** This tool is a direct symptom of fusion—the demand that our Other be "grown up" so we do not have to be. It is a tool used in an attempt to not have to feel separate or vulnerable. The need to trust someone else reflects that we do not have the right to exist and are therefore dependent on our Other. Trust

implies that the other person will always act in ways that are predictable and that align with what we want. Trust is a fused demand that our Other will never have their own separate needs, feelings or issues, or will sublimate them in order to take care of us.

Babies need to trust their parents because they are totally dependent and unable to take care of themselves. They cannot speak or advocate for their ideas or needs. When we trust someone else with our well-being, we are putting ourselves in the position of a baby with a parent, looking outside of ourselves for our needs and safety. The problem is that all of us are babies. All of us get triggered and react, feeling vulnerable and desperate. We cannot trust someone to not have their basic human issues stirred up. We all get triggered all the time and to expect that our Other will be the exception overlooks this reality of the human journey.

When we become the parent for our own Self, we accept our right to exist and trust ourselves to take care of us, to watch out for our well-being and to speak up when needed. We are the perfect parent for our own Self. No one else can know as quickly or as accurately what we are feeling or what our needs are. The goal in a significant relationship cannot be to parent each other—after all, we are not adopting each other!

Example: *"I can't trust you because you only think of yourself"* translates to "I can't trust myself to speak up for my needs so I want you to anticipate my feelings and take care of me."

Example: *"I can't trust you to have a friend of the opposite sex"* and *"I can't trust you to go out with your friends"* translate to "I feel vulnerable and scared that if we separate, you'll become fused with someone else and I could lose you."

6. **Victims:** Victims are terrified of acting on their own behalf, and in their fusion, they see their Other as controlling and not caring about the needs, feelings and thoughts of the victim. With no

right to exist and no ability to separate, victims are trapped in a self-made helplessness, too afraid to speak for themselves. Victims unwittingly create their "victimizer" by their inability to make room for themselves. Even if their Other wants their existence, the victim's fear interferes and the blame is put on their Other. If their Other is oblivious to this struggle, they may think that the victim is just easygoing and coincidentally happy with whatever they want.

Many children are not taught that they have the right to exist. Their parents either did not realize their child's struggle to feel important or they were themselves unequipped to pass on this right to their child. Few of us have fully claimed this right and probably do not even recognize it as an issue.

There are also true victims. Children who have been sexually molested or emotionally or physically abused have definitely learned that they do not have the right to their own life. They have been taught that they exist for the purposes of someone else. Many of us hold the same belief that we have no right to our own feelings, thoughts, needs and wants, even though we may not have been through such a trauma. While all of us struggle to some degree with setting boundaries and speaking up for ourselves, those of us who have been through traumatic childhoods—abuse, neglect or living with angry or alcoholic parents—unconsciously expect to be victimized by our Other and can set up this dynamic in our relationship without anyone realizing this is happening.

Some of us go through life with so little right to exist that it feels impossible to ever speak up for our needs and ideas. We either do not believe that our needs are as important as the needs of everyone else or we are afraid of being punished for having them. Since we do not have our own right to exist, when our Other has a need, we experience them as being angry and controlling. Our Other might say, as sweetly as could be imagined, "Darling Sweetheart, if it isn't too inconvenient, would you please pass the salt?" and we hear, "Give me the salt, #%*ch!"

Jan: I said this once to a really sweet woman who struggled with her right to exist, and she couldn't stop giggling, realizing how true it was for her!

Having been victimized as children, some people may cower in fear, but as adults, many are angry. They long to exist but are too frightened to say what they feel, so they blame their Other for their sudden, uncomfortable experience of separateness, accusing them of being "selfish." They attack, criticize and rage at their Other when their Other dares to speak up with their own needs. They use the tools of criticism, complaint and blame in an indirect attempt to make space for themselves so they do not have to separate and feel vulnerable. When this anger finally emerges, their Other, not realizing the impact of a childhood of victimization or the lack of the right to exist, may be bewildered and stunned at the anger that meets a simple statement or request.

People who have been victimized feel helpless and unempowered. They have never learned and internalized the fact that they have the right to exist. Their only recourse is to be wounded or angry and in this way try to make their Other pay attention to their feelings. They are frightened to separate, fearing punishment or abandonment. They do not want to lose their Other but want to be able to stay in fusion with their Other without totally disappearing themselves.

Most of us experience times of feeling like the victim of our Other. Afraid to separate and claim our own power, we can correctly and endlessly recount our accurate experiences of their "wrongdoings." This will not enable us, however, to see the reason for their behavior or our part in it.

Some books analyze and characterize the "dysfunctional" behavior styles or personality "disorders" of the opposite sex. This puts the readers of these books in the false position of innocent victims who are oblivious to the influence of their own unconscious patterns on their Other and to their own power to grow and effect changes in their relationship.

The biggest challenge for all of us in our relationships is not our Other. It is supporting ourselves to work through and transcend the lessons and the patterns of response we learned in our childhood. Because we are brought to attention by the reactions we have to our Other, our tendency is to focus on our Other's "bad" behavior. The intensity of our reactions reveals our own fusion. Our job is to separate so we do not create a false victimizer or become self-created victims, ourselves.

It is nobody's fault

When we are at peace with our separateness and vulnerability and have the right to exist with our own needs and feelings, we do not use words or tools of fusion. We are able to ask for what we want and make suggestions directly. The use of these words and tools is like a flashing neon sign alerting us to what is going on in whoever is using them: "I am afraid to reveal who I really am. I don't feel like I am important and have the right to exist. I feel too vulnerable and scared to be separate, so I'm hiding and trying to get the focus on you."

We are all desperate to be seen and heard for who we really are. When the language of fusion is used, when someone misinterprets or misunderstands us, we can go into an instant panic reaction. No one wants to feel like something is wrong with them. The language of fusion does not address differentness—it tries to assign wrongness. We become like two kangaroos, fighting. Have you ever seen such a thing? Heads back, they stand close together and bat at each other with their little arms. You can almost hear them saying, "It's *all* your fault!" "No, it's all *your* fault!"

In a fused interaction, people focus on their projections of their Other, reacting to their own creation of reality—their assumptions, interpretations or fears about what their Other is feeling or doing. In an interaction from a place of separateness, people focus on understanding what they themselves are feeling and ask questions so they can also understand their Other's reality.

It is hard to remain separate when we are accused with words of fusion but we must remember that this language comes out of ignorance and the illusion of powerlessness. An empowered person does not complain or criticize, lay down the law or turn over their well-being to someone else. An empowered person takes action to attain their goals and speaks from their hearts, for themselves, not about or against anyone else.

When we separate, we can see that when someone is not speaking with true feelings and with the power of their right to exist, they are stuck in fusion and do not realize it. They are suffering and struggling, unable to act from a place of love if they are fighting for their existence. While we might be the catalyst (the trigger) for our Other's reaction, the nature of their reaction—the feelings that they have and the way they express themselves—is not about or because of us. It is the result of their struggle with their right to exist, their own fusion-separateness issues and their issues with vulnerability and helplessness.

As reactive as we might also be, if we pay attention to our emotional alarms, we can try to separate and not take their words personally. It may seem as though they are speaking about us, but we can remember that their words only reveal their own struggle. We can even remember that the worse we feel as we listen to their words, the more desperate they must be to be using those words. If we remember these truths with compassion for how frightening it is for all of us to feel vulnerable, we can support each other in learning to speak with words of separateness instead of reacting, ourselves, from our own fusion, perpetuating the ignorance and pain we all have. We are each always doing the best we can do, given our level of development at this point in our lives.

When we separate, we can see that the concept of "fault" is irrelevant.

CHAPTER 8
Tools of Separateness

Jan: When startled into my separateness, I now know what to do. I know how to take the appropriate action to center myself and get reconnected with Al. A child might calmly get up from his desk, get in line and march outside in an orderly fashion with his class for a fire drill and yet still have his heart pounding, feeling frightened. Similarly, inside of me, I am screaming in protest against the shock of being suddenly separate but I have learned to continue with an approach that always works. During the screaming phase, until the shock subsides and we begin to reconnect, inside me I'm "rolling my eyes" (it's a trick I have!) and saying, "I hate you! I hate you!" because my vulnerable feelings just hate being separate. I don't hate Al. I hate not being in fusion. "Calm" is a place to work toward and I always get there. But I rarely start there.

There are tools we can use to help us stay separate. They can give us a way to support ourselves as we work to shift from a state of fusion into a state of separateness. These tools can give us relief by providing concrete steps to take so we do not unconsciously and desperately flail around in our emotions. They give us something to do when we are startled.

Having the tools will not stop our vulnerable feelings from getting triggered, however. It is still quite jarring to suddenly experience our separateness, for all of us tend to walk around in at least semi-fusion. Even if we stay fairly separate and alert at work (unless this is where our Other is) or in times of crisis, we tend to relax and unconsciously revert to a state of fusion when we go home.

Our separate adult Self may feel comforted in knowing how to handle situations, but this does not mean that we will like the experience of being separate. Our fused Self, most likely, will still hate going through what we call a "Separateness Interaction." We refuse to call them fights or problems because that makes it seem like they should not occur. They occur all the time, even in the most minor and insignificant of interactions. We are always having subtle reactions to our Other and interpreting what they are "really" doing or feeling. In order to go beyond our reactions and interpretations, we need to take a step back to separate, calm down our jarred body and prepare to be scientists, exploring together what really happened for us and our Other in the interaction.

When a Separateness Interaction occurs, we can each do the following steps:

1. Slow down and breathe deeply.
2. Put your hand on your heart to comfort yourself.
3. Be kind and calm yourself, and
4. Separate—tell yourself "We're just having a different experience" and "I need to be a scientist and discover what just happened."

A "Separateness Interaction" according to Jan

Al: "We have to drive that check over to the bank."

Jan: "I already took care of it."

Al: "What do you mean?" (in a voice that sounded, in my ears, tight and challenging.)

Jan: (inhaling deeply and looking to the Heavens for calm) "I talked to them and they were fine with us just mailing the check."
Pause while we both quickly run through the four steps listed above.

Al: "What was the feeling in your voice?"

Jan: "Defensiveness. I know that I like to ask you questions and get the details about things that happen, but I automatically reacted as if you were challenging me, not just asking me a question. It's totally reasonable for you to ask questions. But I didn't understand the sound in your voice. It didn't sound like relief that things were taken care of and curiosity about how. It sounded tight and challenging."

Al: "I didn't feel that way at all. I had been thinking we needed to deliver the check, and I was startled when you said we didn't. I couldn't switch my brain fast enough to comprehend the fact that the problem was taken care of."

Assumptions corrected. And without any yelling! Hooray for us!

Nothing worth happening can happen without our taking these four steps first. We need to take our time! Feeling the sudden disconnection from our Other can be so distressing that we panic and, desperate to reconnect, race headlong into an interaction that quickly spirals out of control as we try to get our Other back into a shared reality. This will never, ever work and will further increase our distress by bringing up feelings of hopelessness and despair. Aware of our innocence and feeling helpless and hurt by the words of our Other who is just as desperate and bewildered as we are about the intensity of our reaction, we can suddenly feel as though our world has ended and our relationship has no hope.

Breathe! Be kind to yourself. Tell yourself that you are just being called into "Relationship School." Nothing is wrong. Once you can get calmed down, there are some tools to use in order to successfully talk through your Separateness Interaction. The wonderful thing is that both you and your Other have the power to positively influence an interaction and stop an old pattern from being repeated. If your Other forgets, you can remind them. If you forget, your Other is not your victim but can also step in to change the direction of an upsetting communication.

While you read this chapter, you might find it valuable to share with your Other which of the following tools have the most meaning or feel like they would be the most comforting or helpful for you if your Other used them during interactions with you. Because we are different, we may like different tools.

Tool 1: Remember we are both vulnerable

It is so hard to remember that we are all beginners. No one knows how to do relationships. Where were our role models? Was any of this ever addressed in our families or at school? How could we have learned? A significant relationship is the school where we will have the opportunity to practice. We may know this and yet, when something happens that startles us out of our fusion, we forget that our Other is vulnerable and ignorant, too. We look at them with horror. We are so shocked that we see them as deliberately and selfishly thinking only of themselves. How could they do this to us? What were they thinking? Why didn't we realize what angry, uncaring and critical people they are? We feel unimportant and we panic. The intensity of our reaction betrays that it is our desperate baby who is suddenly in charge.

The unspoken demand we each make is that our Other be an adult. In our shock, we forget that they are a baby, too. They, too, do not know what to do with their hurt, their fears, their assumptions. They also struggle when their issues get triggered. When we have an emotional alarm go off, we need to remember that this is hard for everyone. If we could do it better, we would. If the words of fusion are spoken at us instead of the language of separateness—regardless of how awful it feels to us—it is because the other person is lost and hurting. The worse someone acts, the more they are suffering and ignorant.

> *Jan: When I first realized how completely vulnerable I am, I had an image of two people standing together, in tux and bridal gown, saying their marriage vows. As soon as the minister pronounced them married, they both turned around, but instead of being two adults, joyous in their new union, they dissolved into two little toddlers, swimming in their bridal finery. Two adults may choose to get married, but two children run the show if we do not do this work of learning.*

Tool 2: Remember we are both innocent

Al: During the years before Jan was able to connect the underlying terror that she always felt with the fact that her biological father was an angry and violent man, it would have been really easy for me to think that she was just an angry person. It could have been easy to build up my own resentments and live in anger and criticism of her. But I knew how vulnerable she was so I knew she was struggling, even if I didn't understand why.

While we might not understand our Other's feelings, we can know that something is going on. We can either personalize their behavior and go into a fused reaction to them, judging them, feeling hurt, victimized or self-righteous, or we can separate and look for their innocence. The way people act gives us an indication of the struggles they are having. If they are not talking from separateness with true feelings, they are suffering. We cannot emphasize it enough: the worse someone acts, the more they are suffering and ignorant.

No one wakes up in the morning and says, "I think I'll go out and have a car accident, today." That is why they are called "accidents." We do not want them to happen. They just do, even if we are doing our best to avoid them. This is equally true for emotional accidents. We do not wake up and think, "I think I'll make my Other feel miserable today." Yet when we express ourselves to each other in a conversation, it is very likely that we will have an emotional accident—we will each say something that will trigger an emotional alarm for the other.

Al: I have a friend who has a lot of chronic physical pain. One time, I came home, after seeing him, and told Jan that I felt so sad and helpless. She immediately responded by asking if he had ever tried some treatments for his pain that she had heard about.

Crash! An accident. I just wanted caring for my feelings so I would not have to be alone with them. Jan was feeling sad and helpless and wanted to help. Not being me, she responded from her needs and didn't go automatically to the response I wanted. Not being her, I had no desire for what she was offering in that moment. I felt annoyed and she felt hurt. It was an accident because I didn't want her to feel hurt, and she didn't want me to feel as if she didn't care.

Accidents happen because people are separate. It is important to recognize them as just being accidents, a function of two people being in different emotional spaces, each having different feelings and issues triggered. As in a car accident, the most important thing to do is to make sure everyone is okay. There is no need to sit around and blame each other for whose fault it was. It just happened. Emotional accidents inevitably happen in the most significant relationships.

When we have an accident, the important thing is to stop. Just as you would not keep ramming into a car that hit yours, do not keep going, trying to talk with your Other. Stop and get connected with yourself. Identify your original goal and intent.

Knowing the outcome of your first attempt, identify what you might say that would more accurately reflect what you are feeling and wanting, and trying to communicate.

Tool 3: Remember we are both right

Al: Jan's Mom, Bette, and I really loved each other. She had a beautiful gold pocket watch that had belonged to her father. One year, she gave it to me because she wanted me to know how much she loved me. Several months later, she came to me in tears and told me that she felt like she had made a terrible mistake, that she should have offered the watch to Jan's brother, Bruce, because it was his grandfather's. She felt so upset about asking for it back because she didn't want me to feel hurt. I had cherished the feeling of the gift and was also already attached to the watch, wearing it every day. I didn't want to give it up. But I also wanted her to have it. We both sat there, crying and holding each other. There was no good or bad, right or wrong—it was just painful.

When we really use the tools of being separate, there is no fighting. There will be struggle and emotions inside of us but no contest between us. Arguing implies objective reality, which means someone is right and someone is wrong. Separateness acknowledges subjective reality, which means we are both right, and we just need to figure out what to do with having different needs and feelings.

> *Al: The end of the story is that I gave the pocket watch back to Bette and she gave it to Bruce. Rather than it turning into a situation where I felt resentful, this interaction created more closeness and connection between Bette and me. I could feel and understand her need, as she could feel and understand mine. It just made us love each other more.*

From a place of fusion, when we have different needs, feelings or thoughts, we will either think something is wrong with us or something is wrong with our Other. From a place of separateness, we can look for the rightness, not the wrongness, in what each of us is experiencing and acknowledge it to each other. Even if what our Other thinks is not true to us, in that moment, although we may not yet understand why, it is true to them.

Separating allows us to hear our Other's words without making them about us, even if our Other is using words of blame or criticism. If our Other had a high fever and said that we hated them, we would not become offended—we would realize that they were in a different reality than we were. Anytime someone does not understand or describe you correctly, they have a different reality than you do. Their assumption or interpretation may not be fever induced, but it is valid to them, given what they are aware of. We need to hold onto our separateness like a lifeline in a stormy sea: "This is *not* about me!"

Each person has their own truth based on their own history, experience and feelings. Only they can know it until they communicate it. We can trust that although our interpretations of each other or a situation may not be correct, there is something valid for each of us in our own experience. It could be that an old memory or wound—a place of pain or fear—has been inadvertently touched by our words or in the interaction. If we take the time to keep exploring and revealing our intent, experience and feelings, we will be able to understand each other and find a way to compassionately make room for each person's reality and to clarify any misunderstandings that have occurred.

It is crucial to remember that although we speak the same language, the meanings words have can be very different for each of us. It is as if we were coming from totally different cultures and need to learn each other's language and customs. A word that seems harmless to us may be full of hurtful associations and have a totally different connotation to our Other.

We live in an either-or, win-lose world and people tend to get into competitions and arguments about who is right for no one wants to be at fault or wrong. It is a revolutionary concept that there is no right or wrong when it comes to feelings, no competition for which of us wears the bad guy's black hat. We are both right. A world based in separateness is a win-win world.

Tool 4: Acknowledge your Other's reality

Jan: When our daughter, Megan, was a teenager, I bounced downstairs, one day, to ask if she'd like to have lunch with me. She turned to me and said, "Why are you always angry at me?!" I was stunned, absolutely shocked, to be seen so incorrectly. Her words felt like a blow, and my automatic impulse was to say, "I'm not angry!!! How could you think I'm angry?!" but for some reason (maybe I was so stunned that it took me a moment to catch my breath) I didn't protest and try to get her to see my reality. Instead, I let her know that I saw her reality. I sympathized, "How awful for you to be innocently doing your life and have it feel like your mom would come down and yell at you for no reason. I'd hate to think that my mom was angry at me all the time. I'm so sorry it felt like that." (The words I stressed in my response to her did not accept responsibility or blame for behavior I did not do, but rather emphasized that I understood her experience.)

As I spoke, I could see the tension leave her. And I could understand that from her perspective, involved in her own activity and thoughts, the sudden appearance of my bouncy energy must have felt assaultive—an experience she interpreted as anger. When I saw her relax I added, "What I was actually feeling, though, was happy and I just wanted to have lunch with you." "Oh," she replied, and we went up and enjoyed being together. I didn't have to argue or debate realities. I just had to let her know I understood what her experience was for her.

Acknowledgement is other another way to avoid the panic reaction of broken fusion. It gives us time to catch hold of ourselves and separate at the same time that we look for the rightness in the experience of our Other (Tool 3, above). When there is an emotional "accident" and we are experiencing different realities, if our first step is to acknowledge the feelings and experience of our Other, we also stop ourselves from personalizing their reaction.

> *Jan: When I was able to realize that what Megan was saying was not about me, I could easily listen to her, for there was no threat or hurt. What she was saying described her inner experience and interpretation—she was not describing me.*

Freedom comes with not taking things personally.

> *Jan: A long time ago, I worked with a very sweet couple who loved each other very much and lived together peacefully . . . until anything happened that made the man feel helpless or separate. Then he would become so increasingly enraged that the woman would finally have to flee their home for hours, giving him time to calm down.*
>
> *I finally suggested to the woman that when he got upset about something, she should get upset, too, but just a little bit more than he was. If he was upset, she should get really upset. If he was really upset, she should get really, really upset. She tried it. It worked.*
>
> *"The goats got out of the pen!" he exclaimed with irritation.*
>
> *"The goats got out of the pen? That makes me so angry!" she replied.*
>
> *"I hate it when you don't close the gate properly!" he accused.*
>
> *"I can't stand it when I forget to close the gate the right way!!!" she responded.*
>
> *And do you know what happened then? He felt heard, and that his feelings were understood and cared about. He had never had the support to learn how to ask directly for the comfort and caring he needed, but when she acknowledged him, he immediately felt seen, loved and connected to her and was able to return to his sweet and loving Self.*

When we do not feel seen and that our feelings are cared about, we often become frantic. Acknowledgment eases us through the desperateness we feel when fusion is broken. It brings relief for the panic we feel when we are not seen for who we are and for what we may be struggling with.

Even if our realities are different, we do not feel so utterly alone, for at least we are understood. Acknowledgment gives us the opportunity to catch our breath, calm down, share our realities and then see what, if anything, needs to be done.

> *Al: Men often feel speechless when women talk about their feelings or what they need. They feel responsible to "fix" the woman or her problem. What I tell them is that when they are doing a mechanical job and they have a universal wrench, they're confident that they'll be able to fix anything requiring a wrench. Acknowledgement, I tell them, is the universal wrench of relationships. No matter what needs or feelings or wants a woman expresses, if you acknowledge what she has just said, she will feel comforted and feel better. Because a woman does not want to feel alone with her feelings, many times acknowledgement is more important than fixing the problem. When we are responsive, we don't have to feel responsible.*

Acknowledging our Other's feelings can be extremely painful, if we realize that we have caused them hurt. If we are at peace, however, with our right to exist and our right to grow and learn, we will not panic when we are seen in our humanness. There can be nothing our Other can tell us that will threaten us. We do not have to judge ourselves or defensively blame our Other that it is really their fault (somehow) to avoid being accountable for our own behavior. We can have compassion for both of us as we struggle along, doing the best we can.

> *Jan: Once I snapped at Al in a mean way. I instantly heard how horrible my words were and apologized, letting him know what was really going on for me. But the words had already done their damage and he withdrew to recover. I didn't want him to suffer alone and I didn't want to lose him while he recovered, so I told him to talk to me about his feelings instead of going away to deal with them. He did. It was awful. I remember standing there in agony as he got angry at me. But then it got worse, for he quickly moved into feeling the hurt my words had caused. He began to cry as he described how painful my words had been. I know it lasted only minutes, but it felt like forever. But then it was over. He felt heard and cared about, and I survived.*

We were able to move on with our day, connected once again. And I didn't die.

Tool 5: Believe your Other

When someone tells us something, our first impulse is to see if we can intellectually understand what they are saying, or if we can identify with their feelings, finding similar feelings or needs in ourselves.

> *Al: We have two dogs that we both love very much. When we're going out and Jan thinks they might enjoy being with us, even if they have to stay in the car, she'll want to take them. When I try to understand that it could be fun for the dogs, I can't get it. I try to identify with the feelings of wanting to make sure the dogs have a chance to do something that might be fun for them, but I don't feel that way. The only thing I can do to assist my separating is to tell myself that I believe her. I can't find "fusion" with her in my thoughts or feelings, but I believe that it is important to her and it might be to the dogs, too.*

Sometimes it just is not possible to understand a situation or have feelings that are the same as those of our Other. Sometimes all we can do is separate and believe that what our Other is saying they are experiencing or going through is true for them. Knowing that we are separate, we can be prepared to have different experiences, feelings or thoughts.

In separateness, there is no conflict, because we know that each of us has a separate and valid reality—there is nothing to argue about. There is no right or wrong—it is just a matter of creating a way for us to coexist.

While interactions of fusion are based on understanding and identifying, interactions of separateness may additionally be based on faith and belief. Acceptance of separateness allows us to open to possibilities beyond the limitations of our own individual awareness and history. Separateness serves as a catalyst for each of us to explore possibilities that we have not conceived of and to gain a greater depth of understanding. Like the blind men who each felt a separate part of an elephant and thought his experience was reflective of the whole ("An elephant is thick like a tree trunk." "No! An elephant is broad like a wall." "What are you saying! An elephant is long and thin like a rope."), we unconsciously assume our perception and interpretation of life is the only perception and interpretation possible.

None of us is unlimited in our understanding and wisdom. When we are unable to understand or identify something because it is outside of our experience, we can accept the possibility that our Other has a different reality that is equally valid. We can believe them.

Tool 6: Announce your intentions

When we have an issue to bring up, sometimes we take time to carefully think about how best to say it. Other times it takes all of our strength and courage to blurt it out at all and we feel proud of ourselves for being able to do so instead of silently being miserable or resenting our Other. Having taken the initiative to speak up, we usually feel vulnerable and exposed, and anxious about what our Other's response will be. Unconsciously, we are usually in demand that our Other be able to receive our words from a place of separateness and not be shocked or reactive, even though they might have been startled out of the fusion that they were in before we spoke.

While we had time to prepare for this conversation, they did not. They had no inkling that anything was even going on inside of us until we tell them (which can feel to them like an assault) so there is a good chance that they might not react in a separate and adult manner. Not realizing that we have been preparing ourselves to bring up an important issue, their minds are most likely rudely in their own reality! We, in our fusion, act as though they should be sitting attentively in a calm and separate emotional state, waiting to see if there is anything that we might bring up.

> *Jan: These principles apply to relationships with puppies, too! One day, I was calling our puppy, Maya, so we could go home. She was busy in a sniffing exchange with another dog. I called a couple of times without her responding at all. I finally walked over, took her head between my two hands, turned it so she was looking at me, and gently said, "Maya, let's go." It was fascinating! It was as if I could actually see her eyes slowly focusing on me, shifting away from the reality she had been engaged in. I could practically "see" my words suddenly registering in her mind.*

Although we want to be important to our Other, most of us would probably go crazy and feel suffocated if our Other were constantly focused on us. It would begin to feel like a burden to be the center of their life. The fact that is, though, they are the center of their own life (thankfully!) While this is a relief, it also means that their thoughts will not be focused on us, but will be roaming around according to what is on their mind.

> *Jan: My experience with Maya made me aware of how my mind works. Sometimes when Al says something, I may be only vaguely aware of it, as I am usually lost in my own thoughts. I am not looking attentively to him just in case he might have something to say or has some needs to express. The second time he tells me what he has to say, I feel pulled away from my train of thought and needs and begin to shift my focus to him. I begin to understand what he's talking about. The third time he says it, I can usually hear him and his message, and respond fairly appropriately to him, realizing he is bringing up his need, for himself. So I have learned that it is a good idea to prepare myself to be vulnerable three times when I have something to say. I have to be ready to repeat myself so Al has a chance to pull himself out of his thoughts and catch up with me. I call this the "Baseball Approach to Communicating": give each other at least three strikes before we're out!*

Talking about something with our Others will be easier if we can find a way to get their attention and let them know what we are doing, rather than assuming that they will be clear, separate and ready to hear us on command, without a moment of preparation. With our Other, we can create an announcement—words that are easy for both of us to say and to hear. The announcement can signal, like a ritual, what we are intend and also what we do not intend by initiating the interaction.

In order to bring something up to our Other, we need to take the time to get calm and separate ourselves. We cannot expect to blurt out intense feelings and have our Other not feel assaulted and stunned. There are three important components to a successful announcement:

1. We use the first three tools and speak in a calm rather than an intense way.
2. We focus on our need to talk, not on how our Other should be different.
3. We give our Other the opportunity to choose when we continue the discussion, so they also have the chance to separate and do not feel pressured to talk immediately.

The announcement could be something very simple, such as "You know how I always like to make sure things are really clear between us. I don't want you to feel startled or defensive, because nothing is wrong. Is there a time that would be good for you to talk about how to deal with our budget?" (versus "I'm so angry about our money situation and that you never balance the checkbook!")

With time and patience, we can separate and find words that have the same meaning to each of us and that feel invitational, not blaming. (It could even be a code like "Banana Split!") When we find those words, we have a chance of softening the shock and defensiveness that can occur by just starting an important, potentially emotional conversation out of the blue.

Tool 7: Tell your Other what you want
Ask your Other what they want

Whenever we initiate a conversation, we have a need of our Other or we would not be talking to them. We often jump right into talking, however, without taking the time to identify to ourselves or to inform our Other about exactly what we want.

> *Jan: I already know that Al loves me and hates to see me upset in any way. When I'm upset, what I want from him is to tell me that I don't have to face whatever is going on in my life alone, that he'll be right there with me and we'll face it together. I need to hear that we will be fine, whatever happens. Usually, I also want his ideas—I feel like I'm drowning and want someone—him—to take concrete action to throw me a lifeline and pull me in.*

Al: When I'm upset, I want to hear that Jan cares about me and is sad about what I'm feeling. I don't want to feel alone in whatever I'm feeling. Once I feel acknowledged, I might also want help and ideas, but for me, being acknowledged comes first. Usually, I end up not even needing anything beyond that. But if I do, I know if I ask her, I will get all the help I want. Jan and I actually want the same thing—to not feel alone—but we need to hear different things from each other to get that feeling.

We often want something different from what our Other wants. Even if we have told each other what we want in the past, we tend to assume that they will know what we want without our having to tell them, again. We not only risk not getting what we need but also may subject ourselves to unhappiness from getting what we do not need and then feeling frustrated, unseen or not cared about. (Imagine being hungry and asking your Other to make some food for you without letting them know what you would like to eat. We would either eat food we did not want without ever feel satisfied, or get angry at them that we have to tell them what it is we are wanting to eat because they "should have known.") In our fusion, we expect our Other to know what we want or need. But they cannot. We each come from a different history and experience, and our needs will most likely be different, as well.

Jan: I'm sure my need for company and help comes from my childhood, when I want to be rescued from my angry father. I had no question that my mother loved me—I needed to be saved and to not have to face him alone.

I can't stand it when Al is hurting. My helplessness issues get all stirred up, and in my fusion, I want to jump in and save him from whatever his pain is. When I see he's unhappy, I always forget that he had a different experience in his childhood than I did, and so has different needs now. While my rushing to action may soothe my pain and desire to avoid my helplessness, it makes him feel abandoned and alone, just as he was in his childhood. He doesn't want to be alone in his feelings with no one there caring about him and the experience he is going through. Often, Al has to tell me that he just wants my caring before he even brings something up. That helps me remember and stops my mad rush to action. Or, in the middle of my mad rush, he'll ask, "You're doing this because you love me and care about my feelings, aren't you?" And I'll remember, once again, that he isn't me.

Al: My need to be seen and to not feel all alone comes from my childhood. I never felt acknowledged or cared about in what I was feeling and going through as a child. I wondered if my feelings and thoughts were weird or something. When Jan lets me know she understands and cares about my feelings, I feel a deep sense of relief and comfort. In my childhood, I didn't feel my right to exist, so I always need to start there when I share a thought or feeling.

In my fusion, when Jan is upset, I believe that she needs her feelings to be acknowledged. As she has written, she wants help, to not feel so alone, and to know that we will find an answer to whatever comes up in life, or at least face it together.

When we are on the receiving end of a communication, there is no way for us to be absolutely sure of what the other person wants from the communication. If your Other forgets to inform you about what their need is, you can ask, "What are you wanting from me in telling me this? How can I be most helpful to you right now?" The good news is that each of us has the power to check in with the other about this so we can both feel satisfied by our communication.

Tool 8: Take time alone—or a "time out"

Jan: When our son, Seth, was very young, we recognized that sometimes when very frustrated, he would get a certain look on his face—his right eyebrow would go up, and his lower jaw would slide left—and there was no talking to him at that point. It was already too late. I learned to tell him I needed a time out to get centered and I would leave the room.

When we think about it, we know that there are times when each one of us is just not capable of talking calmly or of using any communication tools, regardless of how effective they might be. Either our feeling of tightness or the expression or tone of our Other is a blaring announcement:

DO NOT PROCEED ANY FURTHER RIGHT NOW!

Al: When I was a child and my parents made plans for all of us to go to a movie or dinner, I would get very excited. Often, though, these plans would get cancelled and I would feel very disappointed. When Jan and I make plans and for some reason she wants to change or cancel them, I still feel like I did when I was a child. I feel disappointed and angry and I want to lash out at her. This is definitely not the time for us to have a conversation. I need to go off alone and remind myself that it's just a change of plans, no big deal. I need to get calmed down and comfort myself before I can go back and talk with her.

Taking time alone is helpful because it gives us another chance to catch our breath, separate and come back to continue our discussion in a non-reactive state. It can be hard to step away and take time being physically separate in order separate emotionally. We need to muster up our best maturity and step back. This is hard for all of us to do. (*You are not particularly "relationship-challenged!"*)

It is so easy to bite the bait and be reactive and defensive. (*Jan: As I told a client of mine, "You're a person, not a fish!" And we practiced saying the mantra, "I'm not a fish! I'm not a fish!" as she left.*) If we ignore the warning—that blaring announcement to not proceed—we can get embroiled in an unnecessary, desperate, panicked war, fused with our Other and tangled up in each other's issues. Definitely not fun!

Just taking time alone is not enough. We can still get stuck in fuming and raging, crying and feeling victimized. There are steps we can take to help ourselves separate, calm ourselves down and prepare to communicate, again.

Steps to taking time alone

1. Ask yourself, "What am I feeling?"
   Al: In the example, above, I felt disappointed and angry. Often we are having feelings that come out of being fused. The next step, therefore, is:

2. Identify the true basic feelings underneath the "false" feelings. *Al: I felt sad and helpless.*

3. Give yourself some caring and compassion for your feelings, just as you would if a friend came to you and told you that they were upset.

4. When you feel separate and ready to talk, go back and share with your Other what you discovered that you were really feeling.

Tool 9: "Do-overs"

Yes, do-overs are permitted and yes, they are a good idea. There is no such thing as "One, two, three! No take backs!" in relationships.

It is one thing to understand concepts of how to have a successful relationship. It is a whole other thing to become those concepts. The understanding happens in our left brain. The becoming happens in our right brain. The power of fusion is enormous and the urge to fuse is embedded in our cellular patterning. Slowing ourselves down to be able to calm our reactions after having been startled by our separateness takes lots of time and practice. When we accept this, do-overs become a necessary and normal part of our communication process.

We *all* learn by hindsight. It does not make any sense to beat ourselves for not having known something beforehand or not having been able to do it better or sooner. Instead of being critical or upset with each other, we can congratulate ourselves for now seeing and knowing more than we did before.

There is no such thing as a mistake. What we call a mistake is simply an unexpected outcome to our actions. (If we knew without a doubt that something would have a bad outcome, we would not have done it.) A "mistake" is the result of not yet having discovered or grown into a better way of handling feelings or a situation. We always have the opportunity of deepening our awareness by using hindsight to reflect on what happened and to analyze what we could have done differently. When we calm ourselves, identify what our true feelings are and how we could express them more clearly, we then have the opportunity to call for a do-over.

A difficult interaction is not a tragedy or crisis—it is just one of the bazillions of times we all need to get a bit more conscious. We have a long lifetime to refine how we think and talk with each other. There is no problem you will not be able to work out together if you love, respect and care about each other and you are each willing to try to figure out how the communication could have worked better. (To be honest, sometimes, in the midst of hard moments, we may *remember* that somewhere inside us we have love, respect and caring, but we are not in touch with it at the moment. But that does not change our job to grow up and become a person we are proud of being. As we work to separate, we can have faith that we will find those positive feelings for our Other again.)

These situations do not have to be disasters—they are simply practice for us in becoming who we want to be. We can look at them as lessons to help us grow closer and become more aware, more thoughtful and better communicators.

Tool 10: Describe yourself, not your Other

> *Al: Jan is naturally curious. I am not. She often asks me questions about what I'm doing, or who I just talked to on the phone, or why I'm so quiet. You get the picture. I sometimes think that she is being critical or distrustful or controlling. I have tested out these paranoid assumptions on her, but they aren't true. She is just curious and wants to feel connected to me. Darn! Now I just have to believe her or sound really mentally ill! If I focus on myself instead of on her, I am aware that I feel vulnerable when she asks me questions, as though she's questioning my right to exist, demanding that I justify what I'm doing.*

Using adjectives to describe someone else is a dangerous way of talking. It is not useful to describe what we think someone else is feeling or doing. Most likely we will not describe them the way they experience themselves (for example, saying someone seems irritated when they actually feel frustrated) and then we are off debating adjectives instead of coming to a deeper understanding of each other. Our hearts are so open to our Other that we are extremely sensitive and therefore tend to overreact to their words. A panic response can easily get triggered when we feel unseen and therefore suddenly separate. We fight as though our existence depends on it, for to feel invisible to our Other is unbearable.

Jan: One day, Seth wanted to show me something in the phone book, but his sister was standing, oblivious, in front of the drawer where it was kept. I saw "that" look on Seth's face and immediately excused myself for a time out. He followed me and told me that he wasn't angry. I told him I hadn't said that he was, but that I wasn't capable of talking about things when he had "that" kind of energy. He started to defend himself and his reaction but I cut in and told him that I wasn't feeling critical of him. It was just that I was not grown up enough to be able to stay calm around "that" kind of energy. I told him that I knew I would eventually get my feelings hurt and get angry and I didn't want to. I was sure Jesus or Buddha would have been able to stay calm and separate, but I wasn't as evolved as they were. "Oh." he said, and stood there thinking about my words. "Well. I don't have that kind of energy, now." "Great!" I responded. "Show me what you wanted me to see." And off we went, no conflict between us, no debate and no hard or hurt feelings.

When we focus on ourselves—our feelings, what gets triggered in us, and what we can or cannot do—we do not have to talk about or describe our Other at all.

Jan: One day, when Seth was a teenager, we had a horrible day. His behavior got increasingly outrageous, and none of my best "good parenting" efforts could reach him at all. Finally, thank God, it was nighttime. I was relieved that the day was over. As I was getting ready for bed, I suddenly realized that the first thing I had said to him that morning had hurt his feelings. Oh, I was so mad! He had been so angry and awful that I didn't want to acknowledge what I had done that had started it all. But, I went to him and said, "I'm not even going to begin to talk about your behavior today. I just need you to know that I realized I hurt your feelings this morning and I'm very sorry. I didn't mean to."

We do not have to become involved in what our Other is feeling or how they are handling their feelings. That is their job to understand and figure out, not ours. Our job is to be connected with what is going on in us and to find ways to declare our thoughts and feelings in a way that we feel proud of.

For someone to ask us a question without declaring themselves can feel as uncomfortable as if someone came over to us with a paper bag over their head and started a conversation. While we might be perfectly willing to talk with them or answer their questions, we most likely would first want to know who they were. When we describe ourselves, we take away the mystery of who we are. This accomplishes three things:

1. Our Other will not be as likely to make an assumption about us based on their fears.
2. We are doing what we are asking them to do—declaring our own reality, not focusing on theirs.
3. We increase the possibility that when we truly want to gather information so we can learn about the reality of our Other, they will feel safe to answer our questions and reveal themselves the way we have revealed ourselves.

Tool 11: Catch your breath, then ask a question

Jan: My biological father acted out his pain in angry and violent ways. Although my Mom and I left him when I was two, my experience deeply affected me, and I grew up very frightened of men. I knew it wasn't logical, but every time there was a disagreement between Al and me, my adrenaline would surge and it felt like I would be killed— so I would become flooded with defensive anger. So many times Al would say something and I would instantly attack him for it. When I would pause for a breath (as he, metaphorically speaking, lay bleeding at my feet from my attack) he would tell me that my interpretation wasn't what he had meant. "Oh . . . ." I would say. "What did you mean?" He would respond with an explanation that revealed his total innocence. I felt terrible for him and worked to calm my own terror so that I could skip the assault and instead of acting on an assumption that came from my fear, I could make my first step be to ask a question.

Questions work miracles on many levels. They immediately give us a chance to separate, instead of leaping desperately into the fray, trying to avoid the loss of fusion. They give us a chance to grab hold of ourselves instead of racing into blind and frantic reaction.

Questions presume innocence. (Remember, we did not come together thinking "I chose you so I could make your life *hell!*")

Questions presume separateness. Rather than interpreting through fusion what we see and hear, as if our experience and assumption of meaning is the only one possible, questions acknowledge that we cannot know our Other's reality and that they might be thinking about or responding to something that we are not aware of. All we can know is that something is happening for them. We cannot know what that something is unless they tell us.

> *Jan: One day, Al was being very grumpy. I tried to be patient and ignore it, but it was getting hard to do. My impulse was to snap at him, but instead, I asked, "Are you having a hard day?" To my surprise, he came over to give me a hug and began to tell me how very difficult his day had been. As I listened and sympathized with him, I was silently giving thanks that I hadn't acted on my annoyance, but had used it as a signal that I needed to find out what was going on with him.*

> *Questions remind us that we do not and cannot know another person's experience, feelings or needs. If we were to go to another country, we would hopefully realize that there was no way for us to know the nuances of language or the meaning of behaviors in that culture. When things we heard or saw puzzled us, we would need to ask what they meant. With our Other, however, we often do not think to ask, for in our fusion, it never even occurs to us to question our assumptions.*

> *Jan: In 1975, Al and I went to Bulgaria. It was still a Communist country, and few people from the West visited there, so we didn't know much about their culture. We would ask people if they could help us, and one after another, they would smile sweetly, but shake their heads "No." We would walk away, and look for someone else to ask, but we kept finding that no one wanted to help us. We were amazed at not only how unhelpful people were but also at how happy they were to be unhelpful! We finally ran into a German tourist who, on hearing about our encounters with these Bulgarians who wouldn't extend themselves at all, explained to us that the head shaking we observed—subtly lowering their ear slightly toward their shoulder, one side then the next—was the Bulgarian way of nodding to say yes. We had to laugh thinking of all the*

friendly, smiling Bulgarians who had happily offered to help us, only to have us walk away in bewilderment!

We each internalize the culture of our natal family with its unique language and rituals. We do not even think that other people have had different childhood experiences and do not share the same understanding we do about words or behaviors. Important relationships are the joining of two cultures and we must be like cultural anthropologists who know that they cannot understand what a native experiences unless they ask.

> *Al: My brother and sister had already left the house by the time I was five because they were much older. From then on, it was just my mother and father and me. We didn't talk—no, really. We did not communicate out loud—no, really. And if I ever did voice an opinion or need, which was not very often, it was dismissed as unimportant.*
>
> *So, when I met Jan's mother and brother, and saw how energetically the three of them talked, I always thought that they were angry at each other and were going to have a big falling out. I was very intimidated. And when Jan would ask me questions about what I was feeling, I thought she was setting me up to answer so that she could criticize or control me.*

> *Jan: I was able to talk about anything with my Mom. Whenever an issue came up, we explored how to handle it to incorporate the needs we both had. When differences arose between Al and me, I naturally assumed that he and I would do the same thing but it was so hard to get him to declare himself. Although he always seemed happy to do whatever I wanted, I knew he had to have feelings and preferences of his own. His silence made me feel lonely, and I just couldn't understand why someone wouldn't say what they wanted.*

Even though we may come from the same country, the emotional culture of each state, each region, each community, each family and even each individual is different. The meanings of words and behaviors will be different in these different cultures and any assumptions certainly will be, as well. If we do not make efforts to remember that the other person comes from a different culture, we will misunderstand each other and make the wrong interpretation of what they are feeling or doing.

Whenever we feel startled or puzzled by the behavior of another person, we are being signaled that we do not know what is happening in that other culture. We need translations of words, in terms of basic human feelings and explanations of meaning and intent, for we cannot know, even if we think that we do. Our tightness and our negative assumptions or interpretations are the signals to ask questions, for they let us know that we are disconnected from our Other and they are the only expert on what is going on in them. If we do not ask questions to learn about their reality, we will be left bewildered or upset, having based our negative assumptions about our Other on the "story" we make up about them from watching their surface behavior. The truth beneath that behavior will remain a mystery until we ask about it.

We must be prepared to ask each other questions endlessly, because things that make us feel disconnected from each other happen endlessly.

When something happens that startles, hurts or bewilders either of us, we can try to help each other remember to bring it up so we can understand each other, not by making an interpretation, but by asking a question, as, "Are you okay?" "What are you feeling right now?" "What's going on for you?" "What did you mean when you said that?" "What did you think I was saying to you?" We are always doing the best we can and we can do better when we commit ourselves to trying to be more communicative, deepening our understanding with questions instead of becoming reactive to our own assumptions.

When facing a discussion in which two people have different ideas or needs, the word *how* is an excellent tool to open communication. "*How* can we do this so we are both okay? So we can take care of what we both need?" *How* is such an optimistic word. It presumes that if we try hard enough, if we are concerned and caring enough about the needs of our Other, we have a really good chance of creating a new way to resolve our dilemma that we will both feel good about. Perhaps we will not be able to find a solution, but *how* opens the door to compassionate exploration and so maximizes our chances of success. If additional needs and feelings are revealed through this process, we need only continue the exploration of *how* to create a satisfying enough resolution that incorporates the most important things that comes up for each of us. In this process, we will both feel heard and cared about.

We must be like compassionate scientists collecting data or like news reporters conducting interviews and investigating a story. Asking questions will allow us to learn the history and meaning of words and behaviors—information we simply cannot in any other way.

Tool 12: Make clarifications, not apologies

"Apologize for what you just did!" are words many of us heard in childhood, as we shamefacedly hung our heads and were forced to admit our shortcomings and acknowledge our unworthiness. We all do things that have unexpected consequences—this is an unavoidable part of being alive and is nothing to be ashamed of. But, as children, few of us had someone to help us understand this, so we may be left with a deep resistance to feeling the shame and judgment associated with apologizing.

Apologizing may be especially difficult to do when we are so clear that we were coming from a place of innocence, having had no intent to hurt anyone. An emotional accident may have occurred, but we do not feel at fault so we feel like there is nothing to apologize for. Apologizing may feel like giving up our power and saying that we are a bad person and are inferior to our Other. For some of us, it can even feel dangerous.

> *Jan: I remember feeling terrified to acknowledge my part of an emotional accident. I would want to describe how I thought the accident had happened, but I would feel like I was standing in a suit of armor, protected against being killed for having been imperfect. I remember saying, from inside my closed visor, things like "I think that when I said 'That's ridiculous' you thought I was criticizing you and you got hurt and defensive. Then you sounded impatient and critical of me and we kept on triggering each other." If Al didn't attack me when I talked about the emotional accident (and he never did) I would feel like I could open up my visor and say a little more to explore what had happened . . . . And eventually work my way out of the suit of armor altogether.*

Especially when we are operating in a win/lose system of relationship, neither of us wants to lose, for that feels dangerous. We may even be horrified at the response our words or actions have caused but we do not want to be judged or feel subservient to our Other.

On the other hand, getting an apology is important to many of us, for we have been hurt by our Other and want them to acknowledge what they did. The assumption is that if someone apologizes, they will not repeat their "bad" behavior, but an apology does not mean that there has been a change or increase in self-awareness and consciousness. And sometimes, a person may apologize just as an attempt to end the conversation.

The hurt person may get some satisfaction or sense of "winning" if they receive an apology but not necessarily an experience of having their hurt healed. This is clearly evident in people who need apologies repeated. Although the first apology did not bring them comfort, they keep thinking they will get relief if only their Other would apologize sincerely or often enough. Even a sincere apology is a different thing from healing. No amount of repetition will satisfy their hurt.

If we accidentally stabbed someone and then apologized, we might be truly and deeply upset that we harmed them but the cut would still be there, needing appropriate medical attention in order to heal. For emotional wounds, the healing usually comes from having our feelings *cared about* by our Other. "I'm sad that you're hurt" may be more accurate than "I'm sorry I hurt you." Aware of our innocence, we may not feel "sorry" for the "terrible" behavior our Other attributes to us because operating from our own pain, fear or ignorance, we were doing the best we knew to do in that moment.

If our Other is able to use true feelings to share their hurt over what had happened rather than using words of blame or criticism, we might be able to feel our sorrow that they were upset or that we inadvertently caused them hurt. We could more easily speak words of sadness and caring for their feelings if we are not defending ourselves from being seen as the bad guy. We can then comfort each other without either of us having to take on blame for not having known how to handle our interaction any better than we did. We can feel *sorrow* without being *sorry*.

When we try to be an adult we can be proud of, especially in a relationship where we love each other, of course we do not want to hurt our Other. Even when we think we want our Other to hurt and we use hurtful words, we are usually acting out of desperation—not wanting to feel helpless or be hurt, ourselves—not out of cold and deliberate malice.

Jan: Whenever our children got into a fight I would ask each of them, "Now that you know what happened, what could each of you have done differently that you might have liked better?" I remember one time when Megan yelled at Seth after he had grabbed one of her toys. After I asked my question, Seth said that he knew it was a special toy and that he should have left it alone. Megan said that she knew he just wanted to play with her and that she should have shared better. They each felt understood and cared about. They hugged and went off to play together. No apologies were offered, and none were needed.

Rather than engaging in a win/lose exchange, we can deepen our understanding of each other's feelings and our knowledge of which of our basic human issues got triggered in the accident. Through clarifying, we can come to know each other better, feeling care and concern for what each of us experienced. We can then explore what we might be able to do to avoid a repetition of the same accident.

Jan: Our children have always been sensitive and loving. And talkative! The worst "punishment" we could give them was to give them a "talking time out." Whenever their behavior was an acting out of unspoken feelings that were going on in them, they would have to be quiet until they were ready and able to identify what they had been feeling, and what they could have done or said that might have been more congruent with their inner experience. When they told us, we would admire their self-awareness and tell them how impressed we were with their wisdom and ability to know themselves. Of course we knew that they were sorry. What was important to us was not that they apologized but that they were able to understand what they had been thinking and feeling, and that they were able to speak with their true feelings. We wanted them to grow in consciousness and strength.

Instead of apologizing for "bad" behavior, we can use the emotional accident as an opportunity to go more deeply into clarifying and sharing with our Other what our experience and intention had been.

A demand for an apology is really a demand that emotional accidents should never happen. While none of us ever want them happen, they are an unavoidable part of life. None of us are or ever will be perfectly evolved beings.

> *Jan: Al and I still have emotional accidents. I have now found that there is really very little for me to say after an accident. I get the point. Every single time, without exception, my part of the accident occurring was that I wasn't separate and so got startled and reacted to him from fusion. My anger or irritation is an emotional alarm letting me know that I was in a state of fusion. If I passed a mirror and saw a hunk of dirt on my face, I wouldn't have to talk about it. I would know immediately what to do—clean it up. Accidents are now mirrors for me. I see myself, what needs to be done, and know that it is always to work on being more separate, to teach about myself and to ask more questions.*

We will always have more growth and knowledge to attain, so of course our issues will get triggered. And, we will continue to get startled and inadvertently hurt each other. If we remember that each emotional accident is a learning opportunity, we can use it to practice our ability to separate and to be the person we want to be, not to exchange apologies that fail to enlighten us about ourselves or deepen our understanding of each other and our relationship.

Tool 13: Teach about yourself

> *Jan: I love pumpernickel bagels, dark and rich, loaded with tons of butter and cream cheese. I've never had better bagels than those from Los Angeles, so when a friend came up to visit us, bringing a big bag of bagels, I was thrilled. Unfortunately, none were pumpernickel. But, brave soul that I am, I courageously buttered and cream cheesed up a water (or plain) bagel. Oh, dear Lord! It was incredible. I staggered into the room where Al was, and orgasmically exclaimed, "I just love water bagels."*
>
> *He turned his little East-coast-where-people-live-and-breathe-bagels head to me and asked, "What do you mean by 'water' bagel?" This was not the response I expected from him. Shocked out of my ecstatic bliss as well as out of my fusion, I was furious! How could a New Yorker not know what a water bagel is?!*

My second reaction was horror. "Oh, my God!" I thought to myself. "He's retarded and I just never realized it until now!" (I kid you not! That was really what I thought!) I felt panicked but calmed myself down with words I use to instruct myself in times less overwhelming than this, "Your job is to teach someone else about yourself, if they do not understand . . . . even if they're retarded," adding the last part for this occasion. So I carefully explained to him that a water bagel has no egg or spices or seeds, no sugars or fruits—just plain old flour and water as the basic ingredients. And, just to see exactly how retarded he was—remember, I'm a psychologist and know how to evaluate these conditions—I asked him what he had thought I meant.

Al began to tell me what his train of thought had been when I made my comment about the bagel. I don't even remember what his explanation was, nor can I honestly imagine, even now, how someone could mistake my meaning . . . . but I do remember that what he said was understandable to me, just very different from how I think. (Maybe my relief about him not being retarded was so great that his explanation didn't stay in my mind!)

Sometimes we are so taken aback by our experience of separateness that we cannot even begin to understand what might be going on with our Other. Our job is to teach each other about our own culture or reality, thoughts and feelings. Remembering this can serve as a lifeline to hold onto and direct our behavior, especially when we are breathless with disbelief.

Al: Jan loves to eat at home. She loves the food we make. I like it, too, but I really like the feeling of eating out at a restaurant. My mother didn't like to cook and was never concerned with what I liked to eat. When I go to a restaurant, I love the feeling of someone asking me what I would like, going and making sure it's prepared the way I want, and then bringing it back and serving me. I get to have the feeling of having a mother, every time I go to a restaurant. Since Jan had a great Mom, there would be no way for her to know why it is important to me, unless I told her. If I didn't teach her, I'd be abandoning myself.

We have the job to advocate for ourselves and our wants. This can take the form of informing and educating our Other about what is important to us and why. It does not have to be a conflict between us, but rather a presentation so we can fully understand each other and find a way for both of us to exist.

Sometimes we do something for our Other because we love them and want to make their life easier or better. (Others of us have needs or feelings we have not taken the time to identify or the risk to express. Thoughtful acts, for us, are actually cries for attention—attempts to get our Other to give us love.) While thoughtful acts can make us feel good, most of us also want a love flow to happen—"I give to you, you receive it, love comes back to me, I have more to give." Thinking we should just be selfless and content with feeling good about our offerings, we may not pay attention to our need to be seen and received, so we may fail to let our Other know about our gift to them. But secretly, we are waiting for acknowledgement and may feel hurt, unappreciated or disappointed if it does not come.

There is nothing wrong with making announcements, with celebrating how good it feels to us to give to each other. A gift is not diminished or lessened if we also teach our Other about our needs. "I'm washing the dishes because I love you. And I'd love a hug!"

In a place of fusion, we expect our Other to just know what we want or feel and why. In a place of separateness, we know that they cannot already know our inner experience but that because we care about each other, they will want to learn about us.

Tool 14: Use emotional aikido

None of us likes to be criticized or blamed or talked to with any of the words of fusion. We tend to become defensive and want to protect ourselves. Most of us have the "No I'm not—you are!" approach to handling criticism. Similar to the martial art of karate, this response is like emotional karate—meet an opponent's movement with a block and/or a counterattack.

Emotional aikido, on the other hand, does not stand in opposition to the attacker but rather steps aside and redirects the force of the attack, dissipating its power. Similar to the martial art of aikido, in which the distinguishing guideline is its concern for the well-being of the other, emotional aikido diffuses the attack so that no one is harmed.

So, you may be wondering, how does this have anything to do with criticism or the other words of fusion? Criticism and blame are communications indicating fusion. When we respond to them with emotional karate, we are also caught in fusion.

Attack: "You never want to do what I want."

Defense: "I'm always trying to please you!" or

Counterattack: "Well, you never come with me when I want to do things! Why should I come with you?"

If we recognize that anyone using criticism or blame is not connected to their true Self, we will not become hooked and triggered by their words. Those words will only be the signal that our Other is unconsciously trying to avoid the vulnerable feeling of separateness.

Imagine someone walking up to you who did not know what they were feeling or were too afraid to say what they wanted. Would you kick them? Whack 'em with a karate chop? Of course not! When we know that someone is feeling vulnerable or lost, it is not difficult to have compassion and encourage them. When we are attacked, however, it is easy to forget that our Other is really just feeling vulnerable.

If being criticized or blamed is so hurtful to us that it is easy to overlook or forget how vulnerable the criticizer is, then it is successfully serving its intended purpose—to protect the criticizer from feeling too exposed and vulnerable. Criticism is a distraction and a defense used by someone who is too frightened and unempowered to be able to simply ask for what they want or say what they are thinking. It is used in an attempt to communicate their needs by beating us down so we rejoin them in fusion and are not a danger. Using emotional aikido, we need only step aside and let the criticism pass us by.

Attack: "You never want to do what I want."

Aikido: "I would love to hear what your ideas are and figure out how we can do them!"

Safe and unassaulted, having gotten out of the way, it will not be difficult to invite our Other to share their feelings, thoughts and needs. Rather than getting hooked by the words of the criticizer, we can compassionately invite them to be vulnerable and support them in having the right to exist with their feelings and ideas.

Jan: A couple I know took their son to a baseball game, and told him that they would buy him one treat from the refreshment stand. He picked a sour candy that they knew he would not like. They tried to protect him from feeling disappointed. They reminded him that he could pick only one treat, but they could not dissuade him. When he got upset about not liking the candy and wanted them to buy him something else, a fight ensued. He begged for another treat. They reminded him that they had tried to stop him from buying that candy, that they had warned him that he wouldn't have a second chance, but that he hadn't listened to them. He got upset with them because they wouldn't change their minds and they were upset with him because he kept trying to get them to, after they had been so clear. They were all caught in fusion.

If the parents had been able to separate, they could have sympathized with their son about how awful it feels when we make a choice and it does not turn out the way we hope it will. There would have been no fight. They could have stood together, instead of turning against each other in a confrontation, facing the bleak reality that we all have faced when we are surprised and unhappy about the result of a decision we have made. Their son could have had sympathy for his disappointment instead of feeling controlled, punished or judged by his parents. The interaction did not have to become a power struggle, with each person wanting the other to agree with them so none of them would have to feel separate or sad.

Fusion: "Pleeeeease buy me another candy! It isn't fair. I don't like this one. I didn't know it would be so sour."

Aikido: "I know! It's so disappointing when things don't turn out the way we want. I hate that too, when it happens to me."

Fusion: "But you can get me another treat!"

Aikido: "I know you want one, but each of us only gets to buy one thing, today. It's so sad that this turned out to be something you didn't like."

When someone blames or criticizes, they do not want to feel their helplessness or their separateness. We do not like those feelings, either, especially as their blaming and critical words make us feel misunderstood or unseen. A desperate battle can occur over whose reality is the correct one.

This is an example of an exchange of emotional karate that is more common among adults:

Criticism: "You're always depressed."

Counterattack: "Well, you're always angry."

Block and counterattack: "I'm not angry. You just never want to do anything except mope around."

Block and counterattack: "I don't mope around. I get upset when you constantly get irritated with me."

When we use emotional aikido, we can address the separateness our Other is avoiding. An exchange using emotional aikido to answer a criticism might go like this:

Criticism: "You're always depressed."

Aikido: "Isn't it amazing that two people who love each other so much can be in the same room having such different experiences? We're both intelligent and yet have such different interpretations of what is going on!"

Attack: "I'm not having a different experience—everyone says how depressed you are."

Aikido: "Wow! There it is again! We are seeing it differently right now! What's actually happening for me is . . . "

Communication is a process of working through miscommunication, misunderstandings and the panic reactions that come from the sudden experience of separateness. When we separate, stepping out of the way of an "attack" that is an attempt to maintain fusion, we avoid being hooked into desperate interactions in which we each try to get our Other to agree on our version of reality. Accepting our separateness allows us to use emotional aikido and be gentle with our Other, remembering that it is hard for all of us to be vulnerable.

Tool 15: Make positive suggestions

Jan: Megan and I were driving together on a winding road in Maui. After a while, we realized that almost everything we were saying was a complaint: "I'm tired." "I'm thirsty." "It's hot." "This is taking a long time." "This windy road is making me seasick." We started laughing so hard at ourselves, but we still couldn't stop complaining! Every time we opened our mouths, out would pop another complaint. It became hard to talk through our choking laughter. We kept feeling them coming, rising up from the depths of our whiny little souls, but we couldn't stop them from coming out. We spent the whole drive complaining, laughing at ourselves—and then complaining some more!

Just as a toddler's favorite word is "No!" not "Yes!" we come into awareness of ourselves through negative experience. We know what we do not want, do not like, what does not taste good, look good, feel good, fit well. The easiest thing for us to do is directly express this negative awareness by complaining, criticizing and blaming.

There are two major problems with this tendency. First, it is an unempowered, passive and fused stance. We are not active agents in making our lives what we want but instead sit back and notice what is not okay for us, as if we were helpless babies and it is someone else's responsibility to make sure that we are happy and getting our needs met. Secondly, people to whom we complain, criticize and blame are also very likely to be in fusion and therefore will tend to internalize and personalize our unhappiness, reacting as though we are saying that it is their fault. They probably do not to want to be burdened with the responsibility to fix our problem.

If we stepped on a nail, we would most likely take quick action to pull it out. We would not stand in complaint, saying, "Ow! My foot hurts! Wow! That nail really went in far! Who could have left it here? Someone really isn't being responsible and cleaning up properly! Look at all the blood!"

When experiences happen in the physical plane, we tend to take quick action. "Here comes a herd of elephants! Run!" We do not stand still and observe "Why are those elephants loose? I want to walk here and they're in my way! I don't think they should be allowed to run free." But when we have an emotional experience, because it is likely accompanied with a sudden loss of fusion, we *do* tend to be surprised, and then complain.

The emotional alarm of tightness, at times like these, gives us the signal to take our complaint, criticism or blame and actively translate it into a positive statement or a positive suggestion. "Please pass the salt." as opposed to "Are you going to hog the salt all day?" We can find and express what it is that we do want, rather than talking about what we do not want.

Example:

Complaint: "I'm so hungry I feel like I'm going to pass out."

Criticism: "This is way too late to be eating dinner."

Blame: "You never want to eat dinner at a reasonable time."

Positive suggestion: "I can't wait to eat dinner as late as you like to. Could we find an earlier time to eat that would still work for you?"

Example:

Complaint: "I feel lonely in this relationship."

Criticism: "Our time together is really empty and boring."

Blame: "You never want to talk about your feelings."

Positive suggestion: "I'd love us to spend time every night cuddling and just being together and talking without the TV on."

Example:

Complaint: "I never get to finish what I want to say."

Criticism: "You always change the subject."

Blame: "You make me not even want to talk to you."

Positive suggestion: "It's easier for me if you let me know you understand what I said before you start to talk about your thoughts."

Example:

Complaint: "You always want to work in the garage and never want to do what's important to me."

Criticism: "You're such a controlling person."

Blame: "The reason we fight is that you have to have your way all the time."

Positive suggestion: "What if we both talk about what we'd like to do on the weekend, and make a plan that works for both of us?" And:

Person 1: "I'd love to go on a bike ride with you today. What do you want to do today?"

Person 2:"There's some work I want to do in the garage."

Person 1:"How about if you work on your project in the garage this morning, and then we can go for a bike ride this afternoon?"

Translating our negative awareness into a positive suggestion is especially important when we are talking about how we deal with the patterns of our interactions and emotional issues in our relationship. Instead of talking about what did not happen or what should have happened, we can simply suggest what we would like to have happen. We can engage each other as a team to try a better approach, inviting our Other to our vision of how things could be, instead of focusing on what everyone did wrong and what did not work. Together we can focus on improving the situation—exploring possibilities and attacking the problem, not each other.

Every relationship is a unique system that both people have had a part in creating. None of us are victims in a relationship. The particular system of our relationship could not have developed without our participation, even if that participation was done in ignorance or desperation. (And, we will always be ignorant and subject to desperation! None of us will ever arrive at perfect wisdom or maturity.)

Many people confuse responsibility with blame. But with responsibility comes the power to make a difference, instead of feeling like a helpless victim of our Other's wants. We each have the power to step in and stop self-defeating patterns.

All of us have ideas of what might make our relationship better. When we learn to take action on our emotional alarms and identify our feelings and wants, when we can separate and translate our negative awarenesses into positive suggestions, we will each be able to claim our power and be a leader and a teacher in our relationship.

Tool 16: Make an agenda

There are many reasons that we quietly accept or endure each other. We may have compassion for our Other and so do not bring up or point out minor issues when they come up. Sometimes we do not want to spoil a good time or risk having conflict. We may feel frightened or undeserving to bring up our needs or our unhappy feelings or we do not want to be a complainer.

But, just let our *Other* point out minor issues or spoil a good time or confront us or not suck it up (like we're doing, but complain, instead) we feel betrayed, totally unseen and totally unappreciated. We swallowed our feelings with the unspoken expectation (or secret contract) that our Other would, too. Now that the secret agreement has been unwittingly violated by our Other, we suddenly have plenty to say! For every point our Other makes, we have ten! We feel the innocent and self-righteous victim of our Other. "You never" and "I always" becomes the language we desperately use in our attempt to be seen and appreciated. These interactions can become childlike tit-for-tat experiences that spiral deeply out of control.

At times like these, it is especially important to make a list, at least a mental list, and take one issue at a time. (*Jan: The rule I operate under is that whoever was brave enough to bring up an issue gets to go first, instead of me piggybacking on their courage to start a conversation. Believe me, I never forget what it is I need to say!*)

Tool 13 is a process that two people can use to avoid the problem of spiraling out of control.

Tool 17: The Separateness Communication Process

Step 1: Explain the issue and express your feelings.

Step 2: Acknowledge the issue and the feelings. This may be all that is necessary to address the issue in Step 1.

Step 3: Use Tool 15 - Make positive suggestions. (If necessary, either suggest an action plan or begin an exploration about what would work for both of you.)

Step 4: Acknowledge feeling heard and seen. (Let your Other know you have nothing else to say about the issue.)

Here is an example of this process:

Step 1: Explain the issue and express your feelings.

Person 1: "I'd like to talk about having dinner together more as a family instead of watching TV while we eat. It feels good to me to sit around the table and share what everyone did that day and how they're feeling. I want us to have that closeness and make those kind of memories with our kids."

Step 2: Acknowledge the issue and the feelings, and Step 1: Explain the issue and express your feelings.

Person 2: "I know that's important to you. I kind of like the break, though, when I come home from work, to just be able to chill out and not think."

Step 3: Make positive suggestions.

Person 2: "How about if we start doing it, but just on the weekends?"

Step 4: Acknowledge feeling heard and seen. Let your Other know you have nothing else to say about the issue.

Person 1: "That would be great. Thanks. I feel really good about that idea as a start. I don't have anything else to say about it right now."

Step 1: Explain the issue and express your feelings.

Person 2: "Having talked about that, I realize that I have something that's bothering me. I get frustrated when I'm trying to balance the checkbook and you didn't enter the check numbers or amounts in it because then I don't have the information I need."

Step 2: Acknowledge the issue and the feelings.

Person 1: "Yea, I keep forgetting how important that is to you. I know that's frustrating for you, and I'll try harder to do it. It doesn't occur to me because it's not that important to me."

Step 3: Make positive suggestions.

Person 2: "Could you write in the numbers at the same time you write the check, so if I want to work on the checkbook when you're not around, I can?"

Person 1: "Sure. I'll do that."

Step 4: Acknowledge feeling heard and seen. Let your Other know you have nothing else to say about the issue.

Person 2: "Thanks. I know it isn't the way you'd do it, so I really appreciate that. I don't have any other feelings about this."

In this process, both people get to express their issues and feelings. Both people get the experience of their feelings being important. They are each acknowledged and understood. The action plan acknowledges that the issue has been taken seriously. Because the issue is presented using the words of separateness, it can be resolved without either person feeling criticized.

It is important to remember to listen to whatever the other person is saying to hear their need and not make it about us. What are they wanting, feeling, needing, suggesting?

We may have many topics to discuss, but if we do not take them one at a time, we will descend into an interaction in which neither of us ever feels acknowledged or understood and both people become frantic to be seen.

The Separateness Interaction Process is also an excellent way to deal with "The Time Lag Phenomenon." This is a bewildering experience that happens to all of us. When we do not address issues and feelings in a way that is satisfying in the moment, those issues and feelings do not just disappear. They will come out when our Other triggers them but has no idea that we are actually responding with emotions that belong to a situation from the past. Whenever you have the thought that your Other is completely outrageous, a jerk, overreacting, and you feel absolutely and totally innocent and they seem crazy, remember that The Time Lag Phenomenon may be operating. Instead of becoming reactive, yourself, ask what your Other is needing or feeling in this moment. Do not focus on the past, even if it was just one eye blink ago. Acknowledge how awful it must be for your Other to feel so upset and invite them to engage in the Separateness Interaction Process: "What can we do now that will work better? What are your needs, concerns, ideas? Here are mine. How can we put them together—like a picture puzzle—so we both feel okay?"

Discussions do not need to be wars. There does not need to be a winner and a loser. Both people have their correct perspectives. The needs of each of us, while different, are all valid. The issue is not whose needs are valid but how do we integrate those needs so we are both okay.

We each pay attention to different aspects of reality and so we are each correct about our own inner experience. We may not be correct, however, about what really happened, as our perceptions are colored by our own feelings, history and issues. If we employ the tools of separateness, we will not need to feel either defensive or critical of our Other or of ourselves. We can focus on the issue in order to find a satisfying resolution that takes care of the needs of both of us instead of feeling as if we are fighting to not be seen as the "bad guy."

Tool 18: End a Separateness Interaction with a hug

We might be fine and feel like our issue is resolved with our Other, after having a Separateness Interaction, but our bodies might still feel tight. The adrenaline that was released in the moment of our shock over feeling separate may take longer to dissipate than our discussion takes. One way to help our bodies relax—and know that the "danger" is over and that the adrenaline that surged to help us meet this danger is no longer needed—is to hug each other.

> Jan: Al and I would often feel very awkward after a Separateness Interaction was over. I have distinct memories of us just standing and looking at each other, not quite sure what to do. Somehow we happened on the idea to say, "We should hug. Not because we want to, but because it's good for us." That always made us smile, and made the distance between us go from seeming insurmountable to being nothing, as we each stepped forward. When I hold Al and feel him holding me, I feel and can know in my body that he loves me—I don't just know it in my mind. Hugging is a good tool to use all the time, not just after a Separateness Interaction, to help us feel connected to each other.

Our minds might know something, but the knowledge might get stuck up there because our bodies are still braced to defend and protect ourselves from hurt. When we touch each other, especially in a long, uninterrupted hug, we can allow what we know to be true to go down into our very cells and transform us—not only for that moment but in our ability to really feel and remember that we are allies with our Other and that we are safe.

Tool 19: Create a new vision together

Because we come from different cultures and are separate, unique individuals, we are each aware of different aspects of every experience. Just as our brain knows how to integrate what our two eyes see from different angles into a more complete whole, together we can take our different awarenesses and create something bigger and richer than what either of us could have conceived of alone. Remember, we picked our Other because what we have to offer each other creates a balance between us. Each of us has insight and wisdom that the other does not yet have. We can strive to develop a way of going so deeply into issues that we come out with a plan that honors both of our perspectives. Despite any initial negative reaction to broken fusion, if we take the time to really understand each other, we will usually find that we have complementary visions that enrich each other. When we can tolerate our separateness long enough to work to integrate the strengths we each have, a stronger whole is created.

> *Al: Jan, her mom and I took a trip together to Europe. We were all so excited to be on an adventure together. Really loving each other, we were each eager to make the other two happy. Focusing on each other, we neglected to pay attention to our own needs.*
>
> *About a week into the trip, things blew up. Focusing on pleasing each other, we were each upset that we hadn't been making sure we were speaking up for what we wanted for ourselves. Irritations and hurts had built up and it felt like we needed to call the trip off and just go home.*

Problems in relationships do not always come from negative interactions. Sometimes we want so much to please and show our love for our Other that we sacrifice our needs for our Other's happiness, not realizing that a successful relationship requires the full presence of both people. From a place of fusion, we can become hurt or angry, passively unwilling to talk about our ideas, for that would mean having to sepa-rate, which is against all of our instincts. From a place of separateness, however, we can share our vision of how things could be with each other and find a solution that integrates our most important needs.

> *Al: Finally, great psychologists that we all are (!) it occurred to us that surely if we tried hard enough, we could figure out how to communi-cate and make this trip a good one. We decided that we would have a family conference every morning, to talk about what our ideas and needs were for the day and make a plan. Then, we'd have another family conference, at night and talk about how the day had gone.*

Any time people are coordinating their lives, whether they are at work, in their family or at play, clear and regular communication is essential. For example, all organized sports teams have timeouts, conferences, huddles and team meetings. It is not realistic to think that we will not need to have them in a relationship. Needs change. Moods change. External events and situations change. Football teams meet (huddle) after every play. They make a plan for the next play based on the in-formation they exchange about what they are aware of and what is happening in the game. In a relationship, we need to huddle regularly for the same reasons.

When we can identify our feelings, solutions are really rather sim-ple, thank goodness! If we can accept that any two people are going to have different needs, different reactions, different ideas and different solutions to issues, then we do not have to think in terms of right and wrong. We can merely acknowledge that we are just different. And those differences are even part of the reason we are drawn to each other.

> *Jan: When Al and I were writing this book, whenever we came to a part where we had different approaches or ideas, one of us was always tempted to give in to the other. But we determined that we would not do that. Instead, we kept discussing and describing what our thoughts were until we were able to get to a new and more complete understand-ing of the concept and an integration of our perspectives that neither of us had been able to see on our own. It was interesting and exciting*

to have those discussions and to be able to create something between
us that neither of us had ever conceived of on our own! We think our
book is all the better for it, too.

Accepting that each of us has a unique and valuable perspective to add
to the relationship allows the possibility of conversation and sharing,
and coming up with creative ways to make room for the needs of both
of us. Separating and creating a life together is an exciting and dynamic
process. It is much, much easier than trying to live in fusion, which
makes us unhappy and distant from each other, for we each repress and
give up who we really are in order to keep our Other.

> *Al: In the past, Jan and I had different needs about socializing. She liked*
> *it. I didn't. This kind of situation can easily turn into arguments when*
> *people are stuck in fusion. Not being willing to accept the differences, each*
> *person tries to convince their Other to do it their way. Jan could have*
> *said, "Why don't you just be more open to meeting people?" I could have*
> *said, "Why don't you like to have meaningful time alone with me, more?"*
> *Instead, when we went to parties, we figured out that we could bring two*
> *cars. I could go home when I was done socializing and Jan could stay if*
> *she wanted to. Pretty simple, but we could only create the solution when we*
> *separated and tried to figure out how we could both be okay.*

Often discussions become fierce as people desperately try to convince
each other that their way is the right way. Fused and thinking there can
only be one reality, they become stuck in a contest of whose reality is
going to "win." The alternative is "losing" and giving up what we want.

When we separate, we have the opportunity to create a new type of
culture in our relationship, a culture in which we are both are valuable
and what we each need and want is important. We can create a new
pattern of talking with each other in which we both keep sharing our
needs, feelings and concerns, brainstorming until we are successful in
finding solutions that work for both of us. We just need to keep faith in
the process, knowing that a situation in which we have different needs
is just an opportunity to be creative and that we do not need to feel
defeated or give ourselves up.

Tool 20: Allow yourself to be playful

Al: As I have described, I came from a childhood that was both negative and lonely, so it is a challenge for me to think in positive and collaborative ways. This makes it very difficult for Jan, as well, for she wants us to grow and learn and improve our communication. She doesn't want me to get stuck in feeling overwhelmed or self-critical.

After a Separateness Interaction, one way that I relieve any tension that might be lingering in my body is to tease. I might respond to a question Jan asks that may be completely unrelated to the interaction we just had. Once, when asked, "Would you like syrup or jam on your pancakes?" I responded, "I would like to have whatever is the most positive and collaborative." My teasing makes both of us laugh, but in fact, it also makes it easier for me to think about our conversation. In this playful way, I am reminding Jan that I have taken our discussion very seriously and am really keeping in mind what we talked about. And, periodically through the day, I may use the words "I want to be positive and collaborative" whenever I want to say, "Yes."

We might feel awkward about how to resume our time together after a Separateness Interaction. One of the best ways to try to create a sense of ease is to be playful as a way to dissipate the tension.

Jan: One thing I love about Al is that he can always make me laugh. I remember one time, after we came back into a group of friends after stepping outside to settle a disagreement, we held hands, but he trailed after me, holding his eye as though I had punched him. Everyone has Separateness Interactions, but he makes it all feel normal and okay.

Tool 21: The Emotional Bill of Rights

Jan: I remember one of my students raising her hand during a class I was teaching. With a look of shock on her face, she said, "Jan, you're not teaching psychology—you're teaching revolution!"

When we accept ourselves as evolving human beings, we create a new world for ourselves, one that has no rules or judgments that we must adhere to. It can feel both liberating and disorienting to step into freedom. As an artist might feel overwhelmed standing before a blank canvas or God might have felt overwhelmed at the vastness and emptiness of space before Creation, we also might be breathless when we behold the enormity of our right to exist. Only when we accept and come to peace with our right to exist can we become the creators of our own life, looking not to someone else to be the experts on us, but rather looking inside our own hearts for guidance and truth as we face the vastness of possibility.

In this process of creating ourselves, we have the necessity and the right to be separate and different, even from those who mean the most to us.

We want to offer you The Emotional Bill of Rights:

1. You do not have to make logical decisions.

    Jan: When I go to a restaurant, I do not study the menu, computing the nutritional content of the selections. I see what I feel like having.

The idea that you must follow logic is an illusion. Logic does not necessarily make better judgments than any other approach can make. Thinking and logic are tools of the left brain and are extremely valuable in gathering information and brainstorming possibilities. But being logical limits you to things you understand, for often solutions cannot be accessed by the left brain. Logic is only one of the brain functions and addresses only one dimension of reality. To treat it as the best brain function and think that it addresses the most important dimension of reality is limiting. Valuing logic above all other forms of decision-making is an opinion or judgment. It is not a fact that logic is a superior method to use. Our right brain, the source of emotions and intuition, also provides valuable and valid input to guide us in decision-making.

2. You have the right to not understand something.

    Jan: I remember the first time I was able to ask someone what a word meant. It was an exhilarating experience. I could acknowledge being less informed than they were without feeling inferior to them! What freedom!!! Not knowing and not understanding something always made me feel too vulnerable—as though I would not be valuable anymore if I weren't perfect. Being at peace with my human limitations and my right to exist has made me impervious to criticism! No comment about me can cause me to have a reaction of fear, shame or self-judgment.

It is our birthright to be learning, growing, evolving beings. If someone tries to shame or criticize us for living our birthright, they are revealing information about themselves—that they are not at peace with being an evolving being. They are telling us nothing about us!

3. You do not have to care about everything.

Al: There are many things that I have cared about in the past that I just don't have the energy to care about right now in my life. For example, I have always been a person who loves babies. But now I hardly pay attention to them at all when I am around them. Nothing wrong with the babies, but I am focusing on different aspects of my life right now and just don't have too much space for them.

You have the right to choose your own priorities. And, you have the right to choose not only what you care about but also when you care about them. There are endless possibilities in life and not all of them will be important to you. We usually do not even have the time and energy for all the things that are important to us. If someone points out how you could improve, or what you could be or should be doing, you are NOT obligated to do anything about it. They are talking about what is important to them. You have the right to ask yourself "Am I satisfied?" and then let your own inner truth be your guide.

4. You do not have to offer reasons or excuses to justify your behavior.

Al: Again, sometimes I get calls from friends who say, "I haven't heard from you for a while. What's up?" Nothing is up. I just may not be feeling like socializing, at this point in my life.

You have the right to examine your own heart and choose your behavior based on what you find there. You are not responsible to others for your behavior and therefore do not need to justify it to anyone. "How can you refuse to give reasons to a friend?" Consider this—why would your friend require reasons? You may want to share your feelings and thoughts, but no one has the right to demand answers or justifications from you. It is simply not their business.

5. You are not responsible for someone else's problems. You are only responsible for yourself.

> *Al: There are times when a friend or relative is having a particularly difficult challenge in their life. Sometimes all I have to offer in response is "I love you" or "I feel sad that you are having such a hard time."*

Even if someone presents their problems as if you have the obligation to help them, you do not have that responsibility. You may feel sad for them but it is not your job to fix them or their life.

> *Jan: My friend, Lesley, once told me something brilliant, as we were talking about our children. She said, "I've learned that I have to stand back and allow someone the dignity to fail or they'll never discover what muscles they need to succeed." I had never thought of it that way. Hearing her words made me realize that often when I jump in to help someone, I am really trying to fix them so I don't have to tolerate my helplessness or feel my pain that they are struggling.*

6. You have the right to change your mind.

> *Jan: Whenever I teach, at the end of every term I tell my students that I brought something for each of them. I then dig through my purse trying to find the gifts. Finally, triumphant, I pull out a huge handful of imaginary "magic erasers," telling my students that if ever they did or said something that didn't feel right to them, they had the right to correct themselves to reflect their true feelings. They only needed to pull out their magic eraser. No one could ever tell them "You said it and you can't take it back!" because their magic eraser proves they have the right to change their mind*

whenever they want to. They can even announce that a "doctor" gave it to them! Every single student always comes up and takes one!

All of us have had the experience of saying or doing something and then immediately feeling that it did not correspond to our inner truth. Sometimes we just cannot realize what is true to us until we take action and find that it does not feel right. "No take-backs!" does not apply in life. We are all groping our way as best we can and never need to feel trapped or apologetic when we find our initial thoughts are not our most accurate thoughts.

> *Jan: Once we went on vacation to France, and paid for our Gramma, Marge, to come with us. The flight was fine, but as soon as we got to the hotel, Marge said, in great distress, "I need to go home!" I was stunned but said, "Okay." What else was there to say? I didn't want her to be unhappy. I was terribly disappointed, having looked forward to this family vacation for months and having invested a lot of money for her ticket, but I also realized that she couldn't have foreseen every feeling she might have about being away from home until she lived through the experience and discovered what her feelings were. (End of story: After calling home, she felt reconnected to her husband and happily continued with us on our trip.)*

There is never a reason for us to feel guilty or responsible for the feelings and reactions of someone else when we become more clear about our needs and change our minds. We can be emotionally responsive to our Other without changing our behavior as if we were responsible for them. We can give them caring for their feelings but we are not obligated to keep them from having those feelings by sacrificing what is right and true for us.

7. It is your right to make "mistakes."

Because we are evolving beings, we will always be learning. Sometimes what we do will have unexpected consequences, but that does not mean that we have made a "mistake"—we are simply engaged in the human process of exploration and growth. There is no way we can know for certain what the outcome of our acts will be. And, like scientists, we persistently experiment to try to make our life work. Did Thomas Edison make mistakes when he had to make one thousand prototypes before he successfully made his first light bulb, or did it just take time to find the exact solution?

We do not need to feel ignorant or guilty when the outcomes of our acts surprise us. It is your right to do experiments and just be in response to them—to make adjustments and learn. Without shame or judgment, experiments can even be interesting!

8. Not everyone needs to like you.

> *Al: This is a particularly hard "right" for me to claim and an extreme-ly important one for all of us if we are to feel separate in a relationship. Sometimes, when Jan and I are having a difficult discussion, I have to remind myself that although I wouldn't want it to happen, Jan may not like me and maybe she won't even want to be with me anymore. When I can accept this, I can operate with more internal freedom in our relationship. I want to be with Jan and I want her to like me, but if it doesn't work out that way, I'll still be okay. When I remember this, I am able to be more separate and not lose myself trying to keep her.*

Not everyone will be a match for us. There will be many people to whom we are drawn and for whom we may even feel love, but only time and experience will reveal if they are doing life in a way that is complementary to our own path. It is the same process as doing a jig-saw puzzle—we see many pieces that seem similar—the right squiggle and curve in the right places, a patch of color that corresponds to what we are looking for. But as we bring the pieces closer together, we find subtle differences that make them clearly not a match. Imagine if, not wanting to feel our disappointment, we refused to accept the mismatch and pounded, pushed and cut the pieces to fit. We would wind up with one funny looking, distorted puzzle picture.

In relationships, if we do not accept the possibility that we will not be a match with someone we care about, we will wind up pushing and contorting ourselves and them to be people we are not, trying to avoid feeling our sadness and disappointment. And, as with the distorted puzzle picture, we will wind up with a relationship that simply cannot work.

When we separate, we will be able to remember that this does not mean something is wrong with anyone—we are each just focusing on different aspects of reality, valuing and attending to different tasks in life, with different styles. There is no right or wrong, good or bad.

We are the only non-negotiable in our own life. We might be sad if other people go away, but if we abandon ourselves to try to keep someone else, what do we have left?

9. You have the right to be the one in charge of your life.

> *Jan: I read, once, about Death sitting as an advisor on our left shoulder. That was a powerful image for me. Sometimes when I am trying to find my own truth, to make a decision about what feels good and right for me to do, I imagine myself on my deathbed. How will I have wanted to live?*

Each of us has one life to be responsible for—our own. We each get one body and we have the right to make decisions and create the life for ourselves that we want to have. The only person we have to live with from birth until death is our own Self. Because we need to live with ourselves, we need to be in peace inside—setting our own standards, being kind to ourselves, motivating and supporting ourselves to grow when we need to work on something. To some extent, even if we love them, everyone and everything else is irrelevant and must come second to our own conscience and our right to exist.

10. You have the right to forget your rights and come back and read this over and over.

Tools in Review

1. Remember we are both vulnerable.
2. Remember we are both innocent.
3. Remember we are both right.
4. Acknowledge your Other's reality.

5. Believe your Other.
6. Announce your intentions.
7. Tell your Other what you want and ask your Other what they want.
8. Take time alone or a time out.
9. Do-overs are permitted.
10. Describe yourself, not your Other.
11. Catch your breath then ask a question.
12. Clarification, not apologies.
13. Teach about yourself.
14. Use emotional aikido.
15. Make positive suggestions.
16. Make an agenda.
17. The Separateness Communication Process

   Step 1: Explain the issue and express your feelings.

   Step 2: Acknowledge the issue and the feelings.

   Step 3: Use Tool 15 - Make positive suggestions. (If necessary, either suggest an action plan or begin to explore what would work for both of you.)

   Step 4: Acknowledge feeling heard and seen. (Let your Other know you have nothing else to say about the issue.)

18. End a Separateness Interaction with a hug.
19. Create a new vision together.
20. Allow yourself to be playful.
21. The Emotional Bill of Rights.

A Separateness Interaction is not a "problem"— it's a growth opportunity

We all get startled and scared when we experience separateness. When we get scared, our minds, out of a need to protect ourselves, quickly get active, so by the time we are ready to talk to our Other, we have filled ourselves with scary stories, frightening possibilities and protective boundaries. When we can stay separate, however, we can also experience curiosity—we can become compassionate scientists.

In relationships, we must keep growing. With the tools of separateness, we can remember who we each are and keep creating until we have compassionate understanding for each other and can come up with a solution that takes care of the needs both of us have. That may take some time and discussion, but there is no need to panic! If we are good allies to each other, we will find our way.

We are a team with our Other. We are not enemies. We did not choose each other to make each other unhappy. We were drawn together because we glimpsed who we each could be—and loved what we saw.

A relationship gives us companionship on the journey of life as we make discoveries about our own Self. The most important qualification of that companion is that they be willing to openly explore whatever comes up in them and in the relationship. If we are both are committed to our own growth and to going into our hearts in vulnerability and honesty, without judgment, we will be unable to keep from getting to a wonderful place, for where our hearts meet is Heaven.

Thriving, not just surviving

We are all extremely sensitive and so we notice and are affected by our Other's subtle tones of voice, facial expressions and body language. We cannot help but react to what we see and so we start to adjust our own behavior and reactions, subtly distorting who we really are, unconsciously attempting to protect ourselves against hurt.

Without even realizing it, we also start to protect our relationship, enduring things that do not feel right and acting in ways that repress or deny what we want or feel—all in the name of love or peace or to avoid the threat of loss. Without the tools of separateness, we are scared to bring things up. We do not want to jeopardize our relationship or spoil our time together with discord. We become afraid to look at the reality of our relationship and reactions out of a fear that we will discover something we cannot overcome and will have to lose each other. We hold on because we do not know what else to do.

To some degree, we all negotiate, compromise or give up needs we have in our relationships. We all tend to do things for each other that we do not talk about. Our experience is that our Other benefits from our sacrifices. We do not realize, because we are not them, that they are probably doing the same thing and are having the same experience that they are sacrificing for our benefit.

In our fearful avoidance, we live with misunderstandings, and distance increasingly grows between us. When an issue finally is brought up, usually when someone is so hurt that they get angry, it can rapidly escalate into a war. Each of us feels hurt and misunderstood, innocent and aware of what we have endured that felt painful to us and what we have tried to do to try to make the relationship better. Desperate to be seen, we both get lost in attack and counterattack. We get stuck in fusion and fight to be acknowledged, appreciated and loved.

The tools of separateness allow us to walk without fear into every interaction that makes us feel disconnected from our Other. Having the courage to face every issue gives our relationship the best chance of not only surviving, but also of thriving. When we slow down and separate and remember that we are scientists breaking new ground in the study of human relationships (our own!), we can discover the truth of what each of us feels, wants and thinks. We do not have to live in fear, resentment or hurt, trying to "read" our Other and interpret what they really mean by their words or actions. We can stay connected to them in the truth of who they are.

The tools of separateness will empower us to connect with our Other as we both overcome our ignorance and grow.

It's *not* too hard!

If emotional ignorance could be remedied by our left brain simply learning and remembering, it would be easy to have good relationships. The ignorance we are talking about in this book is a very different matter, for in the absence of knowledge we have all experienced hurt, confusion, desperation and fear, and these have made a lasting impact on us. We are all reactive and vulnerable in our important relationships, so slowing ourselves down to be able to use the new tools is a challenge—a worthy one, but a definite challenge.

It is an illusion that some things are too hard to face. We really do have the strength to look at any reaction pattern and discover the understandable human feeling or need behind it. Only then do we have a real chance to support each other in becoming our best and strongest selves. Only then can we have the opportunity to rid ourselves of fears from the past, grow together and create a new vision for our relationship without needing to leave each other.

If we remember that we are allies, both hoping to find a way to keep our relationship without having to sacrifice ourselves as individuals, then we can face with confidence the feelings and situations that inevitably come up in every relationship. We do not have to be frightened. We will know that we are just being called to action—it is time to get down to work so that we can each become more aware, more empowered, more free and therefore more able to feel the love we have for each other.

Our reactiveness and old patterns can be changed but there are no shortcuts, no easy or fast ways to learn and mature. We must always remember the fact that it takes patience, practice and compassion for both our Self and our Other, for it is in our important relationships that we are challenged to grow the most. With kindness and with determination we can remind ourselves that it may be hard, but it is not *too* hard.

Separating allows us to know the reality of our Other. The more deeply we know someone, the more real they are. At the surface level where we first meet and see the potential of each other, and at heart when we are at our most vulnerable, people can be pretty wonderful. But, oh! That space in between! Tolerating broken fusion long enough to create real connection is a challenge but with the help of the Tools of Separateness, it is a challenge that is absolutely possible for all of us.

It is our job to be an adult and to separate. Our Other has his own inner reality *that is valid*. You may both be absolutely innocent but you *will* be the catalyst for your Other's pain, fear, memories and historical way of reacting and adapting. It is simply unrealistic to demand that they be so evolved, so mature, so separate that they are without their own issues. A demand that your Other be the all-loving, perfect parent, perfectly grown up so you don't have to struggle to separate is the demand of a baby. (*Jan: Don't feel bad. I'm the biggest baby I know!*)

We are never too hurt or too shocked to stop and separate. This might mean asking what is going on with the other person, giving ourselves a time out so we can recover from our own startled reaction, or telling our Other that we cannot talk about any issue with this kind of intensity between us. It may be hard to do, but it is not too hard!

Jan: Al and I just had a fight. We even got angry. It seemed so silly! I wasn't hurt or frightened one bit. I kept thinking, "We're going to get to a great place by doing this." And we did. We kept looking more and more deeply into our feelings, finding our misunderstandings . . . and it was no big deal. WOW!

CHAPTER 9

Practicing Separateness

Jan: When Disneyland first opened, they sold ticket books—"A" tickets for the rides no one really wanted to go on, "B" tickets for somewhat better rides, all the way up to "E" tickets. You didn't get many of those, but were they ever special. They were for the most exciting rides—elaborate, really beautiful or designed to scare you with witches or ghosts suddenly jumping out at you. Sometimes they made you feel like you were going to throw up from the wild movements of the little cars.

It is difficult to navigate the tumultuous and surprising waters of the Journey Through An Emotionally Intimate Relationship—a definite E ticket ride, complete with things (feelings and issues) that seem to jump out at us out of nowhere. We are emotionally thrown around, sometimes feeling like we are going to throw up! This ride makes it challenging to find and hold onto our true selves. Hopefully, you will take comfort in knowing that this is the human journey we are *all* on. Nothing is wrong with you or with your relationship.

Just to illustrate our point that you are absolutely normal, we are going to go through some common situations couples face and common complaints that make us all feel stuck and tangled up in each other's issues—situations where we all are tempted to exclaim, "It's all your fault!"

Every time we talk with our Other about anything, we need to remember to hold onto the Separateness Tool 1: Remember we are both vulnerable (and so can become very reactive), Tool 2: Remember we are both innocent (and do not intend harm) and Tool 3: Remember we are both right (we each see a different aspect of reality).

We come to speedy conclusions in the following examples. In real life, it takes a lot of patience (and deep breathing to stay calm and separate) while we keep asking questions to clarify what we are hearing, and acknowledging our Other's reality. This is the only way to avoid getting stuck in upset reactions before we get to the true feelings we are each having. In all of these examples, we use language that reflects someone having done a lot of practice and work on themselves. This is not realistic! We are all learning and will struggle with our vulnerability and fear as we try to find the words to express ourselves. None of us will use the ideal language of separateness and we should not judge ourselves as we work with these tools and concepts. We need to be patient with ourselves as we overcome our reactiveness.

See if you can recognize yourself in any of these scenarios.

Creating a ritual

Jason and Holly get so easily triggered by each other that they cannot bring up and talk about anything. Afraid of him not believing her, Holly tends to frame every communication in terms of what Jason did or did not do as she attempts to prove her point or make him see that she has something valid to say. This, of course, makes Jason feel unseen in all the caring and generous things he does for her. He becomes defensive, arguing about her description of him or countering with descriptions of her failings. Both of them, hurt and desperate to be seen, are then off attacking and criticizing each other, wanting the validity of their needs and reality to be affirmed.

WHAT THE ISSUES ARE

Both Jason and Holly are stuck in fusion, scared to separate and risk feeling vulnerable. Neither of them feels secure in their right to exist, so they are afraid to declare their feelings and needs, and instead use blame to raise issues with each other.

PRACTICING FUSION

Holly: "Why don't you just sit on the couch all day and I'll do all the work."

Jason: "You didn't even notice that I cleaned up the whole yard up yesterday while you were at work. You never say anything positive to me or give me any affection."

Holly: "You only think about what you need. You never consider my feelings or do anything I want you to. And you act like you're the only one who gets tired."

Jason: "Well, I am tired, but you only seem to think of yourself. And, I would think that by now you should be fully aware of what I need! I've told you enough times."

PRACTICING SEPARATENESS

Here is an example of how Jason and Holly could use tools of separateness to address their issues and create a way of talking they are both comfortable with.

Tool 1: Remember we are both vulnerable.
Tool 2: Remember we are both innocent.
Tool 3: Remember we are both right.
Tool 17: The Separateness Communication Process.

Step 1: Explain the issue and express your feelings.

Holly: "I'm overwhelmed trying to get the house cleaned and making dinner at the same time. Can you help?"
Jason: "Sure. What can I do?"

Tool 6: Announce your intentions.

Together, Jason and Holly also came up with a sentence they both felt good about to announce the speaker's intention. "I would like to bring something up, and I don't want to upset you. I would just like to ask for something, and it doesn't mean you've done anything wrong." Although the sentence was long and formal, it served to bring them to attention, which they both needed in order to avoid their instant defensive reactions. It created a ritual to signal the beginning of an important communication.

They tried using the announcement, and it helped. Jason was able to remember that Holly was feeling vulnerable about bringing up a need and asking for help. This was not about anything that he had done wrong. Having the opportunity to take a deep breath and separate, he felt prepared and was able to listen to her feelings and needs without feeling defensive.

Tool 20: Allow yourself to be playful.

Al: Jason, Holly and I all laughed about taking a morning in which they introduced everything that they said with that ritual announcement:

1. "I would like to bring something up, and I don't want to upset you. I would just like to ask for something, and it doesn't mean you've done anything wrong."
2. (Significant pause for the other to take in their words and get centered.)
3. (And then the message, content or issue to be addressed.) "Would you like eggs for breakfast?"

The response would be in similar form:

1. "I would like to bring something up, and I don't want to upset you. I would just like to ask for something, and it doesn't mean you've done anything wrong."
2. (Significant pause for the other to take in their words and get centered.)
3. (And then the message, content or issue to be addressed.) "I'd love three, over easy. Thanks!"

Jason and Holly's bickering is just another way of them trying to stay in fusion. Underlying the fights that most of us have is a desperateness to reconnect and to be seen. *A fight is a protest reaction to feeling emotionally disconnected,* which triggers abandonment and rejection issues. The underlying fear is that we are not valued and loved.

Although they are still struggling, Jason and Holly are less fearful and have a sense of hope about how they can approach each other with vulnerability and with playfulness, and how, with enough practice, they will be increasingly able to separate, with compassion replacing hurt and connection replacing defensiveness.

Love on demand

Emily wants to feel closer to Nick. She is very open about her feelings toward him. Although she tries to accept the fact that he has a hard time expressing his feelings, she is still very sad and lonely because he does not verbalize his feelings very often. Nick is frightened to express what he is feeling. He feels responsible for her happiness and her emotional well-being. He realizes how unhappy she becomes when he does not express his love to her, but if he tells her that he loves her when she asks for it, he feels controlled and resentful. Instead of just saying it when he feels it, he feels as though he is saying it on demand.

WHAT THE ISSUES ARE

Emily is struggling to feel separate. In her fusion and desire to avoid feeling helpless, she thinks that Nick would respond the way she wants him to if she could just figure out how to express her needs and wants in the "right" way. Although her efforts continue to be unsuccessful, she has not realized that she needs to explore his feelings from a place of separateness.

Nick does not feel his right to exist, so he is hesitant to reveal himself too vulnerably, although Emily obviously values him. When Emily wants something from him, his experience is that only one of them will get to exist and that he will have to become who Emily wants him to be, not who he is.

PRACTICING FUSION

Emily: "I love you, Nick"

Nick: (Squeezes her hand.)

Emily: "Can you tell me in words how you feel?"

Nick: "Why do you always try to control how I express myself?"

Emily: "I'm not trying to control you. But I've told you a million times how important the words are to me."

PRACTICING SEPARATENESS

Tool 1: Remember we are both vulnerable.

Tool 2: Remember we are both innocent.

Tool 3: Remember we are both right.

Tool 6: Announce your intentions.

Emily: "I was hoping we could brainstorm about how to get an important need of mine met. I don't want you to feel responsible or criticized or controlled."

Tool 13: Teach about yourself.

Emily: "Even if I know something with my mind, I feel lonely if I don't hear the words. I know you're more nonverbal than I am, which is absolutely fine, but when we tell each other that we love each other, I feel like we're celebrating how lucky we are and how good it feels. I remember when my Dad died, one of the most sad things for me was not being able to say 'I love you' to him anymore. I want us to enjoy how much we love each other,. and not have a lot of 'I love you's leftover when one of us dies."

Tool 4: Acknowledge your Other's reality.

Nick: "I understand why hearing the words would give you a good feeling."

Tool 13: Teach about yourself.

Nick: "I show my feelings by wanting to be with you or smiling or holding your hand. I feel too vulnerable when I say things out loud. I've done that in other relationships and they ended badly. I feel protective of myself, now."

Tool 4: Acknowledge your Other's reality.

Emily: "Wow . . . . Thanks for telling me that. It helps me a lot to know what you're feeling about all of this. It really touches me and makes me feel protective of you. I don't want you to be scared. It also makes hearing the words feel less important—when you can say them, that would be great, but I'll try to remember that you're saying them by what you do, too."

Tool 20: Allow yourself to be playful.

Emily: "I know! We can come up with a 'secret signal.' Tap your heart and grunt! And I'll know!"

Although interactions will not always go this smoothly (or sound so mechanical and stilted) the security of having these tools available allows us to feel more confident that we will find something that works. When two people want very different things or act in very different ways, there are always reasons—history or fear or pain—behind their feelings and behaviors. If we can avoid the panic that happens when we realize that we are different, we will be able to separate and compassionately learn about each other. We can explore each other's vulnerability, instead of attacking our Other, hoping we can get them to be fused with us so we do not have to feel the vulnerability of our separateness.

Overwhelmed by emotion

Deb is very verbal and passionate. She easily gets triggered into impatience and irritability when things are not what she expects. Jacob is quiet and tends to get frozen when Deb becomes intense. He is childlike and often leaves a mess when he does something. She does not want to have to remind him to pick up after himself and so gets angry, feeling as if she has another child. When Deb becomes irritated and critical, Jacob criticizes her for being too angry and too intense, but because he feels overwhelmed by her emotions, he mostly withdraws.

WHAT THE ISSUES ARE

Deb wants to stay in fusion with Jacob. She has not separated to be able to declare her needs without anger and frustration.

Jacob does not feel his right to exist. He wants to stay fused instead of recognizing that she is a separate person with different needs than his. He avoids separating and declaring what he wants because it makes him feel too vulnerable.

PRACTICING FUSION

Deb: "I don't understand why, when you and the kids have lunch, everything's left for me to clean up. I went for a run and when I got back, the kitchen's a wreck and you're all off doing something else."

Jacob: "I was planning to clean it up. I just wanted to do something on the computer, first. You're always so critical and controlling." (Then he went back to his computer, tuning her out, only answering anything she might say further with a short "yes" or "no.")

PRACTICING SEPARATENESS

At this point, in order to separate so they are not simply being reactive to each other, both Deb and Jacob would both benefit from Tool 8: Take time alone or a time out. They both need to recover from their shock and identify their true feelings. Once they are connected to themselves, they then need to remember the first three tools before proceeding:

Tool 1: Remember we are both vulnerable.
Tool 2: Remember we are both innocent.
Tool 3: Remember we are both right.
Tool 9: Do-overs are permitted.

Deb: "I get angry because I get startled and I feel helpless to reach you. But mostly I just feel sad. It's important to me that you do your share of the parenting. I don't want to feel like I'm always the bad guy who tells the kids to do something. But I wish I had stayed calm and just come in and asked you what was going on instead of getting angry."

Jacob: "It would have been a lot easier for me if you'd done that. And I always seem to forget to tell you what's going on for me. I could have told you right away that I was planning on cleaning up as soon as I finished what I needed to do on the computer. When you get upset, I go straight to feeling attacked and criticized instead of remembering that you're feeling overwhelmed and sad. You're such a strong and cool person that I forget you have those feelings. And I really don't want you to be the bad guy with the kids."

Many men feel overwhelmed and blamed when a woman communicates to them with emotional intensity, irritation or anger. When they hear the true feelings spoken in vulnerability, instead of frustration, they are more open and responsive, instead of feeling defensive and responsible.

Fear of commitment

Matthew is a successful businessman who has never been married and who has no children. He has enjoyed dating Jaiden for five years but whenever the subject of getting married comes up, he is totally unwilling to even consider it. Jaiden wants to settle down and make a family for herself and her two teenage children. They live separately, spending occasional nights together at her home. When the question of marriage comes up, Matthew argues that they have a great relationship and that marriage would only complicate things. Their conversations about this subject have become very emotionally charged, as Jaiden thinks that Matthew is holding himself back from being fully involved with her. He thinks that the only difference between what they have now and if they were to be married is that he would not be able to have the same kind of freedom he has enjoyed his whole life.

WHAT THE ISSUES ARE

Like many men who experienced healthy fusion and unhealthy separateness, Matthew wants Jaiden to fuse with him and accommodate his needs. Marriage feels like a threat that there will not be room for both of them to exist. He is also very fearful of having to be responsible for her needs.

In the beginning of their relationship, Jaiden fused with Matthew by meeting his needs and not considering her own. Although she feels her right to exist, she does not declare her own needs from fear of losing him.

PRACTICING FUSION

Jaiden: "Are we ever going to talk about the 'M' word?"

Matthew: "I told you before we started dating that I was not going to be interested in getting married. If you can't accept how I feel about this, why don't we just end the relationship."

Jaiden: "I didn't ask you when we were going to get married. I asked you when we were going to talk about it. What's the problem?"

Matthew: "The problem is I don't want to talk about it and I don't want to do it."

PRACTICING SEPARATENESS

Tool 6: Announce your intentions.

When an issue is highly emotionally charged, it can be helpful to break the issue down into its component parts, trying to get a deeper understanding of the meaning it has for each of you. Rather than talk about marriage, which is a trigger for Matthew, Jaiden can look deeper and bring up the essence of what marriage is about to her.

Jaiden: "I'd like to sit down with you and have a conversation, that isn't charged with emotion, about what commitment means to you and what it means to me, because I honestly don't understand why you have the feelings you do."

Tool 4: Acknowledge your Other's reality.

Matthew: "I don't want to have a fight, either and I think it's a good thing to talk about if you don't pressure me. I can do that as long as you see that what commitment means has to me is very different from what it means to you."

Jaiden: "I totally understand that commitment means very different things to us."

Tool 1: Remember we are both vulnerable.
Tool 2: Remember we are both innocent.
Tool 3: Remember we are both right.
Tool 13: Teach about yourself.

Jaiden: "To me, commitment is a personal acknowledgement that we are going to have a monogamous relationship and that we're going to face everything life brings us, together. We will make room for our differences and be a team dealing with the world, and we will commit to finding a way for us both to be okay so that nothing can ever come between us. What does commitment or getting married mean to you?"

Tool 4: Acknowledge your Other's reality.

Matthew: "I know that you want to feel like we're on the same team and that nothing can come between us, and that we can work anything out."

Tool 13: Teach about yourself.

Matthew: "I feel like we have that already. I don't think there's a reason to get married. Lots of people get divorced and have all kinds of financial fights and become enemies. I don't want that. Besides, if we're not married, we have a lot of people to satisfy our needs, and I don't like the pressure that I'd always be the one who would be responsible for your needs if we were married."

Tool 4: Acknowledge your Other's reality.

Jaiden: "You're saying that you're afraid of our relationship ending in a bad divorce and that we'd be enemies. You're also afraid that you'd be responsible for satisfying my emotional needs."

Tool 19: Create a vision together.

Jaiden: "In my picture of being married, we already have an agreement we both feel good about for what happens financially if we get divorced or if one of us dies. Also, in my vision of marriage, communication means to just to be there with each other, not a pressure of being responsible for each other. I don't want either of us to have the pressure of responsibility. In my vision, we're both responsible for ourselves, just as we are, now, and I'd want you to tell me if you felt pressure, so we could talk about it and work it out. I want to be with you, not a burden to you. I want that now, too."

This conversation may not give Matthew the reassurance he needs or result in an instant resolution, but it is the beginning of an exploration of what they could create together that might satisfy the needs of both of them. It also models how we can begin to share more deeply about the feelings that are beneath the stands we take with each other.

The pressure men often feel about commitment comes from their sense of over-responsibility. Their experience is one of feeling burdened and trapped. The point of a conversation that is based in separateness is to create space and mutual respect for each other's needs and differences. Many times the fears and assumptions are unspoken, leaving each person feeling helpless and bewildered, and the man feeling like a caged animal who might not even be aware that he has constructed the cage.

The tools of teaching about ourselves and asking questions so we can truly understand our Other gives us the opportunity to clarify these assumptions and explore creating options that take care of the needs of both people. Remember, men are often not aware of choices and so quickly feel trapped. The language of separateness can be particularly helpful for men, especially if women use tools that emphasize choice and acceptance of differences. It is important for a woman to understand a man's fear and to talk from separateness with patience, acceptance and compassion. Over time, this approach may result in a man beginning to feel not quite so alone in his vulnerability and fear.

Moving beyond anger

Danny and Pam have frequent fights that usually start with her reaction to his having gone off to do something on his own. Danny gets angry that she is upset with him because it isn't as though he goes off to do something wrong—he is usually doing something for the family—but she always gets angry at him anyway. He thinks that what he does is never good enough, that every little thing has to be her way and that everything bothers her. He gets angry that she can't let anything go and that he can't ever do anything right in her eyes. Pam just wants to know what's happening regardless whether it is a little thing or a big thing. She gets angry that he acts as if she is not even in the picture by doing whatever he wants instead of checking in with her about her feelings or even informing her about what he is doing so she can feel connected with him. Danny thinks that she will just be critical of what he wants to do or will try to control, change or stop him.

WHAT THE ISSUES ARE

Fused, Danny interprets Pam's needs as her trying to control him. Pam, also stuck in fusion, responds to feeling separate from Danny by getting angry at him. Both Pam and Danny expect each other to remember and accept their needs without their Other having any needs of their own.

PRACTICING FUSION

Pam: "Where did you go? I had no idea where you were until I saw the car was gone."

Danny: "I went to the store. Do I have to tell you every time I do anything?"

PRACTICING SEPARATENESS

Tool 8: Take time alone or a time out.

Pam: "Wait. This is what we always do. I'm getting angry and I don't want to do this again. Let's just take a couple of minutes alone and come back and talk about this."

Tool 9: Do-overs are permitted.

Pam: "Let's start over. It's fine that you go to the store or do whatever you want to do. It's just easier for me when I know what's happening."

Tool 11: Catch your breath, then ask a question.

Danny: "Is there a reason you can't just trust me and know that I'm not going to do anything that would upset you?"

Tool 4: Acknowledge your Other's reality.
Tool 13: Teach about yourself.

Pam: "I totally understand that you want to be trusted. I do trust you. I'm the kind of person who likes to feel like we're on a team together, so I just want to know where my teammate's going. I get really startled and disoriented when I don't know where you are. I don't have a problem with what you do—I just want to feel connected with you by knowing what you're doing."

Tool 11: Catch your breath, then ask a question.

Danny: "So what if you don't want me to go when I say I'm going to the store, and I really want to go right then?"

Tool 3: Remember we are both right.
Tool 15: Make positive suggestions.

Pam: "I know you'd really want to just be able to go to the store, but I might want you to go later, after I've made a list. How about if I were to ask you to wait a minute while I make a list, so I can have input?"

The Emotional Bill of Rights 1: You do not have to make logical decisions.

Danny: "I get that that would work better for you, but I really need to be able to have the freedom to just do what I need to do sometimes. I'd rather go to the store twice."

The Emotional Bill of Rights 2: You have the right to not understand something.

Pam: "Really? And you wouldn't feel resentful? I wouldn't do it that way, but if that works for you, then that's fine with me."

When people are angry, it is important to use Tool 8: Take time alone or a time out. This allows both people to cool down and to find out what they are really feeling. Otherwise, both people will continue to trigger each other indefinitely. There will be more and more hurt feelings and it will become increasingly difficult to find their way out of the tangle they create. Time outs allow each person to identify how to communicate from a place of separateness.

Controlling people fear vulnerability

Jack is a perfectionist and is very controlling. He is critical, demanding and wants everyone to share his high standards and his particular opinions of how things should be. He wants Ellie to be in fusion with him so he does not have to feel either lonely or too vulnerable. Ellie tries to be responsive to what he wants because she wants to please him, but he us so critical and controlling that she eventually gets angry and ignores his demands. She finds herself reacting to him as though she were a rebellious teenager.

WHAT THE ISSUES ARE

Ellie struggles with feeling her right to exist, so when Jack is argumentative or controlling, it is hard for her to respond from a separate and adult place.

Jack is terrified that he will be swallowed up if he makes room for Ellie to exist. In his fear, he tries to control her so he does not have to feel so vulnerable.

PRACTICING FUSION

Jack: "I found the front door open, again, and there are flies in the house. Why do you continue to disrespect me by forgetting how important it is to me that you close the door every time you come and go?"

Ellie: "I leave the door open two times out of every hundred times I go in and out, and I always have a good reason why I leave it open when I do. I'm sick of your being critical and controlling."

Jack: "It's not a matter of being critical or controlling. Who would want to have flies in the house? I've asked you to be aware of this but you ignore my requests and do whatever you want."

Ellie: "I'm not ignoring your requests—I have my own reasons for what I'm doing."

PRACTICING SEPARATENESS

After Jack's initial comment, Ellie has to take the initiative to step back and separate.

Tool 4: Acknowledge your Other's reality.
Ellie: "I understand that you think that when I leave the door open I am consciously and deliberately disrespecting what you want and need."

Tool 5: Believe your Other.
Ellie: "I absolutely believe that for you, there is no other explanation for my behavior."

Tool 13: Teach about yourself.
Ellie: "I love you and I want you to be happy and feel cared about. I want to please you. I'm the kind of person who goes out of my way to try to show love and respect for the people I love and to honor what they need. It's actually hard for me to remember my own needs when I know what your needs are. I do close the door a lot—I just don't care about it being closed as much as you do. But that's not about you."

Tool 11: Catch your breath, then ask a question.
Ellie: "Can you see that for me, it's not about you or my feelings for you that I don't think about closing the door the way you do?"
Jack: "It's hard for me to understand because I don't feel that way."

Tool 5: Believe your Other.
Ellie: "I know that's hard for you to understand because that's not what you would do—but can you believe me when I tell you what's going on for me? You're always going to close the door and I'm mostly going to close the door because I'm not you. But I'm asking you to believe that I'm not doing it to disrespect you."

A person who is very controlling, like Jack, has a difficult time feeling separate. Almost all the tools that were used were initiated and used by Ellie because Jack needs a lot of support and help in seeing that she is actually acting as a separate and independent person—not someone who is doing things to him but who is doing things for herself.

It takes a lot of work to stay patient and compassionate, recognizing that a person who is very controlling must feel very vulnerable and out of control. Many tools must be used to help them understand our reality. We need to use explanations to help them connect with us both logically and emotionally.

Hopefully, by our appealing to their scientific curiosity, philosophy or spirituality, the controlling person will be able to recognize that there are things that happen that are beyond what they know or have experienced—in this case, "Could it be that there is another explanation for a person leaving a door open besides the explanation that they are being intentionally disrespectful? If we are being scientists, given the limitless number of possibilities in the Universe, could there be another explanation besides the one that you already came up with?"

People who are very frightened or wounded often protect themselves by being very controlling. They do not want to experience their vulnerable feelings because it seems as if that would be too painful and too dangerous. When they were vulnerable before, perhaps when they were babies or children or in a previous relationship, they were wounded, so they are trying to avoid re-experiencing that vulnerable state. For them, it seems safer to stay in logic. Ellie was trying to connect with Jack's logic and his adult Self, for to ask Jack to reveal his baby or vulnerable Self is asking more than he can do at this point in his development.

Controlling people resist feeling vulnerable and instead create a false "logic"—one that makes assumptions based on their fears. Operating within that self-created reality gives them the feeling of safety. While a person may ferociously resist being vulnerable, they do so out of fear, not an evil desire to be in charge. The hope is that by repeated use of the tools of separateness, in a calm, reassuring and logical way, controlling people may begin to think of vulnerability as a logical part of being human and feel less threatened.

Over time, hopefully the awareness that all humans are vulnerable replaces their early teaching that vulnerability is dangerous and should be avoided. They may also begin to experience a healing process as they receive acceptance, compassion and understanding for their experience and needs. With this acceptance and compassion, they also may begin to feel not quite so alone in their vulnerability and it may become increasingly possible for them to reveal themselves.

Don't ask, don't tell

Aaron and Molly have been married for over thirty years, have grown in ease and comfort with each other, and have become an extraordinary team. Since they are both retired, their life has simplified and they support each other in doing the activities that interest them. They love each other deeply, are thoughtful of each other, kind and are each willing to do anything to make the other happy. Molly is outgoing and energetic and loves to talk. Aaron is more introverted. He came from a home where there was very little communication about feelings and was drawn to Molly because of her vitality and affectionate nature. Molly was drawn to Aaron because he was loving, undemanding and made her feel safe. Her father had been in the military and she grew up afraid of him.

Molly once needed to have her husband be somewhat withdrawn in order for her to feel safe, but as she overcame her fear of men, she started to feel lonely. She has been unable to find a way to have the deep emotional connection with Aaron that she now longs for. Whenever she talks about this, Aaron feels bewildered and hurt, not understanding how she could doubt his love. He always just explains that he doesn't like to talk much or be touched. She has never wanted to upset or hurt him and so they slowly began to have emotionally and physically disconnected lives. She is afraid to ask him to open up and he is more comfortable keeping his thoughts and feelings to himself.

WHAT THE ISSUES ARE

Aaron is content in his fusion and hopes Molly will be happy in this fusion, too. He does not want to see that she has different needs than he does. Because he does not know how to be separate, he is afraid that he will have to choose between attending to her needs and honoring his own. In his quiet place of fusion, he is loving, but not vulnerable.

Molly loves Aaron and does not want him to feel bad. Instead of focusing on her own needs and how to declare them, she fuses with him and does not exist as a separate person.

PRACTICING FUSION

Molly: "I don't want to hurt your feelings, but it feels like you are not interested in me anymore and that you really don't want to be close to me."

Aaron: "I can't believe you would say something like that. I'm telling you how much I care about you and love you in everything that I say and do. Because I don't show it the way you want me to, you accuse me of not caring?"

PRACTICING SEPARATENESS

Tool 15: Make positive suggestions.

Molly: "I'd really like us to talk more and share what we're thinking about and feeling so I can feel more connected to you. I want to spend more time talking with you, and I also miss having more physical contact with you."

Tool 13: Teach about yourself.

Tool 5: Believe your Other.

Molly: "I feel lonely a lot in our relationship, and I don't want to. I know that you love me and that you have a different experience than I do but we've always sat down together when either one of us is feeling unhappy and talked about what we can do so that we both feel good."

Aaron: "But I think we have a great relationship just the way it is."

Molly: "I know this works for you, but it only partly works for me. A lonely person is lonely because they need more verbal and physical contact. There's nothing wrong with you—you have a different need than I do. I don't expect you to understand why I feel the way I do or to feel what I feel, because I know that our relationship is just what you want. I'm asking you to believe me that it isn't bad to me, I just need more."

Tool 19: Create a new vision together.

Molly: "I would like to treat this as a relationship project—something we can work on together. I want us to approach it like we do when we're planning a vacation and we talk about what things we can do that will be fun for both of us. You're happy with the way it is with our talking and touching, but what about me? We wouldn't go on a vacation and just do the things you like. You want me to enjoy myself, too. You wouldn't say, 'Well, you got to come with me on the vacation. Isn't that enough?' Well, I like touching and talking."

Aaron: "So you're saying that it's not enough for you that I show my love for you the way that I do."

Tool 4: Acknowledge your Other's reality.

Tool 13: Teach about yourself .

Molly: "I don't doubt that you love me, and it certainly isn't that you aren't enough. I love how wonderful and loving you are with me. But you're right. That isn't enough. I'm just the kind of person who needs more talking and physical affection than you do. The reason I'm talking about this today is not to say something's wrong with you but to ask you what we might be able to do about our differentness so that we're both okay."

Tool 15: Make positive suggestions.

Tool 20: Allow yourself to be playful.

Molly: "I know! How about whenever we pass each other in the house, we hug each other!"

Aaron: "Oh, God!"

Molly: "Or, I've heard that in India, people wash each other's feet as an expression of respect and of affection."

Aaron: "All right! We'll hug!"

Aaron wants Molly to do their relationship the way that he feels comfortable. She has been willing to do that for a long time, partly because she did not know how to try to change things. She came to a point where she felt too lonely to continue, and wanted him to reciprocate—to consider how she needs to do a relationship. She remained in this non-communicative and nonphysical relationship for many years, but she now wants him to venture into her territory and find a way to be more verbally expressive and physically affectionate.

Remembering that marriage is a project, we can open discussions and start to explore how we can make changes that take care of the needs we both have without saying that something is wrong with either of us. It may take time and experimentation, as well as patience and compassion, to create a system that works for us both, but it can be done.

Hot issues mask vulnerability

Diana works long hours and likes to come home and have a drink to relax. Her husband, Jimmy believes that Diana loses track of how many drinks she has and does not realize that she has at least two or three each night. He often brings up her drinking. When he does, she feels like a chastised child and resents the implication that she cannot make her own independent adult decisions. This issue has been a sore point between them for years and both of them are pretty angry about it. She feels criticized and controlled and he thinks she is not taking her health and drinking habits seriously.

WHAT THE ISSUES ARE

Diana struggles with her right to exist. Instead of asking for what she needs and finding a way to talk about her feelings when Jimmy is critical of her, she goes away and soothes herself with alcohol. She does not feel loved for who she is and feels too vulnerable to talk about that.

Jimmy is critical instead of being vulnerable and expressing his fears. He tries to control her rather than separate and talk about his feelings and needs.

PRACTICING FUSION

Jimmy: "You can't keep drinking like this."

Diana: "I'm not going to do this with you again tonight. I'm sick of you acting like my father. I'm fully aware of how much I'm drinking. I've talked to my doctor about it and he doesn't think it's a problem."

Jimmy: "I can't do this marriage if you're not going to take your health seriously. You say you're aware of your drinking, but you're not. You drink every day."

Diana: "And you eat junk food every day even though you have high cholesterol, so I don't get how you can be in judgment of me and say I don't take my health seriously."

PRACTICING SEPARATENESS

   Tool 1: Remember we are both vulnerable.
   Tool 2: Remember we are both innocent.
   Tool 3: Remember we are both right.
   Tool 10: Describe yourself, not your Other.
   Tool 13: Teach about yourself.
   Jimmy: "I need to talk about feeling really scared about something. I watched my mom drink herself to death when I was a teenager. (He is now crying). I'm just terrified that I will have to walk through that pain again with you. I can't bear it."

   Tool 7: Tell your Other what you want, and ask your Other what they want.
   Jimmy: "I can't stand feeling so scared and alone, and I just need to hear that you understand why I feel this way and that you don't want me to feel scared and alone."

   Tool 4: Acknowledge your Other's reality.
   Tool 13: Teach about yourself.
   Diana (taking his hand) "I didn't know about how frightened you were. You always talk about it as though it's about my problem with alcohol. I want you to love me for who I am and when you always talk about my drinking, I feel like you don't see me and care about what's going on for me. I had no idea you were having these feelings.
   "I know that I drink to wash away my own pain from my work. I'm so afraid that my supervisor will say, someday, 'You're a fraud! You really don't know how to do this job.' During the day I just put my head down and work hard. When I get home, I feel so overwhelmed from just holding on all day, so I drink." (She begins to cry.)
   Jimmy: "I always feel so lonely and unconnected to you, and I've never known what to do about it except try to get you to stop drinking."
   Diana: "I always feel the same—lonely and unconnected to you, and really hurt by all the criticism. This feels better to talk with you and know what's really going on and feel you caring about me."

Tool 18: End a Separateness Interaction with a hug.
Jimmy: (Hugs her.)

Couples very often get into a power struggle over an issue. It could be, as with this couple, the behavior or habits of one of them. Alcohol, money, weight, hobbies, parenting styles, where you squeeze the tooth-paste—all can become hotly debated issues in relationships and the conversations go nowhere. These subjects are not the point. They do not address what each person is really feeling, so it is impossible for the conversations to have a satisfying resolution. In this situation, the point was that they were both feeling vulnerable about different things. They each longed to be seen and cared about in their pain but were too afraid to reveal themselves.

When Jimmy and Diana took the risk of talking about their true feelings and vulnerabilities, it became possible for them to connect with each other in caring and compassion.

> *Jan: I think of it this way. Our automatic reaction, when something triggers us, is to take action to stop whatever is triggering us. If a mosquito came buzzing around me, I wouldn't say to it, "I feel vulnerable and really don't like to be bitten. What are you really feeling and why are you focusing on me?" I'd just swat it. But people aren't mosquitoes, no matter how strong our impulse may be to swat when we get stirred up!*

Being *the best* versus being *good enough*

Wayne feels like he continuously must respond to Sheila's list of chores for him. He and Sheila are regularly in disagreement about what needs to be done to maintain their home. Wayne believes that she asks him to do as much as she does because she likes to be in charge and to control him. Sheila believes that everything she asks him to do is necessary. Sheila also thinks Wayne does not spend enough time with their two teenage sons and that the boys are suffering from it. Wayne believes his relationship with the boys is fine, and that they are just going through normal teenage rebelliousness. They fight over these topics regularly.

WHAT THE ISSUES ARE

Wayne and Sheila have completely different standards about work and relationship issues. Instead of having conversations about these two topics from a place of separateness, with each having their individual subjective truths, they argue about who is right as though there is an objective truth. Instead of looking at both their standards as being acceptable, they look for whose standard is "correct."

PRACTICING FUSION

Sheila: "Would you mind replacing the screen door today? I'm concerned about all the holes it has in it."

Wayne: "The holes are really small, and I told you before that when they get bigger I'll replace it. I don't want to do it today."

Sheila: "Look, I don't want to have this conversation again. This is what we do all the time. I can't keep up the house without your help."

Wayne: "I don't think this is about keeping up the house. I think this is about you just having to give me things to do. Like I've said before, it seems like it gives you a thrill to be the boss."

Sheila: "No, actually it gives me a thrill to know that we're taking care of the house so it stays in good condition. And, by the way, when was the last time you spent some quality time with your sons?"

Wayne: "My sons don't want to spend any quality time with me. They want to Twitter and text their friends and not hang out with their parents."

Sheila: "So you're not going to make any effort just in case they'd benefit from spending time with their Dad?"

Wayne: "I've talked to them both about this and they're happy and I'm happy with our relationship. Leave it alone, already."

PRACTICING SEPARATENESS

Tool 3: Remember we are both right

Sheila: "I know the screen door doesn't need to be replaced immediately and that we have very different ideas about when to do things. The fact that I'd like it to get done today and you'd like to just relax is fine."

Tool 13: Teach about yourself.

Sheila: "What happens for me, though, is that when things are done that I see need to be done in the house, I'm able to relax inside and just enjoy being in my home, and I can feel peaceful. That's why I always want to get things done right away, so I can check them off my mental list. And, I want things to be as good as they can be."

Tool 4: Acknowledge your Other's reality.

Wayne: "I always forget that about you so I take it personally and think that you're just incessantly trying to keep me busy and get me to do stuff you hate to do. Then I feel pressured and angry. But it sounds like you have a lot of pressure from yourself to have to get things done as soon as they occur to you."

Sheila: "It is a lot of pressure, and I know that you like to have space without having to be doing chores so you can feel peaceful. If the chores got done, I could feel peaceful, too."

The Emotional Bill of Rights 3: You do not have to care about everything.

Tool 13: Teach about yourself .

Wayne: "I don't want to feel the kind of pressure that you do. It's just not worth it to me and it makes me feel agitated. And, I really don't like the pressure of having to do things so you feel okay. Good enough is good enough for me. I don't want to make things as good as they could be. I feel the same way about the boys. Even if there's more that I could do to be a better dad, I feel like what I do is enough—I don't want to be pushed and stressed to always be better. I don't feel like trying to be better at everything I do. Unless there's a big problem, I want to enjoy my life, not improve everything—or myself, either, for that matter. "

Tool 4: Acknowledge your Other's reality.

Tool 13: Teach about yourself.

Sheila: "Wow. That really is a difference between us. I mean, I understand what you're saying, and I want to enjoy my life, too. But it's also really important to me to grow and try to have life and experiences and things—and me!—be as great as they can be. It makes me feel like I'm really living with richness and to my greatest potential."

Wayne: "I do know that about you. But for me, relaxing and enjoying life without pushing myself is what makes me feel like I'm living a rich life."

Tool 15: Make positive suggestions.

Sheila: "Sometimes I want you to do things like fixing the screen door so the house looks as good as it can and so I can check it off my list. So how about, in those situations, I'll do what I can and if I'd like your help, I'll let you know it's because I want everything to be its best, not because you're lazy or it's wrong to want to let things be. Then you can either help me or tell me that it's my issue and that you don't really want to help, this time."

Wayne: "That'll work. It would help if you remind me, when you're asking me to do things, that it's to get stuff off your checklist or because you just want things to be as good as they can be—not because you're trying to control me or trying to be the boss. I'm happy to help you when I feel like doing things but I don't want to have to have that same goal of perfection you do or to do things just because you're feeling stressed."

Tool 20: Allow yourself to be playful.

Sheila: "That'll work fine. Just make sure you sign your time card so I can know how little to pay you each month!"

The quarreling Quibblers

Noah and Annie constantly bicker about trivial things. They both dig in and stubbornly insist that their version of reality is the correct one and that their Other is wrong. They both are self-righteous and compete with each other constantly. They bicker about anything and everything, personalizing and feeling victimized anytime their Other deviates from their expectations in the slightest way. They are both hyper-alert to any difference between them and seize each difference as a vindication of their own innocence and of how the other person is wrong.

WHAT THE ISSUES ARE

The struggle that Noah and Annie have to accept their separateness is revealed in the unspoken anger simmering right below the surface of many of their interactions. It is difficult for them to accept that they just see and remember many things differently—they are each in demand that their Other be fused with them. They will do anything in their attempt to avoid breaking their fusion. As a result of this unconsciousness about their resistance to feeling separate and the quibbling anger that comes as a result, they have very frustrating interactions.

PRACTICING FUSION 1: THE QUIBBLERS

Annie: "I thought you said you were coming home at seven o'clock tonight."

Noah: "I told you that I would try to be home at seven."

Annie: "Your actual words were, 'I don't think anything will prevent me from getting home tonight by seven.'"

Noah: "My actual words were, 'I don't think that anything will prevent me from getting home by about seven.' It's 7:17! Sue me!"

Annie: "Actually it's 7:26 by the kitchen clock, and I asked you to call if you were going to be late."

Noah: "You asked me to call if I would be very late. It's 7:17!"

Annie: "It's 7:26. That's very late."

PRACTICING SEPARATENESS

Tool 2: Remember we are both innocent.

Annie: "I guess something must have come up for you, but I thought you were coming home at seven o'clock tonight."

Tool 4: Acknowledge your Other's reality.

Tool 11: Catch your breath, then ask a question.

Noah: "Sounds like we had a misunderstanding and you're upset I wasn't home sooner. Did you think I'd be home exactly by seven?"

Tool 13: Teach about yourself.

Annie: "Yes. That's what you said, so that's what I expected."

Noah: "My intention was to be home as close to seven as I could be, but I don't like feeling pressure, so I try to be relaxed about it at the same time. I'd like that to be good enough for you."

Tool 4: Acknowledge your Other's reality.

Tool 13: Teach about yourself.

Tool 15: Make positive suggestions.

Annie: "I don't want you to feel pressured, either, but I also don't like being in the dark about what's happening. What if you called me if you're going to be more than ten minutes late?"

Tool 4: Acknowledge your Other's reality.

Noah: "That's fine with me to call. I just thought that would make me later. But I'm fine doing it from now on."

PRACTICING FUSION 2: RETURN OF THE QUIBBLERS!

Noah: "We need to leave at five-thirty because they're expecting us at six o'clock for dinner. So you'd better start getting ready at four-thirty."

Annie: "It won't take me any longer than forty minutes to get ready, and besides, it only takes twenty minutes to get to their house."

Noah: "I've been married to you for twelve years and you've never once gotten ready in forty minutes. And there's traffic Friday nights. You never think about that."

Annie: "Look—I get myself ready to go out every day. I think I know how long it takes me."

Noah: "Obviously you don't, because we're always late when we go someplace. And even if you are ready, you go in and out of the house a million times getting things before we leave so we need to leave time for that."

Annie: "Well, somebody has to remember things and you never do."

PRACTICING SEPARATENESS

Tool 17: The Separateness Communication Process

Step 1: Explain the issue and express your feelings.

Noah: "I hate to feel rushed or be late, so I'd like to talk about when to leave tonight to get to our friends' house."

Step 2: Acknowledge the issue and the feelings.

Annie: "I know you hate to feel rushed. I don't like it either. And I know how upset you get when we're late."

Step 3: Use Tool 15 - Make positive suggestions.

Annie: "I want to feel relaxed about getting ready to go and relaxed when we're driving. I'd rather be late, if it comes down to a choice."

Noah: "I hate being late, though. Why don't we just plan on leaving some extra time, in case there's traffic?"

Annie: "There are some things I need to get done this afternoon, so I don't want to leave unnecessarily early."

Noah: "Could we think about the extra time as being part of our evening together? Then, in case we get there too soon, we can just take a walk alone, before we go to their house."

Annie: "Oh. I hadn't thought of the extra time that way. That sounds fine."

Step 4: Acknowledge feeling heard and seen. Let your Other know you have nothing else to say about the issue.

Noah: "Great! Okay! We're set!"

PRACTICING FUSION 3: WILL THEY NEVER STOP?!

Noah: "Remember back in 1987 when we went to Colorado to visit your aunt? That was a great trip."

Annie: "It was in '88."

Noah: "I loved staying in that hotel overlooking that river."

Annie: "It overlooked a lake. And I hated it."

Noah: "No, you really liked it."

Annie: "No, I liked the hotel we stayed at on the way home. I think I can remember what I like and what I don't!"

PRACTICING SEPARATENESS

Noah: "Remember back in 1987 when we went to Colorado to visit your aunt? That was a great trip."

Tool 4: Acknowledge your Other's reality.

Tool 3: Remember we are both right.

Annie: "That was a great trip."

Noah: "I loved staying in that hotel, overlooking that river."

Tool 4: Acknowledge your Other's reality.

Tool 14: Use emotional aikido.

Annie: "I remember we both loved a hotel, but I remember it being the one on the way home."

Noah: "Really? I thought for sure it was the one on the river."

Tool 4: Acknowledge your Other's reality.

Tool 3: Remember we are both right.

Annie: "Well, I think the point is that we both loved that one place we stayed on the trip."

Noah: "Yea, it was really nice, wherever it was!"

In the first two instances of quibbling and bickering, Noah and Annie are reacting to their broken fusion. Quibbling takes the place of self-declaration. They would rather quibble than have to feel their separateness and be vulnerable as they speak for what they each want or feel. Quibbling comes fast and easy. Teaching about themselves takes vulnerability, patience and acceptance of their separateness.

The third instance of quibbling illustrates an experience common to many of us. We generally have such an aversion to leaving the state of fusion that often the most insignificant experience of feeling separate makes us angry or critical of our Other. It just feels annoying to feel separate. Because we are made aware of our separateness in our relationship with our Other, our anger can be directed at them—even if it makes no sense, should we pause to think about it. Really, what difference does it make if, for example, we have different memories? But with fusion broken, we can feel our irritation rise up over any minor detail and suddenly find that we are quibbling about something that is irrelevant to the main point of the discussion. For Noah and Annie, as for many of us, quibbling is simply a protest against the loss of fusion.

In these examples, Noah and Annie used acknowledgement as a lifeline to avoid their reaction to broken fusion and to separate at the same time that they looked for the rightness in each other's experience.

When we are both clearly struggling to tolerate the feelings of being separate, acknowledging our Other's feelings and looking for the rightness of what they are saying, not the wrongness, accomplishes two things. It gives us the chance to catch our breath and calm down, as well as making our interactions as kind and gentle as possible. Practicing emotional aikido also helps us separate, stepping out of the way of the quibbling that is an attempt to maintain fusion. When we can accept our separateness, we avoid being hooked into desperate interactions in which we each try to get our Other to agree on our version of reality.

> *Jan: I guess we should have listed one more tool, the one I spoke about at the beginning of the book: Bite your tongue! Biting your tongue is also a great way to stop a panic reaction to broken fusion. Knowing that nothing is wrong and that getting mad at your Other is perfectly ridiculous, biting your tongue is an effective, albeit somewhat painful way to avoid an interaction that you can't even justify to yourself! A big advantage of the tool, biting your tongue, is that it also gives you time and motivation to remember the other, less painful tools.*

Sympathy, sympathy, sympathy, **truth**

Zack and Jamie have been married for a decade. When they met, Zack was a real bad boy type, but Jamie was drawn to him because of his forthrightness and his ability to face disappointments and setbacks without judging or blaming himself or anyone else. Now, however, she constantly is angry at him for all of the ways he disappoints her. No matter what he does or says, she is critical and blaming.

WHAT THE ISSUES ARE

Zack struggles with guilt over his behavior in the past and so personalizes whatever Jamie says, taking inappropriate and unilateral responsibility for everything she brings up in criticism of him. He tries to be truthful and genuine and to prove that he is no longer that bad boy. His guilt prevents him from recognizing that he allows her to focus on him instead of talking about her own feelings. He needs to learn to separate so both of them can explore the issues that they each have. He also needs to accept his right to exist as an evolving being, instead of him trying to be so good that she finally approves of him.

As a child, Jamie was not taught that her feelings mattered and was punished every time she tried to speak up for herself. This has left her afraid to voice her feelings and needs. Not having the right to exist,

Jamie can only criticize Zack for what he has not done. While she can bring up ideas, if Zack questions or wants to discuss them, Jamie feels too vulnerable and quickly retreats into silence, hurt and resentment. Over the years, this hurt and resentment has built up and Jamie and Zack are a perfect example of an angry "victim" and her inadvertent "victimizer" being trapped in an unsatisfying relationship pattern from which neither of them knows how to free themselves.

PRACTICING FUSION

Zack: "I finished up my work and I'd like to come home early so we can spend some time together tonight. Maybe go out to dinner."

Jamie: "You don't want to go out to dinner with me. You only say that because you're trying to make up for being away so much."

Zack: "Honey, that's not true. I love you and miss you when I'm at work."

Jamie: "Oh, right. You just want to try that new restaurant you told me about."

Zack: "Well, yes I do want to try it, but that's not why I want to come home early. I want to be with you."

Jamie: "Then why didn't you invite me to go with you on that business convention?"

Zack: "I did, Honey! But you said you didn't want to go!"

Jamie: "You didn't really want me to go, so I stayed home."

PRACTICING SEPARATENESS

After Jamie's first response, Zack needs to take the initiative to step back and separate, and use Tool 2: Remember we are both innocent.

Tool 14: Use emotional aikido.

Tool 4: Acknowledge your Other's reality.

Zack: "Oh, Jamie, I'm sorry it seems like I don't want to be with you. I'm sure that my being away so much has made you feel that way. What an awful feeling to think that I don't really like to be with you."

Tool 13: Teach about yourself.

Zack: "I really would like to go to dinner with you, though, and have some good, quiet time just to ourselves."

Jamie: "If you really wanted to be with me, you would have wanted me to go with you to that convention because we could have had some fun together there."

Tool 14: Use emotional aikido.
Tool 4: Acknowledge your Other's reality.
Zack: "Honey, I didn't realize that I hadn't made it really clear that I did want you to go with me. It would have been so much fun. I'm sad you thought I didn't want you to be there with me. I would have been hurt, too, to think you wouldn't have wanted me to go somewhere with you."
The Emotional Bill of Rights 7: It is your right to make mistakes.

Tool 12: Make clarifications, not apologies.
Tool 13: Teach about yourself.
Zack: "I know that I used to lie to you and not follow through with what I would tell you, so I totally understand that you must still have a lot of hurt about that, and that makes me feel really sad. But that's not the man I am trying to be now. Being honest with you and with God are the most important things for me in my life. I sincerely mean it when I tell you that I want to be with you."

Tool 15: Make positive suggestions.
Tool 19: Create a new vision together.
Zack: "I'm glad that you let me know you're upset and I really want you to check out your fears with me so I can tell you the truth. How would it be for you, if every time you feel hurt or angry, you ask me if I really mean what I'm saying or tell me that you have leftover hurt feelings or anger about something that happened between us? I'd like that. If I can feel like we're in this together, I don't think I'd ever get tired of letting you know that I feel so sorry that I couldn't have done any better earlier in our relationship, because I am. And I know that you did the best you could do, too."
Jamie: "Well how do I know that you mean it this time? I've felt disappointed so many times."

Tool 20: Allow yourself to be playful.
Zack: "I know! I'll give you a nose-measuring device and permission

to use it any time you want. Then you can measure my nose to see if it grows after I tell you things."

Each of us has a history that taught us how to survive in the world. From early childhood, we make assumptions about our experiences (about what is happening around us, why it is happening and how we should act in response) that seem as if they give us the best chance of surviving. We unconsciously continue these adaptive patterns in every significant relationship.

When Zack was able to separate and accept himself as an evolving, growing being, he did not get stuck in his own guilt about the past and shock about being misinterpreted. He was able to let Jamie know that he cared about how she was feeling instead of getting triggered into reacting defensively to her inaccurate assumptions. When she felt understood and cared about, Jamie was then able to hear the truth of who Zack is now. It did not have to be a debate about which reality was correct. Secure in himself, Zack was able to respond lovingly to her reality, and later share his own.

Being the leader

Neither Jaxon nor Faith feel seen and acknowledged or appreciated for who they are and what they do. Each of them waits for the other to notice them, all the while having hurt and resentment build inside them. They are in competition for who is the most hard working and giving, as if there were only so much love and approval to go around.

WHAT THE ISSUES ARE

Both Jaxon and Faith feel unempowered. Each waits resentfully for their Other to be the approving parent neither of them had when they were children. Neither of them have the right to exist, to separate and speak or advocate for what they need, so they are stuck, each feeling like a victim of the other. Caught in fusion, they both have a fear of the other one "winning," which would feel to each of them as though they were diminished.

In this example, it is possible to see how one person can lead the way in practicing separateness by using the tool of emotional aikido to avoid being triggered and to help the other person attain separateness, as well.

PRACTICING FUSION

Faith: "I wish you'd spend a little time cleaning up around here, since you're home."

Jaxon: "I can't believe you didn't notice all the work I've done around the house this week!"

Faith: "You talk like I don't do anything!"

Jaxon: "Well, you sure don't see what I do."

PRACTICING SEPARATENESS

Faith: "I wish you'd spend a little time cleaning up around here, since you're home."

Tool 14: Use emotional aikido and invite her to use:

Tool 15: Make positive suggestions.

Jaxon: "I did do some cleaning up, but is there something else you'd like me to do? I'd be happy to."

Tool 17: The Separateness Communication Process

Step 1: Explain the issue and express your feelings.

Step 3: Use Tool 15 – Make positive suggestions.

Jaxon: "I've been wanting to tell you about a great idea I came up with for myself. When I was a kid, I was always waiting for my mom to notice me and make me feel like she approved of me, and I think I do that with you, too. So I've decided that I'm going to make a chart of all the things I do and practice showing it to you. I think it will make me really feel good to ask for appreciation, rather than wait and hope that you notice what I've done."

Faith: "I notice what you do. You're the one who never notices what I do."

Tool 14: Use emotional aikido.

Tool 4: Acknowledge your Other's reality.

Jaxon: "I'm so sorry it feels to you like I don't notice what you do. I notice a lot but maybe I don't tell you enough. I'm also sure you do a lot of things I'm not even aware of."

Tool 13: Teach about yourself.

Jaxon: "I really want you to hear that my making a chart has nothing to do with you. It totally is about freeing myself from feeling like I have to be quiet and wait. You aren't the one who makes me feel like that. The point of the chart is for me to be able to speak up. I'm trying to avoid the trap that I always fall into of being so reactive to you and feeling hurt and resentful when there's really no reason to."

Tool 17: The Separateness Communication Process
Step 3: Use Tool 15—Make positive suggestions.
Jaxon: "Why don't we both make a chart? Then I can make sure I do recognize all the effort you put into our family. I hate the thought that I'm missing things you do. I don't want you to feel sad about being unrecognized. This would make sure that I notice!"

Tool 20: Allow yourself to be playful.
Jaxon: "Hey! We can give ourselves stars on our charts every day and at the end of the week take ourselves out for ice cream!"
Faith (giggling despite herself): "Well, that's kind of silly, but, okay. I'll do anything for chocolate ice cream!"
We all make interpretations about the knowledge level of our Other. We look at their large adult bodies and think that they will be mature and wise. Regardless of how they react, we tend to persist in this hope and demand that they be logical and think clearly. Like a child, we approach interactions with the unspoken expectation that if they only saw clearly who we were, then they would be the loving and approving adult we want them to be.

In our fusion, expectation and demand that our Other be a knowledgeable, logical and nonreactive adult, we display who we are. We try to show our good intent and prove our love by actions (which may or may not be noticed), thinking that surely if we do enough or say something the right way, they will then see us the way we see ourselves.

We try harder and harder, refusing to accept defeat, enduring and displaying until we feel beaten down, exhausted, hurt and resentful. The amazing thing is that both people can be doing the exact same thing, feeling misunderstood, unseen and unappreciated for trying so very hard when their Other is seemingly doing nothing. Each person, persisting in their own adaptive behaviors and tenaciously in their demand of their

Other, does not even think to step back and analyze what is going on.

Jaxon claimed his power in this interaction. Instead of being stuck as the passive victim, hoping that he would get the attention he longs for, he claimed his right to exist and declare himself. When Faith reacted in defensiveness, in the typical "only one of us has the right to exist, and if it's you, then I can't" trap of fusion, Jaxon was able to use emotional aikido and step aside. Without entering into a competition for the right to exist, he was free to support her in also declaring her need to be seen and valued.

Jaxon focused on himself, making sure that what he brought up was about himself and his own issues, instead of talking about what Faith was saying or doing. Knowing how much he responds from fusion, he was able to watch for the panic and desperateness he always feels when Faith is critical or negative. Having these tools gave him a practical way to override his usual automatic defensive reaction. Preparing how he was going to explain what he was doing allowed him to talk about his needs and issues without making it seem as though he were using his idea as a weapon to attack or blame her.

Jaxon made sure that he let Faith understand that he does see and appreciate her, and that his need was not her fault, nor did it negate her needs. Aware that Faith also fears that she will not be seen, he made sure to diffuse that issue by acknowledging her. The fact that Jaxon made sure that Faith had a better understanding of his motivation and feelings allowed her to see that his actions were not about her and that he was not trying to make her feel unimportant or at fault.

Knowing that Faith and he were both trapped in the same needs and fears, Jaxon worked to be the leader in helping them both separate.

Vulnerability and separateness make connection possible

Although it can feel like an impossible challenge to stay separate when our Other is reacting in fusion and using words of fusion, it is absolutely possible. We are each absolutely separateness. We may not want to. A voice inside us (hmmm . . . wonder who that might be?) can be screaming, "It's all their fault! They are wrong! They should change!" but the truth is that each of us can give ourselves the right to exist, can accept and take care of our own vulnerability and can be an adult we can feel proud of being.

Exercise: *We have all had the experience of feeling like a mature and logical adult.*

1. In what situation do you feel the most confident and capable? At work? With children? At church? At a social gathering?
2. Now, imagine that someone in that situation is all upset or angry. What would you do? Cry? Blame or attack them? Storm out? Probably, you would realize that they were struggling and miserable and having trouble finding the right way to talk about it.
3. This is the adult you have the potential to be. This is the adult who can work with your Other to create the kind of relationship you would like to have.

In the heat of our reaction to our Other, however, it is hard to remember—or to think at all, sometimes!—that even in the very moment of our being triggered, we have a choice. (As you read this book, perhaps something you read felt right and maybe even familiar. Perhaps you even had the thought that you already knew something that you read but just did not realize that you knew it until we said it. We call this the "Oh Yeah! Phenomenon." It was already a part of you. You already knew it, somewhere inside you. Because somewhere inside of us we know this information, the way we act is always a choice, at some level.)

None of us could hope to be racing around, breathless, distracted and stressed, and be able to stop in an instant and become quiet, centered, still and able to reach into that place of knowing and choice. When startled by our separateness, most of us are swept away by emotion in an automatic response that leaves no room for reflection or conscious choice. But right now, as you are reading, you are not in that triggered state. You are most likely, in this moment, logical, calm and contemplative. This moment is a foundation to build on.

None of us like the feeling of being triggered. Knowing this, we can each make the decision to practice separateness all by ourselves so we are prepared to change the communication patterns in our important relationships. But before we can separate, we first have to slow ourselves down.

Jan: We moved from Los Angeles to a small town, but I soon realized that I was still racing around in my busy, big-city mode, a stark contrast to the peaceful environment of my new hometown. So, I deliberately practiced slowing myself down. I would make myself sit in front of a big window that looked out on a beautiful valley and I would practice taking deep, slow breaths. Every other moment, it seemed, I would find myself jumping out of the chair, thinking, "I have to take out the trash!" "I have to brush my teeth!" "I have to _____ !" (Fill in the blank. I did—with anything under the sun that would keep me from having to be still!) All the busyness kept me from myself, and I realized how resistant I was to just being quiet and connecting with what I was feeling.

So I made a deal with myself to just breathe. I didn't have to think or feel anything. Just breathe. Just be present in this moment. Gather myself up—all my neediness and vulnerability—with my in breath, and hold myself close, like a baby on my chest. When I exhaled, I would imagine blowing out any tightness I had in my body, as well as all the judgments, needs and expectations of everyone else. I could feel myself becoming more self-contained, more separate. I found I began to hold my chest with one hand, while the other stretched out to make a space no one else could invade. I welcomed people coming close to me, but I wanted them to be the caretakers of their own needs and feelings.

Gradually, I grew accustomed to and comfortable with the feeling of peaceful quiet. I found that comforting words would come up from deep within me to calm and reassure myself, words like, "All you can do is be who you are, and that's enough." My breathing slowed down and my sense of peace grew.

What I really liked about this process was that I didn't have to learn a new behavior—I already have to breathe! All I needed to do was slow that breathing down and take in deep breaths through my mouth. As athletes breathe through their mouths to allow them to expend their greatest effort, I found that, like them, I was engaged in a very strenuous activity: battling all my "frightened bunny" impulses to run. Doing this gave me more oxygen and helped me feel calm and quiet inside. The rest followed on its own.

I began to practice breathing like this everywhere I went, regardless of what I was doing. I told myself that my body could be busy and my thoughts and words could be involved with someone else, but my breathing was mine. I envisioned being at the center of a tornado with people, events and words whirling around me. My job was to stay in the quiet center of the storm. If I reached out at all, I would be caught up in the whirlwind, spinning out of control. I was a part of whatever was happening around me, but I could stay safe and separate in that center.

When I would go home, I would pause outside my front door and take a deep breath and prepare myself for anything to happen. When someone would do something that left me clueless about how to respond, I learned to stay quiet and do nothing but breathe. After all, they weren't going anywhere. I could take all the time I needed, waiting until something appropriate came into my mind. I was practicing separating.

I'm still learning to do this with Al. I don't need to rush to act or speak. I can sit and wait for my first surge of emotion to pass. We have been together a long time. I don't need to let fear make me hurry.

Because we are vulnerable to our Other, all of us are very sensitive to their words, tones of voice and facial expressions. If we do not take the time to separate and slow ourselves down, we will find ourselves easily triggered by the slightest of acts,tones or looks from our Other. Even a sigh or raised eyebrow can hold significance for us, when we are that vulnerable. Only by cultivating separateness in ourselves can we begin to practice separateness with our Other.

The examples in this chapter of interactions between couples have one thing in common—they are all expressions of how the fear and avoidance of vulnerability and separateness make connection impossible. When we acknowledge how vulnerable we both really feel and when we use the tools of separateness, we can support each other in expressing our true feelings, replace fusion with real connection and find resolutions that honor the needs of us both. All of this, remember, takes patience, practice and compassion for our Self and our Other, for although this is a worthwhile project, it is a very difficult challenge.

CHAPTER 10

Growing Beyond Adaptation to Transformation or All Right! It's NOT All Your Fault!

Most of us have spent the majority of our lifetime in a prosperous society. Technological advances make our heads spin and we are taught impatience, with advertisements that tell us proclaim, "Get what you want when you want it." Fast food, fast cars, fast Internet, fast electronics. (When we first got a computer in the mid-1990s, it seemed miraculously fast. Now if we have to wait a few seconds for a web page to come up, we get impatient! Ah, yes, we are all children of this culture.)

The teachings of our culture infiltrate our unconscious mind and expectations without our ever being aware that this is happening. Movies and books resolve life problems and relationship difficulties within hours, exercise gurus guarantee dream bodies in only a few short weeks, drugs promise a quick end to every physical or emotional complaint conceivable without having to make a change in how we live or eat (just do not listen to the disclaimers at the end of the ad which tell you how the drug will kill you). Reality shows on television put dreams of quick glory, fame and fortune in our minds, the lottery promises instant riches.

When it comes to relationships, there are lots of books that promise great results—*Instant Relationships for Dummies* or *A Perfect Relationship in 3 Easy Steps*! Well . . . as you may have noticed, we are not writing that kind of book (and your book probably looks pretty used by now, so forget about trying to return it and get your money back so you can buy one of those other books! Besides, we just made up those titles).

When it comes to the world of emotion, there are no easy answers. That is good news and bad news. The bad news is that this is a life-long project, not the effortless romance our cultural mythology promises. Relationships take work and practice and are not a one-time endeavor for which you can learn the rules and then everything will be really easy. The good news is that as you journey, you do not have to feel badly about yourself—nothing is wrong with you or with your relationship. You are completely normal! And the depth of self-knowledge and emotional intimacy you can attain with your Other is limitless. There is always more ease, more peace, more wisdom and more freedom to love lying behind every emotional alarm that we experience. Free from judgment and fear, we need only step up and learn together. No shame, no guilt, just power, strength and love.

It is so important to us that you understand and believe that doing the work of separating in a relationship is natural, inevitable and a life-long practice. If you doubt this truth, you will be left despairing and hopeless as you continue to feel triggered and reactive and encounter challenges in your relationship. You will continue to look for the right relationship book or the right psychologist to make your relationship work easily. If you doubt this truth, every book you read that proclaims relationship "cures" and every new psychologist you visit will slowly bring you to the terrible misunderstanding that your relationship must not be the right one for you, and that you are hopelessly messed up and should just go on medications for the rest of your life—for the challenges are endless. If we accept this truth, however, every time we are triggered, we will remember that we are being given another opportunity to grow, to discover greater wisdom and freedom to be ourselves, and to have a deeper, more loving connection with our Other.

Speaking about being triggered . . .

Jan: Writing this book has been a fascinating experience for us. Al and I have been examining our relationship in far greater detail and have talked together about our relationship dynamics with much more clarity than we have ever had. Having this "scientific" perspective has helped us to have a bit of distance from our reactions so we could investigate, with curiosity rather than unbridled emotion, every situation in which we get triggered with each other. We still get emotional—don't get me wrong! But, knowing what is really happening helps us to avoid reacting from panic. (And, in case you want a reality check, we are both exhausted! It feels like we have been in intensive couple's therapy for months!) What this has led to, though, is a really wonderful realization.

We have always worked hard on our basic human issues. We have always worked hard to use tools of good communication with each other. But until we started to work on this book, neither Al nor I realized the absolute truth that "Every tight reaction I have has absolutely nothing to do with the other person. It is simply the signal letting me know I need to work at being separate."

We might know about but cannot experience fusion-separateness issues unless we are in an intimate relationship, for that is the clearest place for them to be triggered. We cannot wait until we "mature" before we get into a good relationship, because maturing and growth are the result of learning from the experiences we have while we are in a relationship. We either go through serial monogamy each time we grow into a new level of awareness or we support each other through our growth so we can keep going forward together, deepening our wisdom.

We all tend to act and talk from a home base of fusion, as though we were expecting our Other to be just like us. We do not separate and see our Other for who they are—we speak as if they have the same needs, feelings, interests and brain function that we have. But when we really see the vastness of our differences, what then? That is the point where many people become hopeless and give up, thinking that their relationship is just the wrong one.

This is where the realization about our tight reactions having nothing to do with the other person has led to a very clear direction for handling relationship stress.

🌸 Regardless of what our differences are, what would it be like to have faith that those points of despair or hopelessness or alienation or anger are just signaling another "project" to explore together and grow from?

- ❋ What would happen if we could tolerate the disorienting and uncomfortable feeling of not-knowing without having to take action to get away from that feeling?

- ❋ What would happen if we each just went deeper into our own selves to see what was there—which of the three basic human issues got triggered in us?

- ❋ What if the task were simply to observe ourselves and then to share what we were feeling or discovering and see what happens from being self-aware and hearing each other?

- ❋ What transformations might occur if we allowed ourselves to fully take in the experience of feeling and understanding what is happening for each of us?

- ❋ What if every tight feeling just signaled another stage of self-discovery and there was no threat that we would lose our Self or our Other?

Steep in the dilemma

Jan: Once I had a small cut on my hand—not very deep or at all serious. But it was just painful enough to keep pulling my attention to it. I couldn't sleep, aware of it hurting. For some reason, in my exhaustion, I started to visualize what was going on in my body. I "saw" the white blood cells scurrying around, cleaning up the cut and knitting it back together. I watched the flurry of activity for a while and suddenly was aware that my cut wasn't hurting anymore. The intensity of the feeling was no different, but now, instead of being the sensation of pain, it was the activity of healing.

To all of us, pain feels like a signal that something is wrong. Our automatic animal response is to avoid it but not even all physical pain is life threatening or wrong. The pain that accompanies the birth of a baby is not an easy thing to endure, but it signifies the beginning of a new life. Similarly, the emotional pain we feel as we struggle in our relationship signals healing and growth, the beginning of a new way of life. It is an inevitable part of the process of our transformation as we internalize a deeper understanding of ourselves and of how relationships work and as we learn to use the tools of separateness.

Pain is the greatest force of liberation. It says "No!" to enduring. It demands change. It is the source of the courage and fortitude necessary for change. Pain is the call from our very core to wake up, to take ourselves seriously. It is the call to awareness and freedom. It signals an opening of possibility, a crack in our unconsciousness, a window of opportunity.

Reminding ourselves of this will both provide comfort through the struggle to become who we want to be and will inspire us, for we will know that we are growing and are creating the relationship we all want to have. Rather than reflexively attacking or pulling back from the discomfort of separateness, we will be able to tolerate the process of discovering and working through whatever issues come up for each of us. We can allow ourselves to steep in the unresolved dilemma that precedes growth instead of reacting to get away from uncomfortable feelings and end our having to feel separate at any price. Just as a tea bag steeps in hot water to create something new—not just water, not just tea leaves—we can steep in the not-knowing, exploring our feelings and human issues so we are able to truly understand ourselves and each other and create something unique that honors the reality of both of us.

Jan: A few months ago as we worked on this book, Al and I looked at each other and felt lost. Why were we together, anyway? I felt so lonely and so hopeless. But, in faith, I repeated our realization to myself, believing, because I had experienced it so many times already, that continuing to look inside myself, instead of reacting to get out of my unhappiness, would take me to a place I could not yet even conceive of. And it did. I can't even tell you now what had caused me to feel alienated from Al, because staying with myself and sharing what I discovered made that experience a fleeting one. What I am left with is the success of using our realization. The problem was just an exercise calling for me to practice going more deeply into myself instead of taking external action and striking out,. (Oh, my! I have changed! And if I can, anybody can!)

Attaining the oneness we all long for

The pull of fusion—a natural, comforting and human desire—is strong and there is nothing wrong with wanting to be in fusion. The pull of separateness—a natural imperative of life and growth—is also strong and there is nothing wrong with wanting to separate. Our ability to move fluidly along the fusion-separateness continuum allows us to be whole and complete individuals as well as to be connected in close and loving relationships.

The exquisite paradox is that the experience we seek, thinking we will get it through fusion—oneness, closeness, intimacy, a feeling of connectedness—can only be attained through healthy separateness. It is impossible to be close to, connected with or intimate with someone unless there is a "someone" who is separate from your own Self. In fusion, there is a sense of wholeness, of being one with something larger. There is a safe and delicious sense of oneness and sameness, and all experience is shared. But unbroken fusion in a relationship only belongs to the time before we were born. While we will enjoy moments of it with our Other, fusion is inevitably broken every time we become aware of our differentness.

In separating, we become self-contained. We can witness without attachment, not needing to personalize and react to the behaviors or emotions of our Other, for we know they are a separate being. We can feel safe in our right to exist and so can accept our own Self and our Other, seeing the truth of who we both are, in all of our vulnerability.

From this place of peace, we can see that we are all a part of a larger whole. We may be involved in different tasks, but we are all on the same human journey. Each of us may be having a different experience, but each experience is like a different facet of the same diamond—we are each working on our own facet of existence, meeting the challenges of where we are in our personal development. Side by side, we are all involved in the same work of growing, each with a slightly different focus or challenge. Connected but not fused, we can feel the sense of oneness for which we instinctively long.

When we are in healthy separateness, we do not need to act in panic when we have a startled reaction to our differentness. We trade the undifferentiated sameness of fusion for the intimate connectedness of two people who are whole and complete beings in their own right, and who come together to experience closeness, belonging and the human journey of growth. When we are fused, separating is a threat. In separateness, our safety comes from accepting our vulnerability and our right to exist. When we are separate, we can come together into periods of healthy fusion and enjoy the sense of oneness, but we do not have to get stuck there. We do not have to sacrifice our Self in order to have the love and connection we want.

Radical personal transformation is The Way of All Relationships

The very fact that we are exploring our relationships is due to a wonderful and incredible advance in the development of human consciousness. We are like scouts pushing back the frontiers of unconsciousness, making inroads against a cultural ignorance about the true nature of relationships.

These explorations also lead us to inevitable personal change. What we might never have questioned on our own—behaviors that seem natural and normal to us—become glaringly illuminated in the context of a relationship where suddenly someone else has an entirely different idea or reaction than we would have or expect. From a place of fusion, we are often left thinking that our Other is wrong or simply crazy, and we tend to do a combination of either adapting around or trying to change our Other. Neither of these approaches can be successful in the long term. Lost in our ignorance, we can mistake helplessness for hopelessness and so despair that there is any chance our relationship can ever be one in which we can find the peace and love we long for.

Eventually, we are faced with having to either leave the relationship or look at our own Self—if we are among the fortunate ones who think of this possibility—questioning our own assumptions in order to understand how two people could possibly be so different. We cannot easily just walk away from a significant relationship when difficulties and stress arise, as we can in a more casual relationship. There are strong reasons to try to stay—necessity, children and bonding. If we are among the fortunate ones, we realize we are just engaged in a project to learn how to communicate, how to watch our own patterns and processes, and how to find a way to be the person we want to be, discovering and overcoming our self-defeating impulses and unconscious tendencies.

We serve as teachers for one another. We are like mirrors that reflect issues back to our Other that would otherwise go unnoticed. We are dynamic learning partners, forced to confront assumptions and patterns that unconsciously run our lives. This exploration lifts us out of the world of frustration, anger, helplessness, hurt and blame, and gives us the tools to create a new type of relationship and a new, more peaceful and more empowered Self. We are equipped to become the adult we once demanded our that Other be.

As we journey through life—through the challenges of childhood, school, vocation and relationships—we gain experience and opportunities to become more self-aware and more whole. It is in the most significant and intimate relationships that we are touched so deeply that the most primitive, unevolved and undeveloped parts of ourselves are revealed. In these relationships, we have the opportunity to accept our humanness and the inevitability of growth and change—not as problems, but as the next step to our freedom.

Since there is no problem, there can be no fault. Because we are all innocent, there is no need for blame. With compassion and patience, we can strive to free ourselves from the ignorance and unconsciousness that has trapped us in pain and reactiveness. We do not have to settle for adaptation to life but can grow beyond it to personal transformation, freedom and peace.

Don't wait

Jan: Washing up for the night, some years ago, I was rubbing my face in my towel, so annoyed with Al over some minor transgression, when it suddenly hit me—if he were dead, I'd love him so much. None of the minor irritations and habits that bothered me would matter at all. (Not even finding those mysterious holes in his jeans just above the right knee. What does he do to get them in all his pants, anyway? Does he creep stealthily out of bed in the middle of the night to drag himself along the floor till the fabric is shredded? That's the only theory I have been able to come up with, anyway.)

An invisible wall fell away for me, in that moment. I didn't want to wait until he died to love him like that. I wanted to love him without restraint, now.

If we were perfectly developed beings, we would not become triggered or startled by interactions with our Other. We would just calmly and compassionately take the appropriate action or speak the appropriate words. Knowing that whatever happens in our important relationships is exactly what we need to face in order to continue with our growth into wholeness, we do not need to react in fear that something is wrong with either of us or with our relationship. Even if we cannot put words to it, we can remember that that each of us struggles with ignorance and the basic human issues—helplessness and vulnerability, separateness and the right to exist—and that the worse our actions are, the more we are suffering and lost.

Knowing that this is a natural and inevitable part of the human journey, we can redefine marriage from a problem to a project and allow ourselves to have hope, again, of having the relationship we long for. Having acceptance and compassion for ourselves as we continue this journey together, we can be free to love each other again. Fully. Totally. Now.

One valuable lesson from a fairy tale

In the depths of the struggles, when we feel lost and vulnerable, we can follow the model of Hansel and Gretel. They, too, felt lost, not knowing what to do or where to go. They, too, were alone in the dark. But they had each other and they huddled together in faith that the morning would come, the light would break and they would find their way.

In our times of darkness, we can huddle together with our Other and take heart and comfort ourselves by remembering these five things:

1. I really love you.
2. You really love me.
3. This is hard.
4. We are just lost, *right now*.
5. Step by step we *will* find our way.

Keep faith with each other. Keep looking deep inside your heart for your truth. Morning *will* come. The darkness *will* fly away and you *will* be able to love again.

Jan: I remember the young faces we looked at as we stood together as newlyweds, brushing our teeth—hopeful, innocent, vulnerable, anxious at times, sometimes angry or with nothing to say to each other, full of illusions and dreams. Over the years, those faces in the mirror have changed, lines marking experience, eyes more clear with true vision as illusions fell away, comfortable with each other, sometimes leaning together, shoulders touching as they ended days that challenged them. Now those faces are more peaceful—not afraid and not needing to be defensive anymore. Their love is easier now, and deeper. They look back at us with bemusement, wondering where the time has gone, but oh, so glad to have gone through that time and still be here, together, the four of us. They have gone through the lessons, the struggles, the celebrations, the fights, the self-discoveries. Wearier, wiser, more contented, they're still here. Glad to be together. Happy for the memory of all those years the four of us met up in a bathroom every night. And glad to be facing the future together. At peace and in love.

Al and I wish you many happy, peaceful years with the faces in your mirror.

About the Authors

Jan Harrell, PhD has been in practice as a psychologist for over thirty-five years, experiencing meaningfulness and joy she never imagined could be a part of "work." She taught at UCLA Extension and Southern Oregon University.

Alan Robins, PhD worked for the Los Angeles YMCA's before beginning his career in psychology. He also was an amazing comedian, forming two a cappella comedy quartets that performed in Oregon, the Cook Islands, New Zealand, Russia and Europe.

Jan and Al married very young and were blessed with a long and loving marriage that ended in 2015 with Al's death. They worked together and share their journey of growth and discovery in this book.